VOLUNTEERING

Melanie Oppenheimer currently teaches twentieth-century Australian history at the University of Western Sydney. She became interested in volunteering in the mid 1980s when writing about her grandmother's experiences as a Red Cross VAD during World War II. She is the author of *Oceans of Love*, a biography of a nurse in World War I, the edited volume (with Jeni Warburton) *Volunteers and Volunteering*, and *All Work. No Pay: Australian Civilian Volunteers in War*, which was shortlisted for the 2003 New South Wale

VOLUNTEERING

Why we can't survive without it

MELANIE OPPENHEIMER

To my mother
with love

A UNSW Press Book

Published by
University of New South Wales Press Ltd
University of New South Wales
Sydney NSW 2052
AUSTRALIA
www.unswpress.com.au

© Melanie Oppenheimer 2008
First published 2008

National Library of Australia
Cataloguing-in-Publication entry

Author: Oppenheimer, Melanie.
Title: Volunteering: why we can't survive without it/Melanie Oppenheimer.
ISBN: 978 086840 986 3 (pbk.)
Notes: Includes index.
Subjects: Country Women's Association of Australia – History.
          Voluntarism – Australia – 20th century.
          Volunteers – Australia.
          Volunteer workers in social service – Australia – 20th century.
Dewey Number: 361.370994

Design Josephine Pajor-Markus
Printer Ligare

This book is printed on paper using fibre supplied from plantation or sustainably
managed forests.

Contents

Preface: Why volunteering?

A civilization flourishes when people plant trees under which they will never sit.

Greek Proverb

I am often asked how and why I became involved in researching and writing about volunteering, something I have been doing now for over twenty years. The answer is not very academic but I can clearly pinpoint the moment. It is connected with a cherished childhood habit. When I was young I used to rummage, which means to search unsystematically and untidily through something. Well into my adolescence I loved nothing better than to rummage through the drawers of my mother's dressing table. This was a dressing table that was never sat at – my mother was far too busy for that, probably volunteering for one of her many causes. Nor did she really use it, apart from the mirror. It was an item of furniture that basically displayed family photographs. But the drawers – there were two on each side – were overfilled with an assortment of items from her past. There was a drawer of costume jewellery; a drawer of scarves; a drawer of belts; and a drawer of gloves, remnants of her heady youth, some purchased in Paris when she was a student at the Sorbonne. These items were rarely worn now but to me they were treasures. I spent hours rummaging through my mother's past, scented with stale eau de Cologne and Arpège perfume. From there I graduated to the barn, where there was a large room of trunks, boxes and suitcases full of the most fabulous stuff that some people would call junk. It was a very cheap form of entertainment for a rural child who did not attend formal school until aged eleven. Hours of musty pleasure with dust, mildew and other people's memories and long forgotten possessions for companionship. Small wonder I became a historian.

On one of these rummaging expeditions when I was older (as they say, old habits die hard but I feel somewhat embarrassed to confess exactly how much older), I found a pair of dark blue dungarees. I put them on and discovered that they fitted me perfectly, noting that their original owner must have had a figure like mine. I took to wearing them everywhere. On noticing my newly acquired wardrobe, my mother explained that they were my grandmother's Voluntary Aid (VA) overalls from World War II when she volunteered for service on the British aircraft carrier, HMS *Glory*, as part of a Red Cross medical team to pick up prisoners of war and bring them home at the end of the war. The overalls were issued to the women – it was the first time women had officially served on board a Royal Navy vessel – so that they could climb the multiple ladders of the aircraft carrier with a modicum of decorum. There were letters, diaries and a photograph album documenting the three-month voyage. I was immediately fascinated by the story and wanted to know more. Coincidently, I was also looking for a thesis topic, as I had recently returned to university. One thing led to another and after completing the Glory study, I enrolled in a PhD at Macquarie University and continued to research and write on aspects of civilian volunteering in wartime (not to be confused with those who volunteered for active service during war).

When I started, in 1986, there was precious little written on the topic. Volunteering was largely invisible in Australian history. Over the years, I have written both historical and contemporary books and articles, including *All Work. No Pay. Australian Civilian Volunteers in War*, based on my PhD, and edited a book with Jeni Warburton, *Volunteers and Volunteering*, which provided a contemporary snapshot of volunteering in Australia.[1]

Today I am regularly invited by a range of volunteer groups and organisations to talk about aspects of Australian volunteering, and people seem genuinely interested in the subject. During 2007–08, I was involved with a series on volunteering, called 'Vita Activa' as part of ABC Radio National's popular *Life Matters* program. I had been spruiking the idea for some time with little luck until Janne Ryan at the ABC suggested I contact Amanda Armstrong, the Executive Producer of *Life Matters*, and the rest, as they say, is history. The success and general response to the program and listener feedback confirms that volunteering is popular, topical and well practiced in Australia today.[2]

Much has changed in the twenty years I have been engaged with the topic. Volunteering, philanthropy and financial giving are now widely discussed and practiced, with the concept no longer tainted by class or fashion. Quite the reverse. But there is still a considerable gap in our historical and contemporary knowledge, and volunteering continues to suffer from a lack of real understanding and recognition. In the academic arena too, volunteering and unpaid labour are still considered 'lightweight', not topics with which serious scholars in the hallowed halls of our universities engage. Although governments of all persuasions are much more cognisant of the value and worth of volunteering and most are actively involved in administering volunteer programs and offering support, volunteering is still on the periphery of mainstream policy and decision making. Its status is not assured, and there is so much we do not know about the role and impact of volunteering in and on our society. This was brought home to me during the 2007 Federal election campaign when I realised that of the main political parties, only the Australian Labor Party (ALP) actually had a policy on volunteering. As I write, we have a new Federal government with a parliamentary secretary responsible for social inclusion and the voluntary sector, yet the official minister for volunteering resides in another portfolio. It is early days but it appears little has changed.

All of the above are good reasons for writing a book on the history of volunteering. But because I come from a long line of volunteers (the question of the existence of a volunteer gene has not gone unnoticed), and because I cannot divorce my interest in volunteering from my family history, or to be precise a pair of overalls, each section of the book is prefaced by a short biographical vignette of a family member who was a prolific volunteer. As Jill Roe once wrote, 'historians increasingly look to biography and culture for answers to the big questions'.[3] Time will tell whether I will find such answers in the volunteering experiences of my family. But family is important and these individuals have certainly had a profound influence on me.

Acknowledgments

I would like to acknowledge the following people and institutions who all contributed to this book at various stages over the years. I was fortunate to receive a research secondment to the Writing and Society Group at UWS in 2005, and I'd like to thank Ivor Indyk for his support and for suggesting the focus on literary volunteers. I was also awarded the National Archives of Australia's Margaret George Award in 2006 which enabled me to spend essential time in Canberra. Many may be surprised to realise just how many files about volunteering matters are held in the NAA. I'd particularly like to thank Derina McLaughlin, Fiona Burn and archivist Caroline O'Connor for her time and knowledge of the collection. Indeed, she is still trying to locate some outstanding 1970s files from the Department of Immigration on migrant organisations for me! Ann Curthoys gave me generous access to her anti-Vietnam War interviews; Marie Coleman shared her knowledge of the Social Welfare Commission, as did Colleen Wardell with the NSW Asthma Swimming Program; Matina Mottee gave me access to the ANESBWA records, now safely deposited in the Mitchell Library; Joy Noble has provided inspiration and support over many years as has my mentor, Bruce Mitchell, who, along with Jeni Warburton, read various drafts of the manuscript; Amanda Andrews and Maria Glaros were excellent research assistants; and the team at ABC Radio National's *Life Matters*, especially Amanda Armstrong, Tracey Trompf and Richard Aedy, who were fabulous in assisting with the volunteering series, 'Vita Activa', where some of my ideas were crystallised. Thanks also to other colleagues and friends including Judith Snodgrass, Mark Lyons, Kylee Bates, Annette Maher, Carol Liston, Erik Eklund, Margaret Tennant, Justin Davis Smith, Louise Hufton and Danielle Roddick, UWS media officer, who has always been supportive of my projects. I have been particularly impressed by the professionalism of the team at UNSW Press and they have been a pleasure to work with at all times. Thanks especially to Phillipa McGuinness who had faith both in me and the project, my excellent editor Fiona Sim, and Heather Cam. Much was achieved in a brief time. And, of course, my family, including Keith and Lorna Guyot, Jillian Oppenheimer who did more than her fair share of babysitting and provided invaluable support, my husband Mark and our daughters, Isabelle, Luci and Camille.

Abbreviations

ABS Australian Bureau of Statistics
ACF Australian Comforts Fund
ACOA Australian Council for Overseas Aid
ACOSS Australian Council of Social Service
ACV Australian Council for Volunteering
AICD Association for International Cooperation and Development
ANESBWA Australian Non-English Speaking Background Women's
    Association
ASIO Australian Security Intelligence Organisation
BLF Builders' Labourers Federation
CFA Country Fire Authority
CFS Country Fire Service
CLF Commonwealth Literary Fund
CWA Country Women's Association
FaCS Family and Community Services
FAW Fellowship of Australian Writers
FECCA Federation of Ethnic Communities Councils of Australia
GNCs Good Neighbourhood Councils
IAVE International Association for Volunteer Effort
ICRA Indo-China Refugee Association
IYV (United Nations) International Year of Volunteers

NAA National Archives of Australia
NESB non-English speaking background
NLA National Library of Australia
NWAC National Women's Advisory Council
RCSD Regional Councils for Social Development
SES State Emergency Services
SOCOG Sydney Organising Committee of the Olympic Games
SOS Save Our Sons
UWS University of Western Sydney
VA Voluntary Aid
VAD Voluntary Aid Detachment
VAOC Volunteer Air Observer Corps
VASC Voluntary Aid Service Corps
VCOSS Victorian Council of Social Service
VDC Volunteer Defence Corps

PART I
INTRODUCTION

Grace Munro:
Foundation President of the CWA

I have only very vague memories of my great-grandmother, Grace Emily Munro (née Gordon); visiting her in a darkened room not long before she died. Indeed, to a young girl she was quite a scary figure. The second eldest of seven girls (and one brother), Grace Munro was a dynamic woman of independent means. So, like many middle class women of her generation born in the latter part of the nineteenth century, she never had a paid job but rather undertook volunteer work for most of her adult life. Living near Bingara in remote north-western New South Wales for much of her life, Grace combined marriage and children, as well as volunteering in a range of voluntary organisations including the Australian Red Cross, St John Ambulance and the Bingara Hospital Board.

However, Grace Munro is best known for her role in the formation and establishment of the Country Women's Association (CWA) in New South Wales in 1922. After suffering the tragic death of her fourth and youngest child from croup, Grace vowed to do everything in her power to address the lack of facilities and opportunities for rural women and their children. Encouraged by the co-operative spirit demonstrated by women's volunteer work during World War I, and motivated by a new focus on the specific problems associated with the isolation of rural women, Grace chaired a committee to establish a Bushwomen's Conference at the Royal Easter Show in early 1922. Within a year, the CWA, a name coined by Grace, was born. She suggested nineteen of the twenty-two rules in its constitution and became foundation president.[1]

Moving through her forties, and with her children grown up, Grace's volunteering increasingly dominated her life. The fledgling CWA was the main beneficiary of her unpaid labour when she crisscrossed the country encouraging women to mobilise together, to help themselves, and form CWA branches. Retiring as president after three years due to a duodenal ulcer, Grace continued to work in a voluntary capacity for the CWA and supported rural women's issues for the rest of her life. She lobbied politicians and bureaucrats to establish baby health centres, maternity wings in public hospitals and improve bush nursing; as well as raising considerable funds for the Flying Doctor Service, the Australian Red Cross, and St John Ambulance. In 1929, she was made an Officer in the Order of St John of Jerusalem, and was awarded an MBE in 1935 for her extensive volunteer work. From 1938, she was appointed to the Advisory Council of the New England University College at Armidale. The CWA went on to become a powerful voice for rural women and children, and by 1947, ran thirteen hospitals, 138 rest rooms and baby health centres, eight holiday homes and hostels and fifty-six libraries across New South Wales.[2]

From all accounts, my great-grandmother was a strong willed, dogmatic woman who polarised people. She played favourites and treated her only daughter (my grandmother, whom we'll meet later in this book) poorly, favouring her two sons. She has even been called a right-wing collaborator connected to the New Guard, and the CWA has been labelled a 'counter revolutionary organisation'.[3] And, of course, she could undertake volunteer work because of her middle-class origins, her wealthy husband and her own independent means, so she never needed to engage with paid work. But one cannot deny the impact and importance of her volunteering. When examining her volunteer work, her organisational and motivational skills, her achievements and what she did, year after year, for the many voluntary organisations she worked for, there is little doubt that Grace Munro set the bar quite high. She is a good example of an early twentieth century female volunteer, an energetic leader of women, who through her volunteer work could mobilise, encourage and get things done.

1 Volunteering: What is it?

*We are fortunate in Australia to have a rich history of volunteering
which has contributed significantly to the quality of our lives and
to the foundations of a democratic, caring and vibrant society ...
that the true value of volunteering has been largely overlooked for so
long belies its significance.*[1]

Joy Noble and Fiona Johnston

We are a nation of volunteers. Over one-third of Australians over the age
of eighteen (that is, 5.4 million of us) volunteer on a regular basis. Across
our vast continent, on any particular day, you will find volunteers working
together coaching local sporting teams, counselling and advocating on
behalf of the disadvantaged, baking cakes for a school fete, patrolling the
beaches, delivering meals to the elderly or planting trees and maintaining
our wetlands. There is almost no area of human activity in which volunteers
are not involved, and volunteering plays an important part in our cultural,
social, political and economic lives. Volunteers are the lifeblood of local
communities in our cities and especially in the bush.

Yet, perhaps surprisingly, we know little about the history of volunteering in Australia and we have only relatively recently begun to research
and write about how and why Australians volunteer. We receive satu-

ration media coverage concerning markets, for-profit companies and paid employment. Daily news bulletins devote extraordinary coverage to 'business and finance', and strange beasts called the Dow, FTSE and Hang Seng seem important to the exclusion of everything else. There is a corresponding silence about volunteering, about unpaid labour and not-for-profit organisations. They are, by comparison, largely invisible. Yet, if volunteers on any single day in Australia decided not to turn up and withdrew their labour, our society would soon feel the effects.

Volunteering has been steadily increasing in Australia. Defined as 'unpaid help, in the form of time, service or skills, through an organisation or group', and carried out willingly without coercion, the Australian Bureau of Statistics (ABS) published its first full-length national report on volunteering in 1996. The report discovered that 24 per cent of adult Australians volunteered. In a second report published in 2000, this figure increased to 32 per cent and a third report in 2007 noted the numbers had risen further to over 34 per cent.[2] At the same time, there has been an increasing public awareness about volunteering through international events such as the 2000 Sydney Olympics and the United Nations International Year of Volunteers in 2001. Debates about social capital, civil society, community building and social inclusion, and the rise of peak organisations such as Volunteering Australia have all provided volunteering with much needed oxygen. Since 2000, state governments, especially the South Australian government, have led the way in establishing offices for volunteers and creating ministers for volunteering. As mentioned earlier, the Rudd Federal Labor government, elected in November 2007, appointed a federal parliamentary secretary responsible for social inclusion and the voluntary sector.

But volunteering is not a new phenomenon. Australians have been volunteering since the first European settlement. So why do we know so little about it? What propelled the sudden interest in volunteering in the last decade of the twentieth century? Why have our governments only now become interested in volunteering? Why do governments not have a philosophy of volunteering? Why are our history books largely silent about this integral part of our western democratic tradition? And where are the stories of volunteers in our national histories?

In this book, I aim to answer some of these questions and to explore the largely untold history of volunteering in Australia, especially from 1945, and the relationship between governments and the voluntary sector. But the question as to why has it taken so long for volunteering to be recognised can be answered quite simply. Fundamentally, volunteering is work that is not paid and falls outside the rubric of our economic structures – that helps to explain its invisibility as our society focuses almost exclusively on paid work. Unpaid work, domestic work, child rearing or 'informal volunteering' (unpaid labour largely carried out in the domestic sphere as caring work) is excluded from standard statistical models operating in Australia and elsewhere, and it is classified as unproductive. So volunteering is, according to these accounts, essentially unproductive, it's not counted and rendered invisible. Because of its 'voluntary' nature, it is less important, has no historical value, and is therefore omitted from the historical record.

Marilyn Waring, a former New Zealand politician and economist, noted this seemingly incongruous situation in her landmark book, *Counting for Nothing*, originally published in 1988. This book was a revelation for me when I first read it ten years ago. Suddenly all my questions regarding the status, or lack thereof, of volunteering made sense. Although Waring was largely writing about the domestic unpaid labour of women around the world, the same arguments can be applied to volunteering. Waring argued much of women's global labour, mostly subsistence farming, was deemed 'unproductive' and thus not included in the gross domestic product (GDP) because in 1953, the United Nations System of National Accounts (which has been adopted world wide as the world system to record economic activity) stated that 'primary production and the consumption of their own produce by nonprimary producers is of little or no importance'. What this means is that within the productivity guidelines, housework, reproduction, subsistence farming, community work and volunteering are not counted. Waring argued that if voluntary and unpaid work were given a monetary value, by the accepted processes of imputation, this work would become visible, thus influencing policy makers and challenging broad assumptions and values.[3]

More recently there have been attempts to argue that unpaid work *is* work because 'it is an activity that combines labour with raw materials to produce goods and services with enhanced economic value'.[4] Economists such as Duncan Ironmonger have attempted to impute a dollar value on volunteering to enable its 'economic' value to be counted. Yet despite this, unpaid work and volunteering still remain outside the defined economic framework of our capitalist system because capitalism has competition and financial reward as its cornerstones and volunteering does not. Having said that, it has been estimated that volunteering contributes about $42 billion a year to the Australian economy.[5] In 2006, about 729.9 million hours of voluntary work were undertaken by Australians.[6] Although attempts to quantify and qualify the financial importance of volunteering in supporting our economic structures and enhancing our social capital continue to be made, it is slow going. And while volunteering remains outside the GDP, it remains 'second class', outside mainstream economic and fiscal policies, with its true value and importance neglected. Governments continue to pay lip service to the importance of volunteering but ultimately deny it official recognition.

Voluntary action and social capital

During my years of thinking about volunteering, there have been several important books that influenced me. One was Waring's. The others were by two British writers, William Beveridge and Geoffrey Finlayson. A Liberal politician and economist, perhaps better known as the father of the British welfare state, Beveridge was the author of two key wartime reports that formed the basis of the welfare reforms in post-World War II Britain. But Beveridge also wrote a little known report, *Voluntary Action. A Report on the Methods of Social Advance*, commissioned by one of the large British friendly societies and published in 1948. Even Beveridge's biographer José Harris, did not consider *Voluntary Action* important and almost completely ignored it in the first edition of her biography, published in 1997. Revealing a shift in attitudes that will be noted towards the end of this book, in a second edition, published in 2003, a discussion of *Voluntary Action* and its repercussions was included.[7] For me, Beveridge's book presents a clear and persuasive articulation of the role of volunteering in our society, especially its importance for our democratic traditions. The report was a prophetic plea for 'voluntary action' (Beveridge's term) not to be forgotten in the wake of the emerging welfare state. Beveridge believed that voluntary action was for social advance in the community, and was made up of mutual aid and philanthropy. He described them as follows:

> It is Mutual Aid when consciousness of a common need leads to combined action to meet that need, to helping oneself and one's fellows together. It is Philanthropy when the driving force is not consciousness of one's own needs, but what I have described as social conscience … To have social conscience is to be unwilling to make a separate peace with social evils, escaping from Want, Squalor, Disease, Unemployment and Ignorance into prosperity oneself, while leaving one's fellows in their clutches.

Beveridge argued that it was very important that 'the vigour and abundance' of voluntary action, 'outside one's home, individually and in association with other citizens' were recognised and supported, as they were 'outstanding features of British life'.[8] These ideals needed to co-exist with the newly formed welfare state, and an environment had to be created in which the state, individuals and voluntary organisations worked together for 'social advance.'[9]

Another phrase to describe voluntary action is the 'voluntary principle' – an integral part of a democratic society. A thriving democracy does not alone depend on an open and free market, a hallmark of capitalism, but also on its citizens acting collectively, in association with each other, for the common good. These ideas were uppermost in Beveridge's mind as he wrote in the aftermath of World War II, a time in which the political ideologies of totalitarianism and communism versus the freedom of democracy and capitalism were being delineated. Beveridge believed that the hallmarks of a free democratic society were a healthy voluntary sector and visible voluntary action.

Historian Geoffrey Finlayson's landmark study of the history of the voluntary sector and the state in Britain, written forty years after Beveridge's report, also profoundly influenced my thinking. Along with

Frank Prochaska who wrote the definitive book, *The Voluntary Impulse*, explaining the historical antecedents of philanthropy in Britain, Finlayson was one of the first historians to examine the relationship between the voluntary sector and governments. He pointed out the overemphasis of other historians in focusing on the role of the state in the twentieth century at the expense of either the voluntary, commercial or informal sectors.[10] Finlayson also used Beveridge's term 'a moving frontier' to describe the relationship between the voluntary sector and the state, and to explain how it shifted and changed over the course of the twentieth century. As will be shown in this book, this concept of a moving frontier is very useful in helping to explain the Australian context.

Richard Titmuss's, *The Gift Relationship*, ostensibly concerning voluntary blood donation, was a key polemic text about the role of volunteering and altruism in modern society. First published in 1971, the book argued that 'a competitive, materialistic, acquisitive society based on hierarchies of power and privilege ignores at its peril the life-giving impulse towards altruism which is needed' for societies to function properly.[11] Titmuss claimed that the desire to help others was a fundamental human trait and that 'if we accept that man has a social and biological need to help, then he should not be denied the chance to express this need by entering into a gift relationship'.[12] Others argued that volunteerism was a basic tenet of democracy, that it was integral to a fully functioning democratic society. As Brian Dixon, a former Victorian State Minister for Social Welfare stated in 1977, 'volunteerism is to democracy what blood circulation is to an organism'.[13]

Although the language has changed, I believe there are close connections between these earlier discussions on voluntary action and the voluntary principle, and what is now called civil society and social capital. From the 1990s, these concepts have been widely used to explore democratic constructs and social networks within local communities. Pierre Bourdieu and James Coleman were joined by Robert Putnam who discussed the decline of social capital and its effects on democratic traditions in his influential books *Making Democracy Work: Civic Traditions in Modern Italy* and *Bowling Alone*.[14] Anthony Giddens, whose work on the 'third way' influenced Tony Blair and New Labour in the early 1990s, provided a wonderful analogy comparing a well functioning democracy with a three-legged stool. The government, the economy and civil society all needed to be in balance. If one dominated over the other, unfortunate consequences followed, as in the former Soviet Union, where civil society was effectively killed off.[15] Even today the Russian government continues to undermine the role of fledgling non-government organisations as they and their volunteers are viewed as extremists and a threat to an 'orderly Russian society'.[16]

Here in Australia, Eva Cox was one of the first to discuss these concepts in her 1995 ABC Boyer Lecture series. Entitled 'A Truly Civil Society', Cox extended Putnam's analysis and gave it an Australian flavour. She argued that social capital referred to 'the processes between people which establish networks, norms, social trust' that were to 'facilitate co-ordination and co-operation for mutual benefit'. We could increase our social capital by 'working together voluntarily in egalitarian organisations to connect us with others'.[17] This began a whole new discussion in Australia in which the idea of social capital became very popular and, combined with notions of civil society, was taken up, and continues to be discussed and analysed at length by journalists, writers, politicians, policy makers, social commentators and academics.

As mentioned earlier, voluntary action, the moving frontier and volunteering remain largely invisible in the history of twentieth century Australia. In terms of social welfare, historians have, to a great extent, focused on nineteenth century philanthropy, and the emergence of state welfare in the twentieth century. Our preoccupation with the 'state' – the role of government – in the twentieth century has been at the expense of the smaller but integral component – voluntary action. In this book, therefore, I want to particularly focus on volunteering and how voluntary organisations developed, especially from 1945. I want to show the importance of volunteering in our history, and how it has helped to shape the economic, social, cultural and political frameworks of Australian society. At the same time, I want to identify and examine some key debates between government and the voluntary sector, and use a series of case studies of volunteer organisations as well as biographies of individual volunteers to chart the history of volunteering in Australia. In doing so, I hope to provide some explanation and rationale of its origin and place in our lives in the twenty-first century.

Types of volunteering

Volunteers do almost anything on the planet. They manage, administer, budget, plant, letterbox, fundraise, sell, send e-mails, monitor websites, type, file, collate, write reports, teach, nurse, drive, build. The range of volunteering opportunities is diverse and largely mirrors paid work in occupation and job description. Volunteering is also culturally based and differs according to place and context. For example, the Aboriginal and Torres Strait Islander concepts of volunteering are very different to, but no less important than, those of other Australians. The action of volunteering has a variety of names for different contexts. For example, lawyers do 'pro bono' work; political activists 'agitate' and 'lobby'; sports coaches and others 'help out', 'donate or give their time' – the language may vary but the action remains the same. It is volunteering by any other name.

There is as yet no universally based global definition of volunteering. In 2001, the United Nations stated that volunteering was not for financial gain, that it was undertaken without coercion, rather of one's own free will, and benefited society.[18] This qualification is important. As Eva Cox pointed out, there is a 'dark side' to volunteering, one of exclusion and potential damage, as organisations like the Ku Klux Klan and al-Qaeda attest.[19] Another problem with definitions of volunteering, outlined by Petriwisky and Warburton, is that some definitions exclude informal volunteering; that is, they do not acknowledge volunteers working outside a formal organisation. Citing the example of the grandparent who watches children in a park after school while their parents are at paid work, they argued that 'although this citizen *has* volunteered their time, energy and child-minding skills, they have not *volunteered*'.[20] While recognising the importance of this type of 'informal' volunteering, this book will be largely concerned with 'formal' volunteering undertaken within an organisation or group. Literally hundreds of thousands of voluntary organisations exist in Australia today reliant on volunteers, with about 30 000 that employ both paid and unpaid staff.[21]

Justin Davis Smith used a typology of volunteering that identified four broad areas of volunteering – philanthropy, mutual aid and self-help, campaigning and advocacy, and participation.[22] Much of this occurs through service-providing voluntary organisations in the social welfare, environmental or change-orientated areas, such as providing information, advice, support and assistance in nursing homes, respite care centres, work with refugees, animal refuges and the like. The premise here is that volunteers in the community identify a need or issue, come together and form an organisation to provide the structures, supports and answers to address that need, whatever it might be. This is not done for themselves necessarily but for others in the community (either local or global), those less fortunate or suffering in some way. The second area identified by Davis Smith concerns mutual aid and self-help, which is about people coming together around a specific need or interest for mutual gain. For example, volunteers who are involved in medical or social support groups, or community-based organisations concerning health, sport or recreation. AIDS-related organisations or Landcare volunteers spring to mind, and of course, trade unions are perhaps one of the largest, original self-help organisations. The third area is advocacy and pressure groups that involve volunteers attempting to achieve change in a particular area. This can extend from the local (such as mobilising to save a precious piece of bushland such as Kelly's Bush on the Parramatta River in Sydney in the 1970s or an endangered river such as the Franklin in Tasmania in the early 1980s) to the global, with organisations such as Greenpeace and Amnesty International. Lastly, there is participation, which is quite simply that – undertaking unpaid labour or volunteering because the job (albeit unpaid) is there and needs to be done. Volunteering for the 2000 Sydney Olympics is one such high profile example.

In the most recent Australian Bureau of Statistics report on volunteering, published in 2007, almost half of Australian volunteers were involved in fundraising of various kinds. Others prepared and served food, provided information, and carried out administrative work and management tasks. The largest numbers of volunteers were found in the welfare, community and health areas, with sport and recreation a close second. Volunteering was higher outside the capital cities, with Queensland and the ACT achieving the highest volunteer rate of 38 per cent. The largest cohort of volunteers was the thirty-five to forty-four years age group, indicating the influence of children in the decision of many Australians to volunteer their time. But when looking at the median weekly hours, those in the sixty-five to eighty years age group were doing proportionally more volunteering, averaging two hours per week. People born in Australia volunteered more than those born overseas, employed people volunteered more than unemployed people, and almost two-thirds of volunteers (or 62 per cent) worked for only one organisation. In terms of why people volunteered, the main reason given was to help others in the community, as well as personal satisfaction. [23]

This book covers a period of great social transformation, from the middle of the twentieth century onwards. With changing demographics, more women in the paid workforce and shifts to smaller families, volunteering provides many Australians with a sort of extended family. Volunteering offers social interaction, connection and a sense of belonging that are integral to our physical and mental wellbeing. Volunteering for an organisation can provide a 'family' style network that, while non-binding, can become our lifeline in a modern society that is increasingly unfriendly, unneighbourly and soulless. As a country of immigrants, volunteering in Australia also helps to provide a sense of belonging. Each wave of immigrants brought with them new perspectives on volunteering. They established a range of ethnocultural organisations to preserve their homeland culture, languages and customs. In time, these organisations have become part and parcel of our way of life.

Additionally our first peoples, the Aboriginals and Torres Strait Islanders, have complex systems of giving within their traditional social structures, and close-knit family obligations that have influenced the Australian way of volunteering. However, as outlined by Petriwisky and Warburton and others, Aboriginal Australians, who for cultural and kinship reasons embed informal volunteering within their cultural practices, are much less likely to be included in current volunteer research and statistics.[24] This is unlike other countries such as New Zealand where Maori cultural behaviour related to volunteering is more likely to be integrated within mainstream volunteering practices.[25]

The shifts and changes in the social and political landscape that over-saw the cultural dimensions and shaping of volunteering in Australia have developed over time. By examining our volunteering history we can better explain the phenomenon of volunteering generally, and provide tools to understand this important aspect of Australian life, both now and into the future. In order to do this, I have attempted to construct an analysis of what I call 'the Australian way of volunteering' and this discussion, along with a brief historical overview, forms the basis of the next chapter. Following on, there is a chapter on civilian volunteering in World War II, a high point in twentieth century volunteering in Australia, which forms the springboard for the story of post-war volunteering. The chapters are then largely chronologically based, using a range of voluntary organi-sations and volunteer case studies to explain the relationship between governments and volunteers, and to show the growth, continuity and complexity of volunteering in Australian history generally. However, I have not attempted to cover all areas of Australian volunteering – that would take multiple volumes.

Many of the case studies come from New South Wales but the identi-fied patterns can be applied elsewhere across the nation. I have also tried to be inclusive and cover a majority of areas where volunteering is integral but it is a huge task and unfortunately not all can be canvassed in the one book. So apologies in advance if your particular volunteering area is not mentioned. I hope that, through reading this book, you will be able to understand the bigger picture and see where your organisation and your volunteering fits into the broader story of Australian volunteering. As will become obvious as you read this book, the field is wide open and the canvas only lightly sketched. I implore other writers and researchers to pick up their pencils and fill in the gaps. This is just the beginning.

2 The Australian way of volunteering

When a man [woman] has a new enthusiasm he [she] buys a twopenny notebook, prints 'Minute Book' carefully on the first page, calls together some of his [her] friends under the name of a Committee – and behold a new voluntary society is launched.[1]

Anne Bourdillon

Historical origins

Australia's volunteer tradition can be traced back to our British origins. Volunteering was part and parcel of British political, cultural and philanthropic customs and institutions originating in the Tudor period, when the state first became interested in the relief of poverty, which up until then had been largely the work of religious orders.[2] Laid down by the 1601 Elizabethan statute or Poor Law, the modern framework of voluntary action revolved around the local parish, funded by local taxes and the *noblesse oblige* of leading families and local landowners. The colony of New South Wales was established by the British in 1788 as a government-run gaol. Convict transportation did not cease until 1840 in New South Wales and 1860 in the west. Despite difficult beginnings when the early convicts and their gaolers almost starved, the colony grew and eventually prospered, boosted by the arrival of immigrants from Britain seeking a new life in the resource rich colonies. It has been argued that these early convict beginnings contributed to the basis of an inherently Australian character: an aversion to authority and a peculiar irreverence and humour, largely attributable to the large numbers of Irish transported to Australia, as well as arriving as immigrants. As a transplanted culture, the Australian colonies inherited not only British forms of government, law, religion and political structures, but also modes of philanthropy and charity; however, because the first white settlement was originally a state-imposed and state-run gaol, governments provided much of the financial and economic direction. Colonial, state and later national governments played a leading role in the development of the fledgling economy and social infrastructure, including voluntary action and volunteering.

From its origins as a convict gaoler, the state either partnered private philanthropy and mutual aid to alleviate distress, or assumed direct responsibility itself. Lacking a mature development of church parishes, a long accepted method of welfare distribution in Britain or established wealth, governments were forced to take a more active role in a broad range of areas including the alleviation of poverty. Although Australians could and did make fortunes, the white population was largely made up of ex-convicts, assisted immigrants and those wanting to find a fortune rather than those already having one to dispense. The first private charity was established in New South Wales twenty-five years after the arrival of the First Fleet. Heavily subsidised by the government, under Governor Lachlan Macquarie, the New South Wales Society for Promoting Christian Knowledge and Benevolence (later known as the Benevolent Society) was formed in 1813. This followed earlier government initiatives such as the Female Orphan School established in 1800 by Governor King to provide a home for homeless colonial girls, a lunatic asylum at Castle Hill in 1811, and later the Native Institution or school for Indigenous children in 1814.[3]

Governors' wives, like Eliza Darling and Elizabeth Macquarie, and other leading men and women of the emerging colony such as Caroline Chisholm brought with them from Britain the views and aspirations of the moral reform movement and evangelicalism of the late eighteenth and early nineteenth centuries. This was combined with the rise of the social philosophies of the emerging middle classes in the Victorian era that incorporated concepts of work, respectability, self-help and the voluntary principle. Philanthropy was a very important part of this ideology, reaching its zenith in the latter part of the nineteenth century, a period of unprecedented charitable action and private philanthropic fervour. The nineteenth century stereotype of volunteers as 'Lady Bountifuls' – that is, middle and upper class women dispensing largesse and carrying out good deeds often for their own aggrandisement – has been hard to dislodge. Satirised by writers such as Charles Dickens with his *Bleak House* character Mrs Jellyby and her 'telescopic' philanthropy – her propensity to ignore her children and the poverty all around her in favour of assisting those abroad, especially in Africa – have only entrenched the stereotype.

The concepts of self-help and mutual aid extended to the working classes in the nineteenth century through the development of fraternal societies, trade unionism, friendly societies, adult education and co-operatives, all of which became key facets of working class culture and volunteerism. British migrants brought the concept of friendly societies to Australia, with the first society established in 1830. Within ten years of settlement, various types of self-help or trade societies appeared in each of the Australian colonies, and by the beginning of the twentieth century nearly half Australia's population was connected to a friendly society. This continued until the Depression of the 1930s, which had a disastrous impact on friendly societies Australia-wide.[4] During the second half of the nineteenth century a wide range of associational voluntary organisations, again following British models, were established and played an integral role in broad aspects of Australian life. In sport and leisure, education and politics, Australians came together in the cities and in the bush to form a range of voluntary organisations to enhance their lives and provide mutual support. From the 1880s onwards, volunteers in the emerging social reform movement and the nascent labour movement worked towards promoting social equality and reform in the areas of workplace reform, women's rights, health and education.

At the beginning of the twentieth century, Australia (and New Zealand) developed an international reputation as the social laboratory of the world. The concept of a living wage (embodied in the 1907 Harvester

Judgment), compulsory industrial arbitration, a system of government pensions and allowances, female suffrage and other social reforms, created the framework for an Australian society that upheld notions of fairness and equality. The framework was often termed 'colonial socialism'. The introduction of pensions and endowments and the development of the philosophy of government responsibility for the social welfare of its people, supposedly pushed philanthropy, self-help and the voluntary principle to one side. But if voluntary action was overshadowed by state bureaucracies and government expansion into social welfare in particular, it never disappeared.

This was particularly noticeable during World War I when there was a large increase in the level of voluntary activity. The period saw the establishment of a range of war related voluntary organisations or patriotic funds, including the Australian branch of the Red Cross Society. This organisation became closely involved in all areas of medical and hospital work, providing medical supplies and volunteer staff, and it dominated in the convalescence of returned soldiers. After the war, the Australian Red Cross reinvented itself and by 1939 had become one of the biggest, and arguably most important, social welfare voluntary organisations in Australia.

During the inter-war period, a large number of diverse voluntary organisations were established or consolidated by volunteers in response to the needs of specific groups in the Australian community. Self-help and social welfare organisations established between the wars include the Rotary clubs, based on the North American movement (1921); the Country Women's Association (1922); Legacy (1923); the New South Wales Society for Crippled Children (1928); the Flying Doctor Service (1928); and Apex (1930), to name but a few. After a Royal Commission into Social Insurance (1925–27) that identified numerous voluntary agencies operating across Australia providing both 'indoor' and 'outdoor' relief, there was a move to co-ordinate these services. This led to the formation of a series of peak bodies, such as the Central Council of Victorian Benevolent Societies in 1929, the Council of Social Service in New South Wales in 1937, and the Council of Charitable Relief Organisations in South Australia in 1939.

I argue in this book that World War II was a key period in the development of Australian volunteering in the twentieth century. British historian Arthur Marwick and others have argued that the war was a watershed.[5] In terms of Australia and the development of an Australian way of volunteering, the war was certainly a high point. The 'all in' spirit that characterised the war years provided volunteering with a springboard into the post-war period. The community action – the 'we can do it' – mentality left over from the war years provided an impetus for increased civic engagement in a wide range of areas, and resulted in a country buzzing with voluntary action. From 1945 onwards, Australia was not a suburban malaise and cultural wasteland as is often suggested but rather a society readjusting to peace and prosperity, a society of renewal, with the next wave of immigrants contributing towards a renaissance of civic engagement. As Anne Bourdillon described at the beginning of the chapter, voluntary action provided a vitality in the 1950s that has not been acknowledged or sufficiently understood.

The strengthening of Australian Commonwealth government powers during World War II, especially in taking control of income tax for example, combined with the extension of the 'welfare state', where governments increased their interest in and support of citizens, also affected the voluntary sector and volunteering. Although the state became the increasingly accepted, and expected, deliverer of many social welfare programs, the relationship between the state and voluntary sector continued to evolve. During the 1950s and 1960s, the delineation between government statutory bodies and voluntary organisations, often referred to as the mixed economy of welfare, became increasingly blurred. While some of Australia's most well established voluntary organisations have histories that pre-date World War II – such as the Australian Red Cross, P & C associations, Surf Lifesaving, Girl Guides and Rotary, to name a few – many others have their origins in the war or the post-war period. For example, the National Trust (1945), Meals on Wheels (Victoria, 1952; South Australia, 1953; New South Wales, 1957), Marriage Guidance Counselling (1960), Little Athletics (1964) and the Australian Conservation Foundation (1966).

If World War II precipitated such a shift in Australian volunteering, the second high point was the 1970s. Along with other broad social, political and economic changes, there was a marked increased in 'change-orien-tated' voluntary organisations, from heritage and environmental groups such as the Battlers for Kelly's Bush to those who identified a specific social welfare need such as women's refuges and community legal centres. Over 30 per cent of voluntary organisations today have their origins in the 1970s, a decade that witnessed a renewed development of Austral-ian civil society propelled by the community strategies of the Whitlam era and the Australian Assistance Plan.[6] Government funding increased and the voluntary sector exploded. This is evident in all areas, including arts and culture, where, for example, the initiation of the Community and Cultural Development Fund of the Australia Council (established in 1973) encouraged the growth of local arts organisations.

According to Cora Baldock's seminal study on social welfare volun-teering in Western Australia published in 1990, only 5 per cent of the organisations were in existence before 1945 and over 75 per cent of the organisations were formed after 1970. She also noted a particular growth of organisations between 1975 and 1980, and argued that this could have been due to 'economic recession and government's inability to resolve the problems' as well as an increase of 'anti-bureaucracy and anti-profes-sionalism' that lead to the formation of a range of self-help and social action organisations.[7] This book will explore what initiated this increase in volunteer activity and suggest explanations as to how it came about.

The second wave feminist movement of the 1960s and 1970s also had an impact on volunteering. Some in the movement believed that volun-teering was simply an extension of women's domestic labour, because most volunteering was undertaken by women, was unpaid and often involved the maternal qualities of nurturing and caring. Some feminists believed that women carrying out volunteer work provided another example of the subservience of women within a patriarchal society. It was argued that volunteering denied women access to the paid workforce. The stereotype of the volunteer as a middle aged, middle class woman undertaking 'good deeds' like Lady Bountiful was accepted as a valid summary. In 1973, the American National Organization for Women (NOW) passed a reso-lution claiming that the only acceptable form of volunteering was that which enhanced women's position in society.[8] It was argued that women's volunteering was 'a form of warehousing, of keeping women safely busy at harmless tasks that do not threaten their husbands or challenge the other power relationships'.[9] On the other hand, many women were involved in what became known as 'change-orientated' volunteering, such as the establishment of women's refuges, women's health centres and child-care centres. This kind of volunteering was deemed acceptable, but no wonder there was confusion. Hardwick and Graycar termed volunteering as 'chimerical, even contradictory'.[10] They even went so far as suggesting that the many self-help groups, rather than being organisations of motivated individuals effecting change and 'providing real alternatives', were simply eroding the existence of the welfare state itself.[11] Not surprisingly, few in Australia were interested in exploring or analysing volunteering.

But all that changed. From the 1980s and until the present, under the aegis of the 'new conservatism' that has dominated the thinking of both sides of politics, economic rationalism and neo-liberalism, the relationship between governments and the voluntary sector, and how people have volunteered has changed significantly. These decades witnessed a fundamental shift in the way the relationship worked, particularly in the area of social welfare with the huge increase in the contracting out of key areas by governments to both the voluntary and the private sectors, the privatisation of services, and development of a 'user pays' philosophy. From the 1990s, through policies such as the Liberal Coalition government's 'social coalition' and 'mutual obligation' the state began contracting out, actively reducing its role, for largely ideological and fiscal reasons, in favour of both the voluntary and business sectors. Flying the flag of free markets, these policies lent further force to changes sweeping through society, and drew responses from many writers and academics from both sides of the political spectrum. The arguments by academics, such as Mark Lyons, for the existence of the third sector soon led to governments discovering the largely 'silent' army of volunteers. We then saw the institution of Australian Bureau of Statistics reports on volunteer activity and other public policies aimed to assist and recognise them.

However, what makes Australia stand apart from other comparable countries is not so much the *type* of volunteering undertaken here but the long-term and close association with governments going back to our colonial origins. Some have even argued that the state was 'the creator of civil society' in Australia.[12] But this is not quite true, and again emphasises the role of government over everything else. Rather, I wish to argue that this close connection with government helped to create a unique, hybrid form of Australian volunteering, that I have called the 'Australian way of volunteering'.

The Australian way of volunteering

Australia shares her volunteering spirit with many other countries, and our patterns of volunteering are mirrored elsewhere, particularly in the former British colonies. For example, in Canada, volunteering and the evolution of volunteerism are considered to be part and parcel of Canadian identity. The United States of America appears to almost believe they invented philanthropy, which of course they did not – it was part of their original British heritage – but philanthropy is highly institutionalised and encouraged through public policy in that country.[13] Our cousins in New Zealand also have a significant volunteering tradition recently emphasised in Margaret Tennant's book *The Fabric of Welfare*.[14] But as highlighted in research from the Johns Hopkins Comparative Nonprofit Sector Project, volunteering has different traditions in Europe, where although there are high levels of volunteering, the state is heavily involved in the delivery of services.[15] This was brought home to me after speaking about volunteering at the inaugural Writing History Festival run by the New South Wales Writers' Centre in Sydney in September 2005. As she described the seemingly endless volunteering tasks at her local school, an audience member stated, 'I just don't get it. I don't understand volunteering – why do people do it – where did it come from?' Originating from Europe (Germany to be precise), this educated, intelligent, thirty-something woman really wanted an answer to something she clearly did not understand, something that, as far as she was concerned was not part of her cultural background.

So if volunteering differs in various cultural and national contexts, do Australians volunteer in a particular, indeed unique way? As a nation of volunteers, have we, over time, developed ideas and methods of volunteering that are culturally and nationally specific? Is there an Australian way of volunteering? These are questions I have become increasingly interested in and pose throughout this book as I chart the history of volunteering in Australia. When assessing and examining the history of Australian volunteering, are there peculiar national characteristics that are inherently Australian? Despite the fact that we have, for obvious historical reasons, been heavily influenced by British traditions, do we, in effect, have a form of volunteering that is a hybrid of British and other influences? If so, then what are its characteristics and how have they been manifested over time?

In explaining this idea of a hybrid 'Australian' way of volunteering, I refer to Paul Smyth and Bettina Cass's 1990s discussion of an 'Australian way' that built on Jill Roe's use of the term to describe the development of Australian public policy in her article 'The Australian Way' published in 1998.[16] Smyth and Cass were using it to find a way to describe the 'subtlety of the middle way which Australians have negotiated between the state and the market'.[17] I will use the term 'the Australian way of volunteering' in an effort to explore and explain the idea of a unique volunteering spirit in Australia that lies at the core of our Australian culture and identity.

There are three main factors that have influenced volunteering in Australian history and created a unique set of circumstances that form the basis of an Australian way of volunteering. The first concerns the historical antecedents of white Australia's foundations, which underpin the unique relationship between the state, the voluntary sector and volunteering. Beginning life as a British government penal colony, the Australian colonies always had a distinctive relationship with government. Unlike the American colonies settled by those escaping religious persecution, or Britain which had a complex and well developed form of philanthropy and charity from the eighteenth century, much of it church based, Australia was different from the start. From its earliest days, the state partnered volunteers and their philanthropic organisations and largely funded them in order to alleviate poverty and distress. The Australian colonies of the nineteenth century never had the sophisticated development of church parishes with their long-accepted methods of welfare distribution and no poor laws. Nor did they have the wealth of the aristocracy and their *noblesse oblige*. In their place was a combination of state relief and subsidised charity. This, in turn, affected the development of voluntary action, a distinction noted by visitors to Australia; for example, in 1948, William Beveridge, on his first and only trip to Australia (and New Zealand) observed subtle differences to Britain in terms of the development of one form of voluntary action – mutual aid and self-help. Trade unionism, Beveridge argued was more restricted in Australia, focusing only on 'industrial arbitration'. 'On the whole', he said, 'there appears to be more reliance on Public Action and less on Voluntary Action'.[18]

The relationship between governments and volunteering in Australia has been, therefore, rather one-sided and in many cases dominated by the state. Volunteering has been subjected to the fads and whims of government that has further affected the relationship over time. Most importantly, however, Australian governments have never developed a clear philosophy or understanding about volunteering and its place in Australian society. Because governments have generally held the upper hand especially with funding, they have used volunteering to suit their own political purposes. The shifting relationship since the 1980s and the 2000 Olympics are prime examples to be explored in this book. The result is a perception that volunteering in Australia is not particularly strong or important, nor indeed an integral part of our history.

But as will be argued, that is simply not the case. The relationship or 'moving frontier' between the state and the voluntary sector is far more complex than previously thought and in spite of the historical dominance of the state, volunteering did manage to co-exist and grow exponentially in Australia. The fact that volunteering lacks an historical past does not mean it did not exist. Indeed quite the reverse applies. Australians, however, developed a more diffused way of volunteering *because* of the apparent dominance of the state – with different nuances, subtleties and characteristics. And here is the paradox. Despite or perhaps because of this, Australians have always volunteered. The seeds of philanthropy and charity, of self-help and mutual aid arrived with British immigrants as part of their cultural baggage, and successive generations (including non-British migrants) moulded and adapted these concepts accordingly.

One does not have to look very far to find examples of Australians volunteering, and of the creation of a range of voluntary organisations by individuals and groups to address particular needs in the community. Australians are innovative and the Australian way of volunteering is associated with pioneering individuals and their ideas. Throughout this book there are many examples of how ordinary Australians identified a need in the community, and then threw their energies into addressing that need, either through developing a unique idea or adapting an overseas model, especially from Britain and America. Whether it was Annie Wyatt with the National Trust, Trevor Billingham with Little Athletics, Doris Taylor with Meals on Wheels, or Brian Kiernan with Clean Up Australia, the Australian way of volunteering is *both* derivative and original. But as we all know, it is easy to have an idea, putting it into practice is the hard bit. That is where working together, forging relationships within communities to make things happen, is also integral.

Much of the Australian way of volunteering developed through necessity. The geography of Australia (like Canada) and the ensuing development of a unique Australian character form the basis for the second major factor influencing the creation of the Australian way of volunteering. Australia is a large and physically unforgiving continent and part of our history concerns stories of adversity, of pioneers battling against the odds, of sparse populations in rural and regional Australia coming together and forging communities. It is in this context that volunteering comes to the fore with a unique form that was both understated and infused with the notion of 'just getting on with it'. It is connected to Russel Ward's concept of the 'Australian legend', which explored the creation of a 'national *mystique*' developed by convicts and later rural and bush workers, which reinforced concepts of mateship, egalitarianism and democratic equality.[19] Henry Lawson's poem, *Fire at Ross's Farm* also clearly articulated this theme, when feuding neighbours put their disagreements to one side to fight a bushfire together.

More recently, these ideas have come to the fore with the development of the Anzac tradition, of a fighting spirit forged on the Gallipoli peninsula in 1915. Helping each other out, providing mateship and assistance is part of the volunteer spirit. Once again, comparisons can be made to a country like America, where historian Merle Curti argued that the 'emphasis on voluntary initiative has helped give America her national character'.[20] But again, it is the *combination* of factors that provides the basis for the Australian way of volunteering. For example, a number of uniquely Australian 'types' of volunteering have been created over time such as surf lifesaving and rural bushfire volunteers. If there is an Australian 'type' – laconic, laid back, reticent, then these characteristics have helped to form and mould our Australian way of volunteering.

When faced with disasters both here and overseas, Australians are also surprisingly big-hearted in donating not only time but money. From the devastating 1939 bushfires in southern Australia and the 1956 floods in NSW, to the destruction of Darwin in 1974 and the Asian Tsunami of 2005, Australians have responded willingly and generously. It is sometimes asserted that Australians are mean spirited and stingy in terms of donations and philanthropic giving, in comparison with other developed countries. Not only do I largely disagree with this view but once again the perception may be linked to the relationship between volunteering and governments, an integral factor determining the nature of the Australian way of volunteering. Because the state has historically been so strong and continues to be significant, there is the perception (again largely erroneous in my view) that Australians wait for governments to act rather than taking the initiative themselves. This has further distorted our view of volunteering.

The third factor that contributes to the uniqueness of the Australian way of volunteering concerns Australian federalism. Although the influences of both British and American ideas in the development of volunteering in Australia are evident, our particular system of federalism serves both to assist and hinder the specific structures of Australian volunteerism. The abolition of transportation, the discovery of gold and large-scale immigration slowly changed the colonial social order, as did the creation of the Australian federation in January 1901. But the lack of a strong local government structure such as existed in Britain, and an increasingly dynamic federal government provided a unique environment for a hybrid Australian volunteerism to develop and indeed flourish alongside and interconnected with the state. An overarching state and federal system, and precious little government at the local level, meant that Australians often had to do it themselves or not at all.

The ongoing debates and problems between the states and Commonwealth, which seem as intractable today as ever, have affected the position and characteristics of the hybrid volunteering in Australia. There are, of course, other examples, namely Canada, which has a successful and reasonably similar federal system of government, British traditions, as well as a strong history of volunteering that they define as uniquely Canadian.[21] Obviously, these characteristics can be shared with other countries but it is the *combination* of factors and historical distinctions that has produced the unique Australian way of volunteering.

As will be seen throughout this book, the story of the development of volunteering in Australia varies according to time and place. In particular areas, especially social welfare, the Australian way of volunteering often relied on governments for financial assistance, not necessarily in the first stage (Australian volunteers have always been full of good ideas and initiatives) but in developing the schemes to the next level. Governments, too, have relied on volunteers to innovate and foster ideas, and then come in and absorbed the concept, with the volunteer influences lost over time. Significant government social policy has been developed around the innovations of the sector, without governments ever having to develop clear, coherent policies towards the sector and its volunteers. This does not apply to areas such as sport where governments are not interested in being too closely involved especially at a micro level due to the scale and cost. But one can clearly observe a pattern emerging over time that has both encouraged and stifled the Australian way of volunteering. Australian governments have also been very good at dominating the historical narrative, at the expense of volunteerism, unless of course it has suited the government's agenda.

What I hope to reveal in this book is the associational impulse at the heart of the Australian way of volunteering. To get things done with or without government help, to gather together and work with other people, the Australian way of volunteering has little to do with class, but is a broad cross-cultural phenomenon. Just as Vegemite, the Hills Hoist and the Akubra are uniquely Australian, so too are Landcare and Little Athletics. They are part and parcel of our identity and culture and are predicated on the Australian way of volunteering.

PART II
WAR AND PEACE
1939–1970

Nancy Nivison:
Commandant of Walcha VAD, World War II

My maternal grandmother, Nancy Nivison, was a volunteer all her life. Like her mother, Grace Munro whom we met at the beginning of this book, Nancy was typical of many women of her generation. She was never in the paid workforce, having both a father and then husband to support her. But that's not to say that she did not want paid employment. From a traditional rural background, Nancy was the daughter of a leading New England grazier and pastoralist, H.R. Munro of Bingara. Nancy developed a passion for nursing, but was unable to pursue it as a career. Strong parental disapproval over her desire to train at Prince Alfred Hospital put an end to any nursing plans in what was considered by her father to be an unnecessary and inappropriate career for her. Young ladies of Nancy's social standing in the 1920s rarely had 'careers' other than marrying and rearing children. With a gentle nature and eager to please, and certainly not wanting to challenge authority, Nancy obeyed her father. She married a young grazier from Walcha who had served in World War I, made a home including a beautiful garden, and raised three children through the late 1920s and 1930s.

But my grandmother was quietly determined and World War II created the perfect opportunity for her to revisit her passion for nursing. Nancy Nivison joined the Red Cross, did her training, and in June 1940, she formed the Walcha Voluntary Aid Detachment (VAD), No. 904, part of the Australian Red Cross. There had been VAs since World War I. They undertook a range of tasks and duties of a largely domestic nature: cooking, cleaning, providing endless cups of tea and sandwiches in hospitals and convalescent homes, as well as quasi-nursing. With basic first aid training, VAs were nursing orderlies doing the menial, but essential jobs. They scrubbed floors, swept and dusted wards, cleaned bathrooms, sorted linen, rolled bandages, emptied bedpans, and washed blood bottles. This volunteer work was 'hard yakka' and VAs had to be fit, energetic and committed.

With twenty-five members, and Nancy as the Commandant (in charge), the Walcha VAD spent the first few months of World War II obtaining the required first aid certificates, St John Ambulance certificates for air raid precautions, and Red Cross certificates for home nursing and invalid cooking. They then spent hours each week providing unpaid labour for the severely short staffed local hospital (many medical and nursing staff had enlisted), raising money to donate equipment to the Walcha, Tamworth and Armidale hospitals, making dressings, driving ambulances and keeping their skills up to speed with stretcher drill and first aid, doing canteen cooking and nursing for an emergency six-bed temporary hospital established in the Walcha Tennis Clubhouse, fully equipped and staffed by the local VAD. The VAs also helped the local Red Cross society with fundraising, assisted with a diphtheria immunisation campaign, and with the Women's Voluntary Service (WVS) sent parcels and special packages to local servicemen and women.

My grandmother proved to be a capable leader and the Walcha VAD twice won the coveted Wilfrid Johnson Cup, an annual competition in which all NSW VADs (over 3000 VAs) competed in 1943 and 1945. Perhaps this led to what was a highlight of Nancy's wartime volunteering career, when she was selected as second in command of a Red Cross relief unit to repatriate POWs on the British aircraft carrier HMS *Glory* from September to December 1945. At thirty-nine years of age, 'Nivie', as her Glory girl colleagues called her, was finally doing what she'd always wanted to do – real nursing with real patients. Following the HMS *Formidable* on a similar mission, HMS *Glory* left Sydney on 26 September with a medical contingent including British nurses and doctors and ten Australian Red Cross VAs, decked out in their uniform that included blue dungarees – the ones I found forty years later in the barn. All the aeroplanes were taken out and the huge hangar was made into a makeshift floating hospital. Picking up over 1300 British and Canadian ex-POWs in Manila, the *Glory* sailed to Vancouver, Canada. Most of the men were in reasonable health but others needed specific care. About 150 patients were divided into two wards. They were suffering from malnutrition, malaria, tuberculosis, tropical ulcers and fevers, dysentery and typhoid. A number were also suffering psychological illnesses attributed to their years of incarceration as POWs.[1]

The work was exhausting, with long hours in the sweltering, sardine-like conditions of the steel hangar. The VAs had little training in the nursing of tropical diseases, nor did they have much experience with psychotic or disturbed patients. Their days were spent sponging, taking temperatures, putting lotion on prickly heat rashes, lancing boils, and serving meals, cold drinks and cups of tea. After Canada, the *Glory* returned to Hong Kong, then to Manila, Balikpapen and Tarakan in Borneo where members of Australia's 9th Division were brought home to a tumultuous welcome in Sydney. Nancy returned home for the first 'peaceful' Christmas in six years. She took off her blue VA uniform, and packed away the dungarees in a trunk. The Walcha VAD was disbanded shortly afterwards. Nivie's wartime volunteering was over but she brought her new skills back to Walcha, and as we'll see in chapter 4, my grandmother continued to devote her energies to the local community in a range of areas.

3 Volunteering for victory

*'Unselfish voluntary service' was the way for Australian women to
'do our share'. Through volunteer war work, Australian women
could 'play our part. Now is the time'.*[1]

Ivy Brooks

When we think of Australian history and World War II, many lasting
images and events spring to mind. We remember the heroism of our
soldiers at Tobruk in the Middle East and on the Kokoda Track in New
Guinea, the appalling treatment of our prisoners of war (POWs) in Changi
and on the Burma Railway, Japanese submarines in Sydney Harbour, the
'all in!' effort on the home front and the new roles women played, the
arrival of the American troops – 'overpaid, oversexed and over here' – and
the destruction created by the atomic bombs dropped on the Japanese
cities of Hiroshima and Nagasaki that ended the war. As a nation we have
embraced our war history, which includes the enduring Anzac legend and
our quasi-national day of 25 April reminds us of our military past and
traditions, and the sacrifices made by all Australians in war.

A less well known story from World War II but no less important
was wartime civilian volunteering. Hundreds of thousands of Australian
volunteers mobilised for the war effort on the home front during the

war. It was a high point of volunteering in the twentieth century and contributed towards the development and extension of the Australian way of volunteering. This chapter will provide an overview of wartime volunteering and argue that this experience propelled the development of Australian volunteering into the post-war period. The focus will be on key wartime organisations and their volunteers such as the Australian Red Cross, as well as the importance of volunteering to the position of women in Australian society.

When war broke out on 3 September 1939, it was just over twenty years since the end of the 'Great War'. Many of the volunteering practices and patterns of World War II had their genesis in the experiences of that earlier war, and most importantly many of the wartime volunteer traditions were part of living memory. Key volunteer workers were still alive, and voluntary organisations born out of that earlier war, such as the Australian Red Cross founded in August 1914, were operating successfully across Australia. It was this combination of memory and experience that was used to re-group and re-invigorate the volunteers when it became obvious that war, once again, was inevitable.

On the outbreak of war, neither volunteers nor other Australians greeted the news of war with great enthusiasm. The memory of war, the carnage and destruction, lingered on. Few families had escaped unscathed. Then had come the Great Depression, the worst economic depression in history, of which some were still feeling the effects, with unemployment hovering between 9 and 12 per cent in 1939.[2] Structured and unstructured community-based efforts were therefore refined during the 1920s and 1930s. Australian volunteers were adept at rallying round sick neighbours, organising money and food collections, visiting and helping the needy and less fortunate in local communities. Crisis management and methods of dealing with tragedy and sudden emergencies were commonplace in mining communities where tragedies often struck; rural communities where floods, drought and bushfires were constant threats; and in urban communities, where struggle was a constant part of everyday life.

The beginning of 1939 saw the worst summer bushfires in living memory. Over seventy people died; towns, livestock and property were destroyed and over 3.3 million acres (1 336 500 ha) were burnt across southern Australia. Australians responded as they had always done in a national emergency. Volunteers and their organisations such as the Australian Red Cross, the CWA and the Housewives' Association, co-ordinated donations and goods and offered help, and relief funds were established by governments to assist those affected by the fires.[3]

Types of wartime volunteering

During World War II, the diversity of volunteering was limited only by people's imagination. Volunteering involved door-knocking for contribu-tions, sorting donations and goods, packing parcels for the troops, learn-ing first aid or air raid precautions, carrying out secretarial duties at night and on weekends for statutory authorities or voluntary organisations, cooking and waitressing at the Anzac Buffet in Hyde Park or the Cheer-Up Hut in Adelaide, or anywhere the troops assembled. Volunteers under-took quasi-nursing in hospitals, collected bedpans, washed blood bottles and scrubbed down wards. Wartime volunteering meant participating on committees or deducting a portion of one's salary to place in a work-based war fund, or organising fundraising events such as concerts, fetes and street stalls. Children collected salvage, bought stamps, sold raffle tickets and performed in concerts. Generally, people who volunteered during the war were men unable to enlist, either because they were too old or medi-cally unfit; young, single, employed women who, until the formation of the women's auxiliary services were confined to the home front; older women, most of them married and at home with family responsibilities; and children. Women's volunteering was generally connected to their home duties and undertaken within their local communities. The range of wartime volunteering, largely dependent on gender, age and location, was extensive and breathtaking in its diversity.

There was considerable pressure on Australians to 'give' of themselves, and to 'give' their money to war-related causes. The idea of active citizen-ship involved patriotism and a sense of duty to one's family, the local community and the nation. The analogy of 'giving 'til it hurts' was used frequently during the war as a means of sharing the experiences of those at the front. I have written about this in detail elsewhere, most notably in my book *All Work No Pay. Australian Civilians in War*, which looked at war through the lens of the civilian volunteer.[4]

There are many examples of wartime volunteering. Ruth Playford Smith, a young energetic woman from South Australia, was typical of her generation. 'We all did voluntary work of some kind' she later remarked.[5] Watching all her male friends enlist, Ruth was 'manpowered' with a full-time paid job in a reserved occupation and was frustrated at not being able to actively participate, as she saw it, in the war. So she did the next best thing – she became a Red Cross Voluntary Aid (VA), and volunteered on the weekends at the local hospital. During the week, Ruth undertook volunteer work at the Cheer Up Hut Canteen in central Adelaide. The Cheer Ups were a South Australian institution, formed during World War I, providing accommodation, refreshments and entertainment for the troops.

Others were like fellow South Australian Joy Noble, who as a teen-age girl spent 'Sunday afternoons holed up by myself in a hut erected in the sandhills outside Port Augusta' plane spotting for the Volunteer Air Observer Corps (VAOC). Thelma Prior's volunteer experiences were common. She worked at the Holeproof hosiery factory in Melbourne, and in her lunch hour wrote letters and sent food parcels to the troops. Women already in paid employment like Thelma squeezed their volunteering in between meal breaks, in the evening and on weekends. This volunteer work was either related to their paid employment (such as typing) or else was domestically orientated, such as mending, cooking, cleaning and waiting on tables. Conversely, women not in paid employment – the vast majority of women – often had more time to devote to wartime volunteering. They made camouflage nets or picked up knitting needles and once more began to knit khaki socks for the troops. 'We did a lot of knitting for the Red Cross', said Shirley whose husband was in the Navy. 'I'd often put the children to bed and sit by the fire knitting'.[6] People knitted everywhere: at home, in clusters in church halls, on trams, trains and buses, in schoolrooms and in business offices. Knitting became the symbol for wartime volunteering.

Corporate volunteering was also widely practiced during World War II, where businesses encouraged their employees to undertake wartime volunteering. It was very common for employers to donate the services of their staff towards specific wartime activities, especially for government or large voluntary organisations. For example, a number of Sydney banks, the Public Trustee Office and State Treasury received an urgent call in mid-1941 from an officer of the Eastern Command (New South Wales) who needed additional staff to compile statistical information for Army Headquarters. The job was finished ahead of schedule mainly by trained banking staff working in a volunteer capacity. The women worked in an unpaid capacity one night a week for two and a half hours. The usual hours for night typists were from 7 to 9.30 pm, with two shillings and sixpence allocated for tea money.

While most wartime volunteering was undertaken by women, men were also involved. Many veterans of World War I joined the Volunteer Defence Corps (VDC) that by 1943 had 100 000 members. Specifically established for civil defence, the VDC also guarded aerodromes, undertook coastguard watching and air raid precautions. Roy McKerihan, the President of the Rural Bank of New South Wales (later called the State Bank) and a senior public servant, was the honorary Federal Administrator for the Australian Comforts Fund (ACF), one of the large patriotic funds of World War II. Called 'the banker with the human touch', McKerihan was a public-spirited man and already involved in many philanthropic organisations. During the war, the ACF executive committee held its Sydney meetings in the board room of the Rural Bank headquarters in Martin Place.[7] More importantly, the ACF had the use of numerous bank clerical and administrative staff seconded to the patriotic fund, in both paid and volunteer capacities.

Children, including boys, were also taught to knit socks for soldiers. But their recollections of wartime fundraising and volunteering are more associated with fun and games. If camouflage net making or knitting were not terribly exciting and required sitting for long periods in stuffy halls and classrooms, then digging trenches in the school yard or competing with other local kids to see who could collect the most scrap metal and salvage in the neighbourhood was much more popular. Girls joined the Junior Red Cross and played doctors and nurses. In their crisp white uniforms, they learnt first aid, trying to see who could most successfully bandage an arm or leg. My mother, Jillian Oppenheimer, who was nine years old on the outbreak of war, enjoyed the competition of penny trails, which involved soliciting money from passers-by to see who could get the longest trail, make the most money and therefore win. Penny trails snaked up and down the footpaths of suburbs and towns across Australia. This type of volunteering not only helped to pass the time for children while waiting for their mothers to finish up their roster on the weekly cake stall (for the WVS or Red Cross or some other wartime fundraising), but it also imbued children of that generation with a sense of community and the volunteer spirit. Today these children are our most senior volunteers, an invaluable cohort who, per head of population, do more volunteering than any other age group.

During the war, there were two major ways of volunteering, either by participating or by donating. I have estimated that over the course of the war, over £28 million was raised by volunteers for the war effort, which is about $1.6 billion in today's terms. This is an extraordinary amount of money, indicating a society not only committed to the war but also used to the regimen of volunteering and giving. Donations of money and goods were as broad ranging and eclectic as they were practical and mundane. For example, £100 was donated by the New South Wales Womens' Cricket Association. The money was initially raised for an international tour cancelled due to the war. Boys from the Boorambil State School in rural New South Wales gave up 4 shillings and sixpence they had saved for a cricket bat, and a Randwick race meeting collected £28000 from one event, with the £1000 profits from one greyhound evening similarly donated. Italian fishermen each donated a day's trawler catch to the Greek Patriotic Fund, and fruit and vegetable vendors formed a fund for dependents of employees enlisting in the services. I am not quite sure what happened to Captain Cox's yacht *Sea Rover*, donated to the war effort, nor the offer of pedigree dogs donated by a lonely widow.[8]

Patriotic funds

The second way to become involved in wartime volunteering was to join a patriotic fund. During World War II, volunteers across Australia established over 8000 wartime voluntary organisations, called patriotic funds. Almost every town or local council had a patriotic fund of some description, as did most large private businesses, factories and clubs. These wartime organisations concentrated on providing a range of services including recreational activities, accommodation and food for servicemen and women, as well as helping out soldiers' dependents and victims of war overseas. Some voluntary organisations, such as the Australian Red Cross, YMCA and Salvation Army were already well established within the community, while others were created for the duration of the war. These included the Australian Comforts Fund, and a range of other smaller comforts funds, some directly linked to individual army units.

Some of the smaller service-orientated volunteer organisations disappeared without trace at the end of the war. For example, Mrs Lilian Savige, the wife of the commander of the 17th Brigade, 6th Division, established the 17th Brigade Head Quarters Fund on 24 November 1939, run out of her own home in Auburn, a western suburb of Sydney. Supported by other wives and mothers, and properly constituted with minute books and its own letterhead, the fund raised money, made a range of foodstuffs and clothing, and sent regular parcels to its boys, who saw action in Libya, Tobruk and the disastrous Greek campaign early in the war. Others were like the Women's All Services Canteen that operated in Central Railway Station, Sydney, offering free meals, drinks, first aid and a resting place for the thousands of servicemen and women who passed through the busiest railway station in the country. Managed by a volunteer committee, over 2000 women worked at the canteen during the war. Each volunteer worked a six-hour weekly shift, as well as raising money for the canteen.

Another type of small patriotic fund established by volunteers during the war was the community-based fund. The Wallacia Comforts Club, for example, was formed on 5 March 1941 by a group of citizens meeting at the Wallacia Hotel (near Penrith, west of Sydney). Forty-eight men and women from the area had enlisted, so the fund raised money and sent food parcels to them throughout the war. Along with an assortment of foodstuffs and clothing, the main treat was a hardy fruitcake, resistant to spoiling in the tropical climate of New Guinea or the desert heat of the Middle East. To make the task easier, a bricklayer's cement mixer was acquired to assist in mixing the ingredients for the forty-eight cakes, which were then transported to the local bakery in an old pram, also donated to the group. The cakes were baked overnight in ovens provided free of charge by the local baker. This ritual went on throughout the war. When the war ended and the troops came home, the comforts fund wound up, but the volunteers, who by this stage were well acquainted with each other and enjoyed the work and companionship created through the organisation, decided to continue. They became a 'Carry On' club and turned their attentions to local community causes. The war provided the impetus for many volunteers to do likewise.

Another feature of wartime volunteering in Australia was the creation of industry- and business-based patriotic funds. Whether large or small, companies such as the hosiery firm Kayser, the cinema chain Greater Union, department stores such as David Jones and Hordern Brothers, the pharmaceutical company Parke Davis, and Kodak, established funds to support employees who enlisted. Employees held dances, card evenings, picture and theatre outings to raise money, all carried out and organised through small volunteer based committees. Sometimes weekly or fortnightly deductions were authorised from employees' salaries. For example, at the Bushells factory, the Bushells Employees' War Fund raised funds by a voluntary weekly contribution of threepence by female members and juniors under twenty-one, and sixpence by male members of the fund. These amounts reflect the pay structures and the inequalities that existed between male and female rates of pay. The minimum weekly male wage in the 'food, drinks and tobacco' manufacturing industry was about £5 in 1940 with the female wage half that amount. The monies went towards assisting dependents of enlisted employees during the war as well as those killed on active service.[9]

One of the other characteristics of volunteering in World War II was the creation of a number of patriotic funds to assist allied civilians caught up in the war. Often organised by consul-generals or commissioners of the countries concerned, Australians supported organisations such as the Melbourne-based Maltese Patriotic Fund established to assist war victims from the siege of Malta. The Greek War Relief Fund similarly raised money to offer support to civilians caught up in the German invasion in 1941. But by far the largest and most popular, yet controversial, fund was the Russian Relief Fund, formed after the German invasion of the Soviet Union in mid-1941. After this unexpected event, Australia gained an ally, although there were no formal diplomatic connections between Australia and the USSR, with British diplomatic representatives undertaking such duties. The Australian Communist Party was banned by the Menzies government in June 1940, and the ban was not lifted until December 1942. However, there were many well-connected Australians sympathetic to the plight of our new allies, including the well-known women's advocate Mrs Jessie Street. So when she applied for registration on behalf of the Russian Medical Aid Committee, which would administer the Russian Relief Fund (commonly known today as the Sheepskins for Russia campaign), Jessie and her colleagues faced difficulties.

Anyone sympathising with communism was *persona non grata*, even after the German invasion. The fund became a political hot potato at both state and federal government level. There were many other 'country of origin' allied patriotic funds as mentioned above, which had no difficulty securing registration. The federal government had even given substantial grants of money and aid to Poland, Finland and Greece totalling over £100 000, but no such generosity was forthcoming to the Russian Medical Aid Committee. Interim Prime Minister Arthur Fadden (between Menzies and Curtin) felt that it was premature for Australians to raise funds for Russia, that it was wasteful, and that the needs of the Soviet people should be ascertained before goods were hurriedly despatched to the Soviet Union. This cautious attitude to patriotic fundraising was never applied to the French, Maltese or Greek funds.

Despite the political problems with which Jessie Street and her colleagues were all too familiar, the Russian fund was registered and the Sheepskins for Russia campaign was very successful. Over £184 500 was raised during four years – more than any other 'foreign fund'. Not only does this say something about the sympathy of many Australians towards the catastrophic situation in the USSR, it is testament to the organising ability of the members of the Communist Party, the tenacity and commitment of people like Jessie Street who worked tirelessly in an unpaid capacity to raise money for the fund, and the Australian way of volunteering.

Jessie travelled around Australia promoting the campaign, raising funds, selecting skins and arranging shipping to Soviet ports. She had a good knowledge of Soviet Russia as she had visited there in the late 1930s. This was a cause where she could display her patriotism to the hilt – doing something that she was well suited to. It is also a good example of the Australian way of volunteering, where despite government obfuscation, Australians continued in their own independent fashion to volunteer for a cause they believed in.

The Australian Red Cross and Australian Comforts Fund

The vast bulk of volunteers in World War II worked for the two largest wartime organisations, the Australian Red Cross and the Australian Comforts Fund (ACF). In terms of money raised, overall community support and numbers of active volunteers, these two organisations were the doyens of the Australian civilian volunteer war movement. Both were originally formed in response to World War I, and operated within a federated structure. The ACF, along with the Salvation Army, YMCA (and after 1942, the YWCA) were officially recognised by the Australian government to look after the fit and well servicemen and women. The ACF was made up of individual state-based patriotic funds that had different names and historical origins. For example, in Queensland the CWA was prominent within the Queensland Division of the ACF, perhaps more so than elsewhere; whereas in New South Wales it was the Lord Mayor's Patriotic Fund run out of Sydney Town Hall and local councils that ran the committees.

The aim of the ACF was to provide 'comfort' items not supplied by the services. Today we see these many of these goods as essentials, and indeed when the American troops arrived in Australia in 1942, it was discovered that most of these items were standard issue for their troops. So, for example, the ACF provided singlets, socks, pyjamas, cigarettes, razor blades, soap, toothbrush, toothpaste, stationery, pencils and postcards. They also provided recreational facilities, rest rooms, cheap accommodation, meals, sporting equipment such as footballs, cricket bats, pads and stumps, nets, and gramophones and records. The figures of goods supplied, all funded and parcelled by thousands of volunteers, are quite remarkable. For example, on twenty separate days between 1 September and 30 October 1940, the 16th and 17th brigades in the Middle East were issued with sixty-eight cartons of comforts sent from New South Wales. This included underpants, handkerchiefs, singlets, sweets, matches, reading material and:

> 10,023 cigarette packets, 5,114 tins and 33 cases fruit, 3,934 tins and 3 cases delicacies, 1,134 lbs and 6 cases cake, 672 lbs golden syrup, 288 tins milk, 17,624 lbs tobacco, 10,000 packets cigarette papers, 1,200 tins vegetables, 35,000 razor blades.[10]

Servicewomen were also provided with the bare essentials by the services. So the ACF provided a kit for servicewomen including sanitary pads, talcum powder, skin tonic and vanishing cream. In addition, the ACF sent regular parcels and Christmas hampers (including a plum pudding, cake, small tin of fruit and Nestlé's cream) to the troops. These goods were generally supplied to each Army unit and then distributed by a number of ACF commissioners. At least fifty-one men served as ACF commissioners during the war. They were all volunteers, working in an honorary capacity, and were generally retired businessmen of independent means over the age of forty. The commissioners accompanied the Australian troops. The first ACF commissioner to sail with the 2nd AIF in January 1940 was Raymond Goward, described by General Blamey as 'a monument to unremitting energy even temperament and cheerful disposition'.[11]

Wherever the Australians troops were based during the war, the ACF commissioners (and the Salvation Army and YMCA) were there too. So, for example, ACF commissioners Charles Rees and HC Reilly, along with two YMCA representatives, were captured and interned by the Japanese after the fall of Singapore. There are photographs taken on the Kokoda Track with small makeshift rest stations where the exhausted, wet and muddy soldiers were provided with a hot drink and biscuit. The work in New Guinea was most daunting. The difficult terrain and often appalling conditions made the commissioners' work extremely challenging. Always in the background, toiling away in a quiet, unassuming way, these volunteer organisations were largely forgotten in the official war histories.

No less challenging was the work of the Australian Red Cross, the largest patriotic fund in World War II both in the scale and size of its operations and the support it received from the Australian people. As the ACF and others looked after fit and well soldiers, the Red Cross cared for the sick, wounded and maimed and their dependents. From a population of about 7 million, nearly half a million people, mainly women, were members of the Red Cross during the war years, which probably makes it the largest volunteer organisation in Australian history. A grassroots, community-based organisation, Australian Red Cross support was in its network of branches that crisscrossed the country. During the war, the Red Cross was supported most vigorously by women living in rural and regional Australia, where volunteering crossed class boundaries. Most towns, be they large or small, either already had a Red Cross branch or rapidly created one (sometimes dormant since the Great War twenty years earlier). Take New South Wales as an example. In 1941, the membership of the Red Cross, excluding the Junior Red Cross, was almost 56 500, with almost two-thirds coming from country branches. The country branches ranged from Tamworth with a membership of 700 to the village of Woolbrook, 50 kilometres north on the New England tablelands, with thirty-five members. The mining towns of Cessnock and Lithgow also enjoyed solid memberships of 373 and 630 respectively from total populations of 13 900 and 21 930.

Volunteers attracted to the Red Cross were generally married women, undertaking home duties, with a husband, children and possibly parents to care for. They were not usually in paid employment, having given up paid work on marriage, the standard social and legal requirement of the day (for example, women had to resign from teaching on marriage). Although the standard profile of a Red Cross leader was that of a woman whose husband or father was a white-collar worker, professional or farmer, it was not always the case. For example, in Coburg, a largely industrial, working class Labor voting suburb of Melbourne, the founder of the Red Cross branch, Mrs Morgan, whose formal education finished in grade eight, was a mother and wife of a printer.

The extraordinarily high Red Cross membership was assisted by national recruitment drives run annually from 1940 and modelled on the American Red Cross. Focusing on the grassroots and targeting local communities, the Annual Red Cross Roll Calls were spectacularly successful, with membership growing from 260 000 in 1941 to 450 000 in 1944. Volunteers flocked to join branches and then began fundraising, hospital visiting, knitting and sewing, and providing comforts for the servicemen and women who were sick and/or wounded. Each state division had particular arrangements with other voluntary organisations. In South Australia, for example, the Red Cross, assisted by the Girl Guides, another key women's volunteer organisation, was in charge of collecting, sorting and selling waste material that, by October 1941, had netted over £8000.[12]

POWs and wartime volunteering

One of the key areas of involvement for the Red Cross and its volunteers was with the Prisoners of War (POWs). As well as hundreds of civilians, over 21 000 Australian troops became POWs of the Japanese and close to 8000 were captured by the Germans and Italians. For the families of those interned by the Japanese, there was little communication for most of the war. This ghastly situation of not knowing whether someone was alive or dead was extremely stressful for relatives in Australia. Many lived with this uncertainty for years, and the Red Cross often became the only avenue of hope for the relatives. As in the earlier war, the Red Cross established Bureaux for Wounded, Missing and Prisoners of War in January 1940. Staffed largely by volunteers, many of them lawyers and wives and widows of POWs, the state bureaux concentrated on dispatching parcels and mail, informing next-of-kin how to contact POWs or internees, and generally managed to keep relatives informed. Because of the unco-operative nature of the Japanese officials, there was little information received about their POWs throughout the war. Very few letters and messages were received, and no agreement regarding parcels to internees was ever secured with the Japanese.

Nevertheless, the Red Cross was the main conduit to the POWs and the Australian public responded very positively to their plight. The POW 'will always be our number one priority', championed the Red Cross in

April 1942. As a result, the fundraising efforts of the volunteers were exceptional. From July 1942, the 'Adopt a Prisoner Scheme' was introduced as well as an idea from New South Wales, where streets adopted a POW. The aim was to raise £1 a week from residents of the street and they received a special street sign to that effect. From 1941 to 1945, the POW Fund raised almost £4.5 million, an extraordinary amount.

The trade union movement, itself founded on volunteer principles of self-help and mutual aid in the latter part of the nineteenth century, formed an unusual alliance with the Red Cross; such were the close links between the Red Cross, the fighting forces and POWs, many of whom were trade unionists. For example, in November 1941, the New South Wales Labor Council adopted the Workers Penny-a-Week Red Cross Appeal. The scheme involved volunteer collectors from various workplaces and factories distributing Red Cross 'passbooks' to workers. Each week, or as often as the worker could afford it, a one penny seal was purchased and pasted into the book. Once twelve seals were in the passbook, the worker was entitled to Red Cross membership. Trade unions also sanctioned regular payroll deductions that at one point were raising over £3000 per month for the Red Cross in New South Wales alone.

Popular Girl Contests, a well-known way of fundraising not so fashionable these days, were organised by various unions in support of the Red Cross. In 1945 with the slogan 'Part of our heart is locked up in Singapore', the New South Wales Trade Unions held its Red Cross Popular Girl Contest. The idea was that different unions nominate a suitable candidate who would then raise money from the trade union community. More than one million votes were polled, for the twenty-one candidates who included Miss Melba Milton from the Hotel and Club Union, Miss Val Kelly from the Boot Union, and Miss Lily Chee Quee from the Australasian Meat Industry Employees' Union. Miss Chee Quee represented 'the justice and freedom for the Chinese' in their fight against 'Japanese militarism'.[13] The union movement also had Red Cross Industrial Organisers. One of the most active in New South Wales was retired federal parliamentarian William George Mahony, who regularly broadcast on Labor radio station 2KY in support of the Red Cross. Mahony also organised the first ever visit of a governor-general's wife (Lady Gowrie) to the Trades Hall in

April 1943. As Patron of the Red Cross, Lady Gowrie wanted to personally thank all the trade unionists for their support of the organisation.

Extending the Australian way of volunteering

The volunteer efforts of the Australian people during World War II were unparalleled, and the wartime voluntary sector became big business. By looking at the number of people directly involved, the broad-based support accorded the large patriotic organisations, especially in terms of monies raised and the sheer scale of the voluntary endeavour, was unprecedented. In these ways alone the Australian way of volunteering was fundamentally changed by the experiences of war.

As I have argued elsewhere, there is little doubt, too, that the Australian government recognised the value of the voluntary effort and used it for its own ends. As one politician Mr Nimmo, the member for Oxley in the Queensland Legislative Assembly, said:

> Patriotic funds have a wonderful effect upon the country
> because they are safety valves ... they give the people an
> opportunity to show that their hearts are with the men who
> are fighting the battle for us. The great thing is to keep up the
> morale of the people, for after all that is what wins wars.[14]

The relationship between Australian governments and the voluntary sector shifted during the war as the state gradually asserted greater control through regulation and legislation. As the war progressed, there was considerable pressure for the patriotic funds to perform generously yet be prudent and accountable with monies donated by the Australian public. So governments at a state level introduced legislation to control the funds, but at the same time ensured that the voluntary spirit engendered by the war was not put at risk.

The war had a defining role in developing a new sense of civic responsibility in Australian communities. Australians in the past came together to fight natural disasters such as drought and floods. They were used to helping each other out, providing mateship and assistance when needed. This was all part of the Australian way of volunteering. The effects of the war on the British people through the Battle of Britain in the early years affected Australians, and they responded by volunteering their services for war-related efforts in their local communities. Once the Pacific war began in December 1941, the fall of Singapore and Hong Kong, and the threat of Japanese invasion heralded dark days of possible defeat. However, Australians showed that they could work together towards a common goal. The 'all in' spirit might have included manpowering, rationing and certain restrictions on civil liberties, but it also provided the opportunity for Australians to actively contribute, to volunteer, and 'dig deep'. Many discovered what it meant to become involved in community action, and how empowering that was. This was particularly evident for women, many of whom joined organisations and became involved in activities such as chairing meetings, running small committees and driving cars, skills they never contemplated before the war. The war strengthened community spirit and encouraged people, especially women, to become involved through volunteering. We have heard many times of the opportunities brought by war with the entry of women into paid employment, but rarely have we realised how many opportunities were created through access to wartime volunteer work.

Even before the war was over, community leaders, bureaucrats, and policy makers were looking to the future and the role that volunteering and voluntary action could play as part of post-war reconstruction. This was the beginning of a new phase in the development of an Australian way of volunteering

4 Citizenship awakening

There has been a great expansion of group activity during the war
for patriotic and social purposes, and there is widespread demand
for continuance of this activity into the peace.[1]

Lloyd Ross

It was impossible to maintain the heightened sense of purpose and focus created by the war. After six long years, people were tired of rationing, making do, being frugal, always fearing the worst; especially those who had husbands, brothers and loved ones at war. They wanted to move on with their lives. With peace came a sense of optimism for the future now that the years of world wars and economic depression were finally over. It would be a new beginning. Australians continued with their volunteering but often directed their energies into new areas. The post-war 'surge in associational activity' seen after World War I was again in evidence after World War II.[2]

For many, like my grandmother Nancy Nivison, the experience of wartime volunteering created new possibilities. All the skills Nancy learnt during the war through her volunteering, especially in committee work and leadership, provided a perfect springboard for her, and she entered the post-war period with new vigour and energy. Still in her early forties,

Nancy initiated or became involved in a wide range of activities related to her local community. Despite the disbanding of the Walcha VA detachment in 1946, local women, including Nancy, continued their activities at the hospital, distributing books and newspapers, arranging flowers, and generally providing a pool of unpaid labour as required. As a result of her wartime achievements, Nancy was offered a position on the Walcha Hospital Board, on which she served for many years, again in an unpaid capacity. In May 1947, along with the local policeman, Sergeant Craig and others, Nancy established the advisory committee of the Walcha Youth Club. Associated with the National Fitness Council, the club wanted to provide entertainment and activities for the children and adolescents of the town and district. She was later involved in raising funds for a swimming pool and in establishing the local historical society.

However, in addressing her lifelong passion for gardens, flowers and nature, most of Nancy's volunteering energy was directed in developing the Horticultural Society. Established in 1948, with around fifty members, Nancy was the inaugural secretary, from 1948 to 1950 and then the president of the Society from 1950 to her death in 1973. The aims of the Horticultural Society were to improve the displays and standard of exhibits in the annual Walcha Show, and to extend horticultural knowledge generally. Nancy and the Society became involved in the beautification of Walcha, in planting trees along the highways and the Apsley River that runs through the town, inspecting gardens, and hosting talks with renowned gardeners and horticultural experts.[3] The Society persuaded the local council to take an interest in the aesthetics of the small town, to plant trees, mow the grass, get rid of the wandering cows and sheep, and establish a beautification committee. Along with volunteers in other towns of the New England region, other horticultural societies and a regional association were formed, extending the care of the environment through tree plantings and beautification of the local townships. This broad interest in the environment and heritage expanded significantly in the postwar period and is a major feature of the story of Australian volunteering from 1945.

Community consensus and commitment to the future and each other was evident in a range of diverse areas such as the establishment of youth groups, libraries, sporting bodies, music and dramatic clubs. In this chapter we cannot explore every niche touched by volunteering between 1945 and 1960 but we can look at selected volunteers and their organisations that help to explain the broad story of how Australian volunteering developed. Because governments were crucial in the development of an Australian way of volunteering, the role of the Department of Post-War Reconstruction, and specifically its Community Activities Section headed up by Lloyd Ross are included for discussion, as well as Federal government initiatives with the voluntary sector in the 1950s.

Planning for peace, 1945–50

Towards the end of the war, volunteers began to focus on their roles and responsibilities in peacetime. The Country Women's Association (CWA) invited fourteen voluntary organisations to a conference in April 1945 to discuss future directions and community building into the post-war period. In this 'people's parliament of reconstruction' as Lloyd Ross termed it, there was a variety of ideas presented for volunteering in both Australia and overseas. The CWA wanted to establish hostels, a housekeeper service, baby health centres and rest rooms in country towns. The Bush Nursing Association wanted to establish base hospitals in rural areas to help stop the population drift to the cities. In Heidelberg, Victorian citizens wanted to build a library and in Lithgow in New South Wales, a community centre was planned. The Girl Guides and YWCA were arranging to send trained volunteers to assist in war devastated Europe. Eleanor Manning, who joined the Girl Guides as a child, and devoted her life to the organisation, travelled to Malaya to serve with the Guide International Service assisting with post-war rehabilitation. During the war, Eleanor used her organisational and administrative skills honed in the Girl Guides to good effect, when she became Deputy Controller of the Australian Women's Army Service (AWAS), one of the wartime women's auxiliary services. Returning to Guides after the war, Eleanor eventually became its Chief Commissioner in the 1960s.[4]

Lloyd Ross and the Community Activities Section

Lloyd Ross, the Director of Public Relations in the Chifley Labor government, and a well-known writer and labour intellectual was observing these developments with interest.[5] Ross was a great supporter of what he called 'voluntary civic activity' and believed that it was important for all levels of government, including the Federal government, to play a role in assisting this voluntary action as a way of strengthening communities. Although Ross was unsuccessful in persuading the Chifley government to support such a program, his responses reveal that the concept of active citizenship and its links to volunteering were identified by a few enlightened government bureaucrats in the 1940s. They recognised that volunteering contributed to the development of Australian democratic traditions and was an integral aspect of Australian society.

In his job as head of the Community Activities Section of the Department of Post-War Reconstruction, Lloyd Ross spent considerable time discussing the roles that volunteers and their organisations could play in post-war Australia, and how governments could assist. Ross believed that community building was integral to the success of the government's long-term plans and should be incorporated into the future direction of Australian social and economic policy. He also believed that the concepts of workplace democracy and voluntary action were complementary and part of the ideals of citizenship at home, work and within the local community. This included the pursuit of cultural activities through local communities and governments working together. 'We can best assist the development of culture in Australia' he argued, 'by building, enriching, expanding the local, voluntary, spontaneous development of our people – though we retain an ideal of a nation linking communities into a national endeavour'.[6]

Little is known about the Community Activities Section, probably because the files were shredded in 1950.[7] The Section established discussion groups across Australia. Through emphasising the 'democratic, local, human approach to the problem of community development', Ross believed that his Section often 'kept alive the flickering interest of the people in community developments when some were becoming disillusioned and tired'.[8] Detailed community service reports were commissioned in Heidelberg and St Kilda in Melbourne, the industrial town of Newcastle and Deniliquin in western New South Wales in an effort to convince the Commonwealth government to provide funds to local community groups as a way of making them more accessible and relevant to ordinary Australians, as well as providing funding for essential infrastructure.

Ross put these ideas of community engagement with the government, and the voluntary sector working together in partnership to build and sustain Australian communities, forward to his boss Dr HC Coombs. 'It is not sufficient to plan merely for economic policy', Ross argued, 'due consideration should be given to ensuring the fullest opportunity for people as individuals and as members of a community carrying on those activities which appear worth while to them'.[9] He spent considerable time and energy developing these ideas. Ross believed that unless the government had motivated and empowered citizens at the local level, it would be harder to implement the Chifley government's post-war agenda, represented in the 1945 White Paper on Full Employment. So, as head of the Community Activities Section, Ross spent much of 1944 and 1945 travelling around Australia meeting with a range of community organisations and volunteers, discussing these possibilities with 'active enlightened conscious citizens' as he termed them. But Federal Treasury opposed this radical idea of Federal funding for community groups and the report, although drafted, was never submitted to cabinet.[10]

This setback reflects a common theme and one of the key factors that created the distinct Australian way of volunteering. The 'moving frontier' as Beveridge (and later Finlayson) termed it, between the voluntary sector and government was slowly shifting, but the issue of Australian federalism, and the sensitive area of federal/state relations and relevant jurisdictions remained a problem for the partnership between the state and voluntary action. A good example of this was the creation of six state-based Lady Gowrie Child Centres in 1938, directly funded by the Commonwealth to the tune of £100 000 and administered by the nationally based Australian Association for Pre-school Development (later called the Australian Pre-School Association). This arrangement set a precedent for Commonwealth/state relations in regards to the funding of voluntary organisations. Keen not to intrude 'upon fields already occupied by State Governments', the Prime Minister Joe Lyons argued that the centres would be established in each capital city to not only look after the needs of young children but also the problems of physical growth, nutrition and development.[11] Administered by the Federal Department of Health, the states seemed happy for the Commonwealth to fund the centres because in reality at the time, the kindergarten and child-care sector was largely run by voluntary organisations with only small state government subsidies. That is, with local government virtually non-existent, child-care was not an area of concern for state governments, and they did not, therefore, oppose the federal initiative.

The establishment of the National Fitness Council in 1939, just before the outbreak of war, was another example where the Commonwealth directed funding to local voluntary organisations. Established to assist state governments set up programs to improve the physical fitness and health of Australians, the National Fitness Council became part of a broad program to develop community centres and local facilities. Under the *National Fitness Act 1941*, funds were allocated to encourage state-based organisations to promote physical education in schools and communities across Australia. But the funding was limited to £50 per organisation, which did not go very far when building a community centre or providing expensive infrastructure. David Maunders believes this funding limit was crucial in determining the success or failure of these embryonic community endeavours. Many communities were simply not 'able to provide their own funding', therefore thwarting the local schemes.[12] Here are two good examples of government using the voluntary sector to develop its own policy agenda, which was, in this case, about addressing the dramatic population decline and the concurrent health problems resultant from the Depression years of the 1930s. This, it was argued, placed the future of Australia at risk.

The community centre movement

Lloyd Ross saw community centres as a key to post-war reconstruction. 'Voluntary civic activity' as Ross called it, was an integral component of this movement that originated in Britain and America during the 1920s and 1930s. Ross saw communities as not only geographically focused but also based on 'groupings of people' who 'must feel their unity; they must act as a team to develop the best that is in their way of living'.[13] With no tradition of strong local government, Australian communities were often bereft of amenities and services, yet as the war experience revealed, there was a 'huge reservoir of energy and voluntary effort waiting to be tapped'.[14] The once flourishing school of arts and mechanics' institutes (in the early twentieth century it was estimated over 2000 existed) were largely moribund.[15] Years of depression, economic uncertainty and war had squeezed out community life, and state government subsidies, once an integral part of the Australian voluntary tradition, had all but dried up. As a consequence, Australia lagged behind other countries such as Britain and the USA. Community centres, it was argued, were a key way to provide facilities such as libraries, youth and sports clubs, music and drama groups as well as infant welfare centres. The community centre model was seen as the 'first rung in the revitalising of languishing democracy' and was integral to family, community groups and ultimately the nation.[16]

Towards the end of the war, voluntary or non-profit organisations such as the National Fitness Council and the Co-operative Advisory Council of New South Wales encouraged the concept of the community centre. Building on the once successful but increasingly languishing mutual aid and co-operative movement, community centres were viewed as a practical and logical way to create change within communities to include a range of facilities under the co-operative model using both local government and active citizens. These community centres were to be non-political and non-sectarian, covering a range of areas including health and fitness, recreation, culture and education, and general social needs. They were not physical buildings so much as 'an organisation by which a community endeavours to provide itself – in its leisure – with healthy mental and physical recreation, leisure-time education, and perhaps certain facilities of public health'.[17] Sometimes these community centres were established and paid for by the locals themselves, but it was noted 'total reliance on voluntary funds and help may … swamp more useful activities'.[18]

The national broadcaster, the Australian Broadcasting Commission (ABC) also played a role in harnessing community action through its publications, broadcasts and listening groups. In conjunction with Ross and his department, the ABC published the booklet, *The Community Can do It. Make a Plan*, in 1945 to accompany an ABC radio series. The booklet focused on encouraging a community spirit and community activities across Australia, and was really a self-help manual that included a range of examples and topics for local communities as well as advice on how to harness voluntary action to build a community centre. The radio series aired from May to July 1945. The topics included examples of community-based initiatives across Australia, from the Burnie Youth Centre and Sandy Bay Child Welfare Centre in Tasmania, to the Red Hill Community Centre in Queensland, and the Housekeeper Emergency Scheme and South Coast Co-operative Scheme in New South Wales.

The series began with the community centre at Nuriootpa in South Australia. Nuriootpa was a town 90 kilometres north of Adelaide nestled in the Barossa Valley with a population of 1500 people. Originally settled by German religious refugees in the nineteenth century, the town had grown and prospered, supported by vineyards and small vegetable crops, sheep and cattle. It was reasonably well served by five churches, a high school, state school and nursery school, a war memorial community hall, co-operative store, community hotel, a large park that included tennis courts, cricket pitches, and a concrete pavilion, a circulating library, and a boys and girls gym run by the National Fitness Council. But despite these facilities, younger members of the community were moving away to Adelaide, so it was decided to focus on renewal and regeneration by creating additional community facilities. These included a swimming pool, a baby health centre, a library, memorial gardens and camping grounds, a health clinic and district hospital, a district ambulance service and clubrooms for servicemen and others. All of this was undertaken by local initiative – the monies were raised and jobs completed by volunteers from the community.

The Nuriootpa experience is a good model for the community movement in Australia as well as being 'one of those nurseries of local self-government which Australia so badly needs'.[19] As mentioned earlier, unlike Britain and the USA, local government was traditionally not strong in Australia. This is one of the factors that contributed to the Australian way of volunteering and ultimately hindered the community movement. Because of the weak local government network, Lloyd Ross believed that if left to the states, the community centre movement would falter and die, which is precisely what happened.

The issue of Commonwealth/state/local funding and jurisdiction over-lap was as complex and difficult then as it is today. The Commonwealth wrestled financial control of income tax from the states in 1942, during the darkest days of the war. At the end of hostilities, rather than return to the pre-war situation, the Commonwealth initiated a tax reimburse-ment scheme to the states, based on an adjusted population formula. State opposition to creeping federal powers was probably a factor in the Commonwealth's reluctance to pursue both the National Fitness Coun-cil's agenda, and the community centre movement. The goal of ongoing Commonwealth assistance through direct grants to local communities was simply not going to be reached. By 1950, the idea of a community centre movement was virtually dead, and it would take until the 1970s and the Whitlam government for these ideas to re-emerge.

Literary volunteers

But if the community movement faltered, other areas of Australian cultural and social life were not so affected. The civic resurgence and commu-nity engagement identified by Ross was also evident in the literary world. Another key feature of the Australian way of volunteering is that, irrespec-tive of government involvement and support, Australians have always gone ahead and created organisations to support various endeavours and ideas. This can be seen in the development of literary organisations. One of the earliest was the Fellowship of Australian Writers (FAW) founded in 1928 to lobby government for patronage for writers and to push for increased assistance for writers through the Commonwealth Literary Fund (CLF) – a pension fund for retired and disabled writers established in 1908. Through extensive lobbying by the FAW, this was extended in 1939 to support and promote Australian literature.[20] World War II was important in initiating new directions and synergies between writers, especially in regards to developing new ways of 'mutual association'. The politics of the war against fascism mobilised writers, as did serving in the armed services, and the war brought writers together as a united front against the threat of invasion. The founding of literary magazines *Southerly* (1939) and *Meanjin* (1940), two towers of Australian literary publishing, against a backdrop of war, brought a 'new sense of democratic co-operation and collectivity in writing'.[21]

The Children's Library Movement

The Children's Library Movement, featured in the 1945 ABC broadcasts, is one voluntary literary organisation that took off after the war and is an excellent case study to make this point. As with many voluntary organisations, the origins of the Children's Library Movement reside with a motivated individual who wanted to make a difference. Mary Rivett came from a family of volunteers – her sisters Elsie and Eleanor were involved in a variety of voluntary organisations in Australia and India. The daughter of a Congregational minister, Mary was educated at Fort Street Girls' High School and the University of Sydney where she graduated in 1918 with first class honours and the university medal in philosophy. This achievement took Mary to Britain and Newnham College Cambridge, where she graduated with first class honours in psychology in 1921. She went on to teach at Bedford College, University of London and later the University of Sydney.[22]

While in London, Mary Rivett went to the house where Charles Dickens had lived – 13 Johnson Street, Somerstown, a poor district of London – which now housed the David Copperfield Children's Library. She was fired up by the idea of a library devoted entirely to the special needs of children, and on her return to Sydney she set about establishing a children's library in the basement of a Quakers hall in Devonshire Street, Surry Hills, then a squalid, run-down area of inner Sydney. According to Mary the Children's Library was:

> an experiment in the attempted giving to children, to whom
> otherwise it might be denied, of something of their rights in the
> form of beauty, happiness, and freedom, in a place which is their

own. Surrounded by colour, introduced to good music, given the stimulus of entertaining and interesting books among which he may rove at will, directed where such direction is asked or needed, with the opportunity to express himself in an art or craft of his own choosing, to talk of what occupies his mind.[23]

The library struggled with volunteer labour and limited funds until 1934 when Ralph Munn, the director of the Carnegie Library in Pittsburgh, USA, toured Australia. He was highly critical of the lack of children's library facilities in Australia. In America and Britain, children's libraries were well established, and an integral part of national youth services.[24] Australia, on the other hand, lagged far behind most other English-speaking countries, with the first children's library established in South Australia in 1915. The published survey of Munn's findings was highly critical of the lack of government funding, stating that 'Australia was better provided with local libraries in 1880' than in the 1930s.[25] As Carl Bridge noted, South Australia was the only state to 'plan' a public library, built up by voluntarism, modest membership fees and some financial assistance from the state government.[26]

The publicity surrounding Ralph Munn's visit gave the Rivett/Matheson sisters (Mary having married in 1934) renewed hope, and they formed the non-sectarian and non-political Children's Library and Crafts Movement in 1934. Two years later, they opened a second centre in Erskineville, another inner-city suburb that was devoid of parks and open spaces but densely populated with poor working-class families and large numbers of children. Within a few years, the sisters had over 4000 children associated with the centre. The momentum continued unabated throughout the war, with centres established in other Sydney suburbs including Gordon, Chatswood, Hornsby, Beecroft, Artarmon, Clovelly, Ashfield, Balgowlah, Pennant Hills, Hurstville, Narrabeen, and in the rural townships of Katoomba, Springwood, Cobar, St Mary's, Mittagong, Woodford and Manildra.

The children's library established at St Mary's near Penrith, on the western outskirts of Sydney, provides an example of real community engagement, with people pitching in to assist in a voluntary capacity with sheer hard work. During the war, a large munitions works was established at St Mary's, employing about 4500 people. About 200 houses, called the Duration Cottages, were built for the factory workers and their families but there were no other facilities provided. Although not wealthy, this small community set up a Duration Cottages' Progress Association, which then organised and funded the building of a library and hall. The women did the fundraising for the tools, materials and fittings, while their menfolk constructed the buildings (on weekends, holidays and rostered days off). All the labour to build the library and hall was voluntary. Organised and managed by the Ladies' Auxiliary of the Progress Association, all of whom were volunteers, it became a Children's Library, with over 1000 books for its 350 child members.[27]

The development of children's libraries through community action and volunteering was accompanied by successful lobbying. Argued as both a right and a necessity for a progressive and democratic society, most state governments eventually enacted legislation for free public lending libraries. By 1949, the Children's Library Movement was the major provider of free children's libraries in New South Wales, along with some State Department of Education and municipal council funding. There were twenty-six centres, many in country areas, with over 11 000 members. Despite the gradual involvement of both local and state governments, the bulk of work was still carried out by volunteers with funds raised through donations from the local community.

The Children's Library Movement flourished through the 1950s, extending to Queensland and Victoria, with a similar program established in Western Australia.[28] However, by the 1960s the increase of municipal libraries, through enlarged local government, gradually incorporated the independent voluntary children's libraries, and they were amalgamated into the local municipal council structures. The Children's Library Movement, initiated by a passionate volunteer in the 1920s from an idea glimpsed in London, and propelled forward by American influences in the 1930s, eventually transformed into a local government enterprise. The volunteers withdrew and the provision for children's reading and literacy needs was taken over by public libraries in the form that we are familiar with today (although many libraries now have well developed volunteer programs in place).

The Children's Book Council

Another children's literary organisation that made an impact in the immediate post-war period was the Children's Book Council, arguably one of
the most important organisations in the development of children's literature in Australia. Here is an example where overseas influences (again
America) and World War II intersected to provide the impetus for Australian volunteers and their voluntary action.[29] The Children's Book of the
Year awards, campaigns for encouraging and directing children towards
reading quality literature – and especially Australian literature, as well as
the publication of good quality books for children, all developed in the
post-1945 period.

But the importance of volunteers in the development of this story is
little understood or sufficiently recognised. Once again, the war provided
the springboard for voluntary action in an area that struggled for recognition. The idea of children being a distinct, important group with their
own needs, desires, and civil rights in terms of free access to libraries
and facilities was a fledgling concept in Australia. But as imports of all
kinds, including books, were disrupted during the war, paper restrictions
affected local publishers. Combined with a heightened sense of 'all in' for
the war effort generally, those interested in the welfare of children in the
arts and educational areas fostered a re-awakening of civic engagement,
community and voluntary action. The idea that books and reading could
contribute to a world focused on peace not war, and that children and
young people had a key role to play in the future of Australia were important concepts that were targeted by volunteers and voluntary organisations like the Children's Book Council.

The main volunteers came from organisations such as the Children's
Library Movement, those interested in kindergarten and primary teaching (for example, staff at Sydney Teachers College) and those involved
in the ABC Youth Education Section. But as is the case with so much
in the history of volunteering, there is no flame without a spark. In this
case, the spark came from workers with the United States Information
Library, established in Sydney to support American servicemen and
women during the war. On its staff was Mary Townes Nyland who was
familiar with the United States Children's Book Council and its annual

Children's Book Week.[30] On learning that the United States Children's Book Week's theme for 1945 was to have an international focus, Townes Nyland and other librarians from the United States Information Library brought together key individuals at a dinner party in Sydney in September, a month after the war ended. The guests included Mary Matheson from the Children's Library Movement, renowned author Pixie O'Harris from the Fellowship of Australian Writers, Ida Osbourne from the ABC's Argonauts Programme, and Charles Bull from the ABC. As Mary later related, 'it was a group of able, enthusiastic persons, most of whom knew each other well. We Americans were amazed, I remember, as the Australians seized upon the idea of Children's Book Week, tossed it back and forth, then were "off and running"'.[31]

The first Children's Book Week was held from 11–17 November 1945, involving over thirty voluntary organisations interested in young people, books and education.[32] These included the organisations already mentioned above plus a number of women's groups and educational bodies such as the Australian Book Club, Bush Book Club, Boy Scouts, CWA, Eureka Youth League, Girl Guides, National Council of Women, National Fitness Council, YMCA, YWCA, Australian Booksellers Association, and the World Council of Churches. The Department of Education and its Correspondence School was also involved and the ABC once again played a critical part in supporting and disseminating the concept of Book Week as well as facilitating Australia-wide coverage through its National Children's Sessions, which reached about 30 000 children.[33]

For the first Book Week, the Children's Library Movement members set up displays in libraries, schools and bookshops; authors from the Fellowship of Australian Writers exhibited original illustrations from children's books in the State Library of New South Wales; bookshops featured special tables of children's books and window features; and children's authors autographed copies of their books. John Metcalfe gave a talk on International Children's Book Week that was broadcast on the ABC.[34] Typically, or perhaps because of Australian federalism and the difficulty in establishing national organisations, Children's Book Week was only picked up in New South Wales, South Australia, Tasmania and Western Australia. From 1945 to 1951, Children's Book Week only ran in these four states.[35] Victorian and Queensland branches were established in 1954 (totally independently of each other) and the national body, the Children's Book Council of Australia (as we know it today), was formed in 1958. Its objects were to encourage children's reading through a comprehensive free library system, promote good books for children, establish awards and organise Book Week and book exhibitions.[36]

The 1950s

In the post-war period, especially the 1950s, Australia has been portrayed as a 'transcendentally dull' country, as the famous ex-pat Barry Humphries put it – a static and complacent place lacking any vitality or originality.[37] Perceived as a period of deadening suburban conformity and cultural malaise, this view is juxtaposed against other social changes such as a vast immigration program and the slow dismantling of the White Australia Policy. As former Labor Prime Minister Paul Keating once said of his political opponents, they 'should be placed in the old Parliament House museum with the cultural icons of the 1950s: "the Morphy Richards toaster, the Qualcast mower, a pair of heavily protected slippers, the Astor TV, the AWA radiogram"'.[38] Alternatively, despite the global uncertainty of the Cold War, the 1950s has been seen as a 'golden age' of full employment, economic growth and political stability, dominated by Robert Menzies. Even with this economic golden age, many agreed with Donald Horne's sentiments in his ironically titled book *A Lucky Country* (published in 1964) where he wrote of a country living off its natural resources 'in a mire of mediocrity'. The main critics of this new Australian way of life in the suburbs, argued Stuart Macintyre, were the modernist intellectuals such as Robin Boyd, the architect who talked of the 'aesthetic calamity' that was suburbia, and others who became ex-pats in London. Household names like Barry Humphries, Germaine Greer, Clive James and Robert Hughes became vocal and persistent in their criticisms of Australia.[39] As Murphy and Smart articulated, 'the decade is a metaphor for complacency, conformity, a kind of cosy comfortableness and an assumed "traditional" pattern of gender relations'.[40]

All of this is probably true, especially for some of those who reached young adulthood in the 1950s, and believed that 'the most important thing about Australia in the 1950s was the leaving of it'.[41] But another perspective, another view, the other side of the coin as it were, reveals a different story that helps to characterise the period, providing more depth and complexity. If one looks at the experience of the baby boomers (children born between 1945 and the early 1960s), their parents and grandparents, another set of experiences is uncovered.

When examining the roles and impact of volunteering, one is struck by the vibrancy and innovation of the period. New advocacy-style self-help groups were formed, such as the War Widows' Guild established by Jessie Vasey, whose husband was killed during the war. 'It is no mean destiny to be called upon to go on for a man who laid down his life', wrote the determined Jessie as she and other volunteers fought for the rights of thousands of war widows in the aftermath of World War II. This was followed in 1949 with the establishment of the Association of Civilian Widows of Australia, which in ten years had a membership of 12 000 widows. These organisations were entirely built on the resourcefulness and volunteer labour of many women and they became powerful advocates for this most disadvantaged group in Australian society.[42]

The 1950s also saw the consolidation of many service clubs such as Rotary, Apex, Soroptimist and Quota. Quota International arrived in Australia from America in the 1930s but expanded in the late 1940s and 1950s. A women's organisation that focuses on creating networks and international connections through concepts of sharing and assistance, Quota has been particularly strong in New South Wales in rural centres on the north and south coasts.[43] The Soroptimist clubs were originally formed in the 1920s in the US and Britain for businesswomen, with the first club formed in Sydney in 1937. Today, Soroptimist International is a global women's organisation working particularly with the United Nations and NGOs to assist women and children around the world.[44]

In terms of religious volunteering, the 1950s was also a period of growth as membership of both Protestant and Catholic churches and Sunday school increased. It is generally remembered 'as a time of confidence and expansion'. The new suburbs and population increases, younger marriages and more children, all required the building of new churches and religious infrastructure, and as David Hilliard explained, incomes of churches improved dramatically with the introduction of American methods of fundraising in 1954.[45] Anne O'Brien clearly articulated in her book *God's Willing Workers*, the integral connections between Australian women, religion and volunteering, especially within religious based voluntary organisations such as the Mothers' Union and the Catholic Womens' Association.[46] It is also evident that considerable female volunteering in religious settings, such as attending to the flowers, cleaning the churches, playing the organ and singing in the choirs, leading Sunday school and bible classes, and fundraising continued, largely unrecorded and unacknowledged.

The 1950s also witnessed a nascent cultural flowering in the performing arts, much of it propelled by volunteers. Although there were small home-grown repertory theatre, opera and ballet companies operating in most states and commercial theatre companies such as JC Williamson's, the clamour for a national theatre grew. The initiation of the Elizabethan Theatre Trust through a national appeal with the objective 'to provide a theatre of Australians by Australians for Australians' resulted in the raising of £90 000 from individuals and groups in addition to £30 000 of Commonwealth monies. The Trust was incorporated under Royal Charter, and over 1400 members contributed an annual subscription of £5, led by a board of directors, with Queen Elizabeth as Patron. One of its earliest successes was the staging of Ray Lawler's hit play *Summer of the Seventeenth Doll* in 1956.[47]

When looking through the lens of volunteering and voluntary action, therefore, one can see a different Australia: an active, not passive society; a culture in transformation. For many volunteers, the 1950s was a period of consolidation and renewal. These traits are evident in the area of social welfare, a traditional site for volunteering in Australian history.

The Family Welfare Bureau

The Family Welfare Bureau is an example of a voluntary organisation formed in war that grew in size and stature as the war progressed, and adapted itself to the post-war period with ease. By the 1950s it was an established and well-respected organisation run by a small number of paid staff including professionally trained social workers and many dozens of volunteers, mainly married women. One could say that the Bureau flourished in the 1950s. It was formed in 1939 by the Lord Mayor's Patriotic Fund and Australian Comforts Fund (ACF) to assist servicemen and their families deal with the dysfunctional nature of wartime service, family breakdown, absence, sickness and all the worries and stress that came with being a family affected by war. The type of assistance provided to families of servicemen and women varied, depending on circumstance and need. Sometimes money was given to buy food. At other times, furniture, clothes, bedding and blankets were needed. A recurring problem concerned illness and the hospitalisation of wives of servicemen. Often left without any support when their husband enlisted, the Bureau provided housekeepers to care for the children and to take over the running of the home until the mother had recovered. The Bureau also assisted in organising hospital care and in some cases funded private hospital beds and follow-up convalescence care. Other problems included finding child-care for working wives or in some cases, temporary foster care for children, providing legal assistance and temporary housing. During the war, similar welfare organisations were established in all states to deal with this largely neglected, but burgeoning welfare problem. The casework teams also dealt with ex-service personnel who were discharged as medically unfit. Often the needs of these men were not being met, either because the Department of Repatriation rejected their application for a pension and they were unable to find a job to support their families, or because the pension was not enough. These were families in crisis, with nowhere to turn, and they often ended up at the doors of the Family Welfare Bureau.

After the war, the Bureau believed there was still a demand for their services. Under the adage 'Happy Families in a Changing World', the revised aim of the organisation was to 'give support and aid to individuals and their families in such ways as will relieve anxieties and increase feelings of well-being' so that people could live 'more satisfying lives'.[48] This focus, to offer a range of support programs to maintain the health and wellbeing of the family unit, was a unique concept. As a 'general family agency', the Bureau filled a niche for both ex-servicemen and civilian families. They tackled issues concerning working mothers, behavioural problems in young people ('teen-agers' was a new category), anxieties over money and budgeting, issues of unmarried mothers, problems associated with mental illness, and general domestic topics of concern for families. These were all issues that came under the rubric of 'family'. They looked after the welfare of dependent children, young mothers, older people, widows, migrants and invalids.

Operating out of premises in Martin Place, Sydney, the Family Welfare Bureau offered a Marital Guidance Counselling Service, a Baby Minding Service, a General Information Service to 'overcome any delays in interviewing distressed people', a Handcraft Centre, and a frock shop. It worked closely with a range of government departments, such as the New South Wales Housing Commission, the Departments of Health and Labour, Industry and Social Welfare, and the Commonwealth Department of Employment, Social Services and Repatriation as well as other voluntary organisations, especially the Australian Red Cross and those offering homes for children and aged care.

In 1954, the Bureau was run by a volunteer executive committee, and had seven paid staff including social workers, and forty-two regular volunteer workers. All workers were valued, be they paid or unpaid. It was reported in the 1955 annual report that 'every job, be it large or small, is important. No one can take the place of the trained worker, but her burden can be lightened by doing the "odd" jobs for her in helping to keep the friendly atmosphere for which the Bureau is so well known'.[49]

A committee and three paid social workers ran the Family and Marital Counselling Service which assisted 1194 families during the twelve months to March 1954. Five hundred and sixty-two were families of ex-servicemen, 620 were civilian families and twelve were families of current serving members of the forces. Financial instability, a lack of adequate accommodation and illness were key problems, with widows and deserted wives with children over-represented in their client base. As a result, the Family Welfare Bureau had many requests to place children in homes. 'We are disturbed by the number of requests to place children in Homes and by the fact that this is sometimes the best solution' but in representing a relatively modern perspective, the Bureau felt 'it would seem better to make it possible for the child to be cared for in his family wherever possible'.[50]

The Handcraft Centre was another innovation for the Bureau where the elderly and disabled were offered classes including basket making and millinery, toy and slipper making, knitting, rug and lampshade making and the like. It was a unique program that provided companionship and social interaction as well as enhancing the quality of life for pensioners through a range of activities designed especially for them. Recognising a need for babysitting facilities in the city for women, the Family Welfare Bureau opened a Baby Minding Centre in July 1951, minding over 3600 babies in that year. Fitted out entirely by donations and volunteer labour, and with one paid staff member (a qualified nursing sister) and a number of rostered volunteers, the centre was a huge success. In association with the Royal Society for the Welfare of Mothers and Babies, they also began antenatal classes two evenings a week. The Bureau continued to offer this service until 1954 when the Sydney City Council opened a centre in Park Street. Here is another example where volunteers and voluntary organisations recognised a need, in this case a childminding centre in the city, and found the money and volunteers to establish it. Later, government, in this case local government, came in and took control of the service. This pattern has been repeated again and again throughout Australian history – which is fine, except that rarely do governments give credit to the origins of such ideas nor does history record, or people remember, how these initiatives came to pass.

All these social welfare programs were expensive and the Family Welfare Bureau was always short of funds. A universal problem, both then and now, was how to keep costs down to the bare minimum without compromising the service. Despite having a dedicated group of volunteers who ran the committees, including a women's auxiliary which raised funds for the Bureau and a very successful venture – the Frock Shop – in Martin Place, and despite the fact that the Bureau really ran on the unpaid labour of its legion of volunteers, finding the ongoing funding to keep their doors open was always a problem. It was estimated in 1954 that the Bureau required £6000 per annum to run their programs. Government grants included £1000 from the New South Wales Attorney-General's

Department and £500 from Department of Labour, Industry and Social Welfare, as well as £2500 from the Repatriation Commission.[51]

In the mid-1950s, the primary expenditures for the Family Welfare Bureau were administration and staff costs. In 1953, the Repatriation Commission queried the increased administration costs. A feisty and unamused May Pillinger, the Director of the Bureau, herself a fully qualified social worker, responded with a detailed submission to the Deputy Director of Repatriation, Mr RW Carswell. As May stated, wages increased substantially after the war, which affected all voluntary organisations. For example, in November 1945, the basic wage was £4 19s. Five years later it was £7 6s; then it jumped to £10 7s in November 1951; £11 17s in November 1952; and by August 1953, the basic wage was £12 3s, an increase of 145 per cent since 1945. May also noted that the Bureau employed fully qualified social workers but they were paid less than if they were employed by government departments, and 'only a few shillings more than the female clerical award rate'.[52] Furthermore, she reminded Mr Carswell that in 1952 there was a 'serious trade regression' that affected many people who lost their jobs. This had a flow-on affect to the Bureau, which saw a significant increase in the use of its services, especially by recently arrived unskilled migrants who were often the first to lose their jobs. By mid-1952, it was reported that hundreds of migrants were sleeping rough, with voluntary organisations such as the Salvation Army Hostel and City Mission full to capacity.[53] In attempting to keep costs down, the Bureau cut back on cleaning costs, postage, telephone and printing so that, despite the wage and other increases, the amount debited to the Repatriation Trust Fund remained constant at just under £3000 per year.[54]

The original monies put aside for the Family Welfare Bureau by the Lord Mayor's Patriotic Fund and ACF when it was wound up in 1949 (and administered by the Department of Repatriation) were fully expended by 1955. May Pillinger asked the Repatriation Commission if any additional funds either from the accumulated interest from the Fund or other monies were available for distribution to the Bureau.[55] She left empty handed. Although one-off grants such as the £1000 received from the *Australian Women's Weekly* Ex-servicewomen's Club and considerable in-kind support from a range of businesses, individuals and other voluntary organisations was received, by 1955 it was noted in the Annual Report that funds were 'chronically low'. As will be discussed in the following chapter, this perilous funding situation continued until the 1960s when the Bureau received a welcome injection of funds from the Commonwealth for marriage guidance counselling services.

Assisting 'New Australians'

In the early 1950s, the Family Bureau noticed an increase in the number of newly arrived migrants using their services or being referred to the Bureau. In response to the 'populate or perish' slogan of the war, the Department of Immigration was established in July 1945, with Arthur Calwell the first minister. 'We must fill this country or we shall lose it', said Calwell dramatically.[56] Looking first to Britain, both free and assisted schemes, including the 'ten pound pom' were introduced, with over 23 000 migrants arriving in 1947. But the numbers were insufficient and soon the migration net was thrown wider, including displaced persons from the refugee camps in Europe. Over 170 000 displaced persons arrived in Australia between 1947 and 1954. The booming economy of the 1950s encouraged further migration programs that targeted southern Europe, especially Italy, Greece and the Middle East. Between 1947 and 1969, over two million people migrated to Australia. Almost half were of British descent (that is, from the United Kingdom, New Zealand, Canada and Ireland), and 25 per cent were from southern Europe.[57]

These 'New Australians', as they were known at the time, arrived boatload after boatload. Some new migrant families suffered considerably. With language and cultural difficulties and few family connections, they ended up at the doors of voluntary organisations like the Family Welfare Bureau. Major problems included issues common to many families – lack of accommodation, illness, unemployment, financial and marital difficulties. It was noted by the Bureau that these migrants sometimes had less access to assistance than other groups in the community as 'residency clauses' in statutory benefits and voluntary organisations limited eligibility. The Family Welfare Bureau, specifically non-sectarian and non-political, prided itself on being available and open to any family. The Bureau also worked with the Geneva-based International Social Service (ISS), a non-government, international organisation established in the early 1920s to assist with international migration. The ISS later opened an office in Sydney with the Bureau to further assist this particularly vulnerable group of Australian migrants.

From the reports of social workers working in the various migrant hostels, the problem of delinquency, caused by youth unemployment and boredom, was a serious one. Although there were supervised recreational facilities for both boys and girls in many of the camps, including Boy Scouts and Girl Guides, junior soccer clubs and church groups, vandalism and truancy were ongoing issues. In her report in the early 1950s, social worker Rosalie James describes an incident at the Greta Holding Centre near Newcastle where a group of boys was banned from dancing classes by the YWCA for misbehaviour and was later caught lighting a fire underneath the hall.[58]

Another feature of volunteering in the 1950s concerned the establishment of specific organisations to look after the interests of migrant groups. The establishment of the Good Neighbourhood Councils (GNCs) confirms the developing relationship between the voluntary sector and the Commonwealth government. Based on the New Settler Leagues, established to assist British migrants in the 1920s, the GNC is an example of the Federal government using the voluntary sector to assist in the implementation of public policies. Arthur Calwell believed that in order to 'Australianise' the migrants, government needed the help of ordinary Australians, for in the end only they 'can supply the need for personal friendship, neighbourly companionship ... and mateyness on the job'.[59] From 1950, Good Neighbourhood Councils, committees and branches were established across Australia, involving a range of local voluntary and church organisations. They were managed and nominally funded by the Department of Immigration. The role and function of the GNC was to assist the new migrants to 'assimilate' into the Australian community and adapt to the 'Australian way of life'. Community groups ranging from women's social welfare organisations such as the CWA and YWCA, to trade unions, religious, self-help groups, and national organisations such as the YMCA, Salvation Army and Australian Red Cross were all involved in meeting the various and often complex needs of arriving migrants.

Ann-Mari Jordens has argued that by enlisting the help of the community with non-British migrants, the government was committed 'from the outset to the social inclusion of aliens' and this 'was the principal cause of the ultimate success of its immigration program'.[60] Conversely, it has also been suggested that the GNC were merely doing the government's bidding, pushing the sensitive political policy of assimilation and 'the Australian way of life', with the 'cultural biases of the many middle-class' aspirational participants, who believed in the 'ethnic and cultural homogeneity' of a post-war Australia still clinging to its British heritage.[61] However, a further interpretation of the GNC experience can be seen through the moving frontier thesis – as evidence of the way governments and the voluntary sector worked together, in this case, to assist newly arrived migrants, especially the large numbers of non-British migrants in the 1950s.

Migrants as volunteers

On arrival in Australia, migrants themselves established volunteer organisations. There has been little research on identifying these migrant organisations but it is clear that as each ethnic group arrived in Australia, associations of various kinds were established in the migrant hostels dotted around the countryside. These ethnic groups offered a range of social and cultural supports to migrants, which refutes the common assumptions that non-British born Australians did not and continue not to volunteer.[62] Ann-Mari Jordens documents perhaps the first attempt to create a list of these ethnic migrant organisations. In 1951, social worker Margaret Ramsay, who was working at the Bathurst Reception Centre in New South Wales, catalogued thirty-eight different clubs and groups representing ten different nationalities living at the Centre. 'Some are welfare groups', she noted, 'while others have a wider programme embracing the promoting of cultural activity and social intercourse'.[63] Most were ethnically or politically based, with seventeen Polish groups including the Polish Welfare Society, as well as a range of Yugoslav, Ukrainian, Hungarian and Czechoslovakian organisations. The Greek Orthodox Church ran Community

Central Offices and assisted with employment and language issues. In terms of assimilating and mixing with other ethnic groups, Ramsay noted the Lithuanians, Latvians and Estonians were the most advanced.[64] Just as the Scots, English and Irish migrants before them, this most recent wave of migrants formed groups and organisations as soon as they arrived in Australia. In the beginning they were informal, based almost exclusively along ethnic and language lines. They included self-help, sport, social welfare, cultural, communal and meeting groups.

By the 1960s, in recognition of the work undertaken by these ethnic groups within their own communities, a grant-in-aid program was introduced by the Department of Immigration. For example, the Italian Assistance Association in Carlton, Melbourne (Co.As.It) which assisted recently-arrived Italian migrants, received funding for a social worker, as well as secretarial and office assistance. Other organisations to receive funding included the Australian–German Welfare Society in Melbourne and Sydney and the Australian–Jewish Welfare and Relief Society.[65] Although there was concern that these migrant organisations were often run along ethnic, political, religious or linguistic lines, which did not encourage either assimilation or integration, government funding indicated recognition that these ethnically based organisations and the volunteers who ran them were very important to the overall wellbeing of migrant groups.

One of the largest 'British' ethnic organisations, operating at the Bunnerong Hostel in Sydney's southern suburbs, was the British Migrant's Association. In the early 1950s, about 800 people (almost all British) were living in the desolate, sandy, windswept and relatively isolated hostel, and most were members of the British Migrant's Association. This group organised all the recreational activities at the hostel, such as pictures, dances and social evenings. At the East Hills hostel near Liverpool, the Brittania Club dominated with its whist and housie games, a regular Saturday night social and football.[66]

The Australian Red Cross

The Australian Red Cross was a major social welfare organisation whose volunteers worked closely with newly arrived migrants in the 1950s. Red

Cross VAs did a great deal of work that was largely unrecognised and now well forgotten, unpaid work that helped to make the migrants' experiences a little less overwhelming on arrival in their newly adopted country. VAs met and escorted immigrants, especially women and children, from ships to either Red Cross homes or to the Eleanor MacKinnon home at Cronulla, run by the Junior Red Cross. Mary Ryan, a VA with the University of Sydney detachment, wrote of assisting the arrival of Hungarian refugees at Mascot Airport, as well as British and European migrants arriving by ship who were initially taken to Immigration Reception Centres. The Australian Red Cross had a well-developed and highly regarded Social Welfare Department that worked in conjunction with other voluntary associations and governments to provide a range of programs.

Although never reaching the giddy heights of World War II, the VA movement continued its quasi-nursing work in hospitals and convalescent homes, as well as the Blood Bank throughout the 1950s. VAs volunteered at polio immunisation clinics, anti-TB clinics and Meals on Wheels. They staffed and ran the Red Cross cafeteria at the Repatriation General Hospital, Concord for patients and guests, had a well-developed program at Heidelberg Repatriation Hospital in Melbourne, as well as other hospitals across the country. A large recruitment campaign in 1957 heralded a renaissance for the VAD movement. Using the catchphrase, 'Be a Girl in Blue – Join Red Cross VADs', and a well-orchestrated television and radio publicity campaign, the VAD attracted a new generation of young Australian volunteers. Enid Singleton was one such young woman, who joined the Marrickville VAD in 1958. As was usual for girls of her generation, Enid had left school at fifteen and began working as a cashier at the Sydney County Council (located in the then rather dilapidated Queen Victoria Building opposite the Sydney Town Hall). Although she had always wanted to be a nurse, the pay and conditions at the SCC were considerably better than those of a nurse, so Enid became a VA in her spare time. Every Monday night she would travel to Marrickville to meet with her detachment of about thirty women, and attend a variety of training classes. Enid's training was reasonably vigorous and included attending a series of lectures and passing exams in home nursing at Crown Street Women's Hospital, Sydney Hospital or an equivalent rural hospital, first aid, resuscitation, hygiene, mothercraft, care of the aged, canteen cookery, nutrition, training in civil defence and emergency midwifery. Much of their training was centred not only on learning specific skills but also on what it meant to be a 'good citizen'. As Mary Ryan wrote later:

> we look back on our training as not only having been
> worthwhile because of our service to others, but it also helped
> to equip us for whatever was to be our role in life with a lot
> more confidence, appreciation of life and leadership.[67]

Thelma Dillon, the Commandant of the University of Sydney detachment, wrote about her VAs responding to the December 1957 bushfire emergency in the Blue Mountains. Along with local Red Cross members and other emergency organisations, and following a long tradition of this type of volunteering, the VAs provided assistance for the victims of the fires, with food, bedding and clothing, as well as caring for those directly affected by the fires. The Red Cross and VAs were also involved in the response to the massive 1955 floods that submerged the Hunter Valley, north of Sydney. On 25 February, dramatic flooding of the Hunter and other rivers to the north created a state emergency in which twenty-two people died, over 10 000 houses were flooded, and 100 houses were totally destroyed. Mass evacuations occurred and a fear of outbreaks of diseases such as typhoid contributed to the enormity of the disaster. Over twenty-five bridges were washed away and road, rail, mail and telephone services were cut. Later, the towns of Tamworth, Narrabri, Dubbo, Gunnedah, Moree and Wee Waa were flooded.

The worst affected town was Maitland. Mary Ryan was one of the hundreds of VAs, and other volunteers called up to assist. Calling themselves the 'Mudlarks', Mary and a team of seven VAs left Sydney in an old bus loaded up with 11 tonnes of provisions, including firewood and disinfectant, tomahawks, methylated spirits and about 360 litres of drinking water. Discarding their blue uniforms and veils, they dressed in overalls and gumboots, and slowly made their way up the Pacific Highway, itself cut in several places by floodwaters. On reaching Maitland, they found the town cordoned off by police, with only permit holders allowed through the roadblocks. All the shops were shut, there was no sewerage or gas supplies, most homes had no fresh drinking water and there was no electricity, apart from in the main street. Mary described the scene:

> As we entered the low-lying areas around Maitland people were already beginning to return to their homes to start cleaning up … silt was not only feet thick over the ground, but the foul-smelling ooze was also all through the houses. The banked-up flood water had been at least ceiling high in most of the homes for some days.[68]

This team of VAs spent twelve days in Maitland. They were billeted in nearby Mayfield, a suburb of Newcastle, and each day they would travel to Maitland to hand out food, drinks, cigarettes and soup. Based at the Court House, which itself had been flooded, they 'cut up many thousands of sandwiches on the legal Bar itself, and kept urns of water boiling on pressure-stoves in the witness box, the dock and even on the Magistrate's bench itself, adorned with the Royal escutcheon' recalled Mary. During their stay, these volunteers served 16 500 cups of tea, 17 500 sandwiches, some 2700 litres of soup, and 450 meals of stew. Kathleen Smith, another VA at the Courthouse said the recipe for the soup was 'take one clean bucket, open a number of different cans of soup and/or meat and vegetables, add water, salt and pepper and stir madly over the primus and hope it is edible'.[69] Other volunteers who did much of the cleaning up outside included miners from the Hunter region. National Servicemen in camp at Singleton and prisoners from the local gaol were also called on to assist. The prisoners even took up a collection for the flood relief, with about 120 prisoners donating £60 to the fund.

Civil defence and fire suppression

The response to the flood disasters proved that the Red Cross and VAD movement had a flexible, well-trained group of women volunteers who could be called on in an emergency to fulfil a wide-ranging set of tasks. At the same time, however, the floods revealed a lack of co-ordination between all levels of government and voluntary organisations. There was considerable confusion, overlap and waste between the armed services, police and the range of local municipal voluntary organisations mobilised to assist, including the YWCA, Salvation Army, National Fitness Council, CWA and Girl Guides. As a result, the New South Wales government formed the State Emergency Service (SES). A year later, in 1956, this organisation was merged with Civil Defence to form one body responsible for the co-ordination of response to natural disasters such as flood and fire, as well as any emergencies caused by enemy attacks. In the depths of the Cold War, there was considerable concern about the possibility of a nuclear attack. Each state established a State Emergency Service but the volunteer tradition, a hallmark of civil defence in Australia both during and since World War II, with a 'predominance of voluntary, community-based organisations' was very strongly embedded in the society and culture and influenced the development of the Australian way of volunteering, particularly during this period. 'The uncertain state of international affairs, recurring national disasters and the every-day needs of the community, all point to the continued need for a trained band of voluntary workers who are willing to give their time and skill to the service of their fellow man' argued Australian Red Cross Secretary General Leon Stubbings.[70] There were significant changes towards the end of the 1960s and into the 1970s, a period termed the 'disaster years', which will be examined further in chapter 6.

Michael Wright has argued that World War II stimulated an interest in civil defence and volunteer fire fighting. For example, in 1940 in New South Wales there were 472 bush fire brigade units with approximately 20 000 volunteers. By 1950, this had expanded to 1378 brigades with a total 'workforce' of over 26 000 volunteers.[71] Armed with a new *Bush Fires Act* 'to fight one of the State's most dangerous enemies … the Red Terror', a Bush Fire Committee was formed in 1949. However, at the same time as the volunteer workforce expanded, there was a corresponding rise in career fire fighters that caused considerable friction, particularly in the new growth areas of western Sydney and in the Blue Mountains. The development of local government and progress associations in the Blue Mountains (Wright estimates that there were at least fifteen progress associations that federated to form the Blue Mountains Progress Association) pitched the local volunteers against the professionals from Sydney.

After a series of disastrous fires in the 1950s, the bush fires services, both volunteer and professional, were placed under the Civil Defence Organisation, which effectively placed all organisations, including police and other volunteer organisations such as the Red Cross, under its umbrella.[72] These changes overhauled fire fighting in New South Wales and laid the basis for the modern organisation we are familiar with today.

Volunteers and the Melbourne Olympic Games

Sport is an integral part of Australian society and culture and Australian sport was built on the concept of amateurism and volunteering. In the early post-war period, the most important and defining event for Australians and sport was the Melbourne Olympic Games, held between 22 November and 8 December 1956. It was the largest, most complex international sporting event ever held in Australia, and placed both Melbourne and Australia on the world stage. Staging the Olympic Games was a crucial event for Melbourne as a city and, as Graeme Davison and others have argued, led to 'the rise of modernist Melbourne'.[73] It outstripped Sydney as the fastest growing capital city, with its high immigrant population, and considerable public spending on infrastructure represented the best of the post-war consumer boom. Melbourne became a hub for the creative arts, as well as a leader in manufacturing. The confidence demonstrated by its civic leaders and entrepreneurs was seen in the decision not only to bid for the 1956 Olympic Games but in winning the bid.

The last international sporting event of this nature was held in Sydney in 1938. The British Empire Games were held at the same time as commemorations for Australia's 150th birthday. The Australian British Empire Games Association (a predecessor of the current Commonwealth Games Association) was in charge of organising the games, and there was limited government involvement at either state or Federal level. Three months before the Games began, the Honorary Secretary and Treasurer, James Eve wrote to then Prime Minister Joe Lyons pleading for Federal government assistance. The organisation only had £35 in the account and they needed to buy uniforms for the 200 Australian team members. He argued that Australia would be on view to the world and:

at the Opening Ceremony of the British Empire Games of 1938
– at which you, Sir, as the President, will play a conspicuous
part – Australia, as host nation to our fourteen guest nations
must take the field properly equipped … we trust from the
foregoing you will be better able to understand our difficulties
and appreciate the part this Association is playing in bringing
before the eyes of the British Empire – aye, the world – the
spirit of Young Australia.[74]

The association received £500 to assist in dressing the Australian team.

The whole event, in 1938, was voluntary. The athletes were not paid (either directly or indirectly through sponsorship), the officials were not paid, managers and chaperons were not paid. Committee members of the Australian British Empire Games Association, who organised and ran the Games were also not paid. The work was undertaken within the 'spirit of amateurism', meaning 'a person who engages in a pursuit, especially a sport, on an unpaid basis'.[75] This spirit of amateurism was a key for sport. The word had a noble meaning, that sport and those involved with sport had *not* been tainted by money or unduly influenced by financial gain. Like many other features of Australian society such as 'philanthropy' and 'charity', the concept of amateurism in sport was part of the social and cultural baggage bequeathed to us by the British. In sports-mad Australia, we embraced the concept of amateurism and tried to hold on to it tightly as a dog does a bone.

The spirit of amateurism underlined the Olympic tradition and was at the forefront of the founder of the modern Olympics, Pierre de Courbertin's, views on sporting traditions. At the time of the 1956 Melbourne Olympic Games, the concept of amateurism in sport was under threat by the encroaching professionalisation in some sports. As the President of the International Olympic Committee, American Avery Brundage said:

In this materialistic age in which we live, there is in some
places more or less continuous pressure to lower amateur
standards. Every organisation connected with amateur sport
and the Olympic Games must not only firmly enforce the
amateur code, but also should initiate and actively promote a
program of education on the advantages of amateurism. If it

were not for the services freely given by thousands of members of clubs or National Federations, International Federations, National Olympic Committees, and the International Olympic Committee, there would be no Olympic Games.[76]

But in terms of volunteers and the 1956 Melbourne Olympics, little had changed from 1938. The Australian athletes were amateurs, not professionals. Their coaches and the officials from the various sporting associations were also unpaid. They were acting in an honorary capacity. For example, both my husband's father and grandfather were closely involved in athletics in Victoria. My husband's grandfather, Bert Guyot, who was associated with athletics in Victoria for over thirty years, was selected as the manager of the athletics team. He was also given responsibility as chief lap scorer for the athletic events. My father-in-law, Keith Guyot, who was a walker and narrowly missed selection in the Australian athletics team due to injury, was also an athletics 'official' for the Games.

There were scores of Australian sporting associations involved in the Games. All their officials (like the Guyots), the coaches, assistants and administrators were subsidised by the Commonwealth government through their voluntary sporting association. Their travel to Melbourne was paid for, they were given board and lodging, and were kitted out with the official uniform. The uniform consisted of a white hat, Olympic Official's tie, white shirt, 1956 Olympic Games Official Blazer (blue double-breasted jacket, gold buttons, Olympic symbol on pocket), grey trousers, black socks and black shoes.[77] These honorary officials were also given 6 shilling meal tickets towards an evening meal. The Olympic movement was keenly aware of the importance of voluntarism in sport, simply to keep the costs of running an event like the Olympic Games down. As Brundage said:

> It would be impossible to pay for these services which are so
> gladly contributed by those who believe in amateur sport.
> Since the Games rest on this solid foundation of interest in
> amateur sport by thousands of voluntary workers, and on their
> contribution of time and energy, it is not right that others be
> permitted to profit there from.[78]

The threat of increasing professionalism in sport was risking the very foundations of the Olympic movement and the ability to successfully host the event.

However, at the Melbourne Olympics there were volunteers as we know them today. Lady Volunteer Car Drivers, described as 'a team of expert women drivers' who would 'be available to chauffeur International Olympic Committee members and International Sports Federation representatives to competition and training venues and official functions' were sought. [79] They wore a specially designed uniform of green jacket, skirt and golden blouse, with the Olympic symbol on their berets. Local oil and rubber companies, motor vehicle distributors and factories were also approached to provide at least thirty-five volunteers (men) for a variety of tasks such as garage attendants for daily washing and servicing of buses and cars.[80] This is what we now call 'corporate volunteering', whereby businesses and corporations 'volunteer' or 'donate' their staff to undertake tasks or to 'volunteer' their services.

But the major source of 'volunteer' labour for the 1956 Melbourne Olympics was the Australian Army. More than 600 regular Australian soldiers were seconded to the Olympics to cover a range of activities. For example, 200 soldiers assisted the rifle range at Williamtown; seventy-five were stewards and scoreboard operators for the Pentathlon; fifty signallers flashed results of the marathon to scoreboards in the main arena; 150 helped control traffic during the marathon and walkathon; fifty had administrative and security jobs at the Olympic village; thirty-five officers and men fired salutes, hoisted and lowered the flags and acted as marshals for the opening parade; and the RAN and RAAF Brass Bands learnt the national anthems of all the countries. The Army also supplied 22 000 sheets, 11 000 blankets and pillowslips; 6000 pillows and 6000 beds for the athletes in the Heidelberg Olympic Village.[81]

Despite a financial blow out, the 1956 Melbourne Olympic Games was a huge success. The event marked a turning point in the development of sport in Australia. Television was introduced into Australia in time for the Games, so the main events were broadcast both nationally and internationally. Athletes such as Dawn Fraser, Shirley Strickland, Betty Cuthbert and Murray Rose became household names, and with a gold medal tally of thirty-five, the Games were the most successful in Australian history. But it was also the end of an era. The 1956 Olympic Games was the last of the amateur Games. From that time on, the cost of hosting the Games escalated enormously due to the professionalisation of sport around the world, the competitiveness of host cities to outdo each other, the growth in the number of sports, events and competitors, the growing influence of TV and advertising, and security issues. All of the above has had a significant impact on volunteers and volunteering in sport.

Conclusion

The immediate post-war period and the 1950s can be seen as a time of paradoxes. On the one hand, it was conservative, insular, stable and politically consistent, at least with the enduring Prime Minister, Robert Menzies. But on the other hand, it was a period of uncertainty and the Cold War, of political disintegration and instability, of huge cultural and social changes brought by immigration, technology and the baby boom. In some areas of volunteer endeavour, the 1950s 'appeared decidedly lean'. Historian Melissa Harper noted the declining membership and lack of interest in the organised bushwalking movement. So much so that in 1956, the New South Wales Federation of Bushwalking Clubs appointed a committee to examine the public's 'perceived lack of interest in walking'.[82] But for most volunteers, the 1950s was a period of consolidation and renewal. In the traditional area of social welfare volunteering, where the relationship with governments was most developed, there were shifts, with the moving frontier advancing especially in areas dealing with migrants. In terms of volunteering overall, the story of the Australian way of volunteering from 1945 to 1959 was one of continuity and growth.

5 New ideas, new directions

They [women] were the backbone of the suburban committees, the local committees, of the different organisations. And in the office of course they did the typing, did the gestetnering, made the endless cups of tea, served in the shop ... and of course the voluntary roster for filling all the envelopes, getting the mail outs done ... it was women that kept the peace movement going really. [1]

Bev Symons

During the 1960s the Australian way of volunteering developed and expanded in a range of new areas. Across Australia, people became involved in greater numbers in a variety of volunteer organisations including sport, the environment and heritage, and especially politics. Although Bev Symons's comments above relate specifically to the peace movement, she was articulating what was commonplace in every political party and pressure group. All Australian political parties, whatever their affiliation (including the organised labour movement), have survived and grown on the tireless efforts of volunteers. But few have viewed volunteering in this way and rarely has it been discussed. Bobbie Oliver's article on the voluntary work of Labor women's organisations in Western Australia, and Margot Beasley's study of the women's committees of the Waterside

Workers' Federation are rare exceptions.[2] Most people also do not recognise that the pressure groups and advocacy organisations established as part of the anti-Vietnam war movement were predicated on the shoulders of an army of volunteers. Volunteering is often perceived as non-political, local and welfare based, when realistically it has always been much broader and more diverse.

Similarly, although people have probably not associated the 1965 'freedom rides' with volunteering, that protest movement was based entirely on the unpaid labour of its active participants.[3] In an effort to fight ongoing discrimination against Aboriginal and Torres Strait Islanders, the freedom rides were undertaken by committed black and white volunteers keen to challenge the endemic racism within many country towns across New South Wales. Influenced by the 1961 American examples, the freedom rides helped to bring on the 1967 referendum that finally gave Indigenous Australians equal rights. Political activist organisations like the University of Sydney's Student Action for Aborigines (formed in 1964 to organise the freedom rides), the Aboriginal-Australian Fellowship (originally formed in 1956 by Pearl Gibbs and Faith Bandler) and the Aborigines Progressive Association (formed in 1964) were all founded and run by committed volunteer activists.

Largely because of Australia's controversial involvement in the Vietnam War, the 1960s were seen as a watershed politically, socially and economically. Home ownership on a quarter-acre block was now an attainable goal for most Australians, with 72 per cent buying their own home by 1966, up from 46 per cent in 1947. The period saw rapid economic growth enhanced by a mineral boom though curtailed by a crippling drought on the east coast. Consumer goods such as cars and black-and-white televisions were within reach for many, especially on hire-purchase or lay-by, and electrical appliances such as washing machines and dishwashers revolutionised the domestic workload for Australian women. Local government developed and expanded, and soon most towns and suburbs had electricity and water connected (but not always sewerage), local streets were bituminised, with footpaths, curb and guttering enhancing neighbourhoods and communities. The result was improvements in the standard of living for most Australians.

The post-war migration scheme contributed to this economic boom, especially with the increasing numbers of women in the paid workforce, at around 25 per cent in the early 1960s. The average male weekly wage could still support a family in relative comfort, so the bulk of Australian women left the paid workforce on marriage to become full-time house-wives and mothers. The main increase in women's paid work came from young women who generally left school at sixteen and worked until marriage, and those aged between thirty-five and forty-nine, women who returned to work when children reached school age. The arrival of the pill in Australia in 1961 gave women access to a reliable and easy form of birth control that enabled them to regulate their own fertility and this had an enormous impact on women and on Australian society generally. The corresponding influence of the pill on volunteering, however, is less well understood. While the pill may have freed up women to enter the workforce, it caused a crisis in volunteering around the western world because, unlike their mothers and grandmothers, women were not neces-sarily volunteering to the same degree or in the same fields.

The Vietnam War, political activism and volunteering

The 1960s was a period of heightened political struggle. Australian politics was not immune to the global fight between communism and capitalism, and although the conservative parties continued in power, even after the retirement of Robert Menzies as Prime Minister in 1966, the ideological battlelines were never more apparent. The Vietnam War caused particular schisms within Australian society and played an important part in the history of volunteering in Australia.

Australia's foray into Vietnam effectively began in 1962 when Austral-ian military advisers were sent in to assist the struggling South Vietnam-ese government. Conscription was controversially introduced in 1964, and the following year the Menzies government committed the 1st Battal-ion, Royal Australian Regiment (RAR), attached to the United States 173rd Airborne Division. Australian troops were later based at Nui Dat to administer the province of Phuoc Tuy, and were there until withdrawn in 1972. The period of the Vietnam War and Australia's role in it has been well documented with a range of feature films, documentaries, books, articles and memoirs published. But the role played by volunteers and voluntary organisations is less well known. In some ways this is curious, as the protest movement, which became such a feature of the war, was propelled by volunteer activism; that is, it would never have got off the ground if it had not been for the passion and involvement of thousands of volunteers across the country who mobilised their efforts, for years in some cases, for the causes in which they believed. The anti-war movement was predicated on people's commitment, their advocacy and unpaid labour, just as the social welfare, environmental and sporting movements were. Political protest and advocacy are forms of volunteering, just as working in an unpaid capacity for Meals on Wheels is considered volunteering.

As the 1960s progressed, there was increasing opposition to both the war and to conscription. Although a majority of the Australian population initially supported Australia's involvement in South Vietnam, there was increasing civil unease and unrest at the ongoing war, conscription and deaths of Australian soldiers. The result was the formation of a number of voluntary organisations, all of them initiated by volunteers, that fall under the rubric of the Vietnam protest movement. There were some peace organisations already established and some with a long-standing history. These include the Women's International League for Peace and Freedom, originally founded in 1915 to unite women who 'desire the settlement of disputes by other means than war and the emancipation of women of all races'.[4] This international pacifist organisation had no political affiliations but aimed to educate and help abolish the causes of war. During the 1950s there was an active peace movement associated with organisations like the United Association of Women that campaigned against nuclear war. But most were labelled a 'communist front' by mainstream politics, which had a negative impact on them.[5]

Other voluntary organisations, such as the Campaign for Peace in Vietnam were formed in an attempt to distance themselves from the older peace movement. A group of concerned citizens, largely based around the University of Adelaide, were called together at a public meeting on 31

July 1967. The organisation had two objectives. Firstly to work towards the end of Australian military involvement in Vietnam, and secondly to work towards an end of hostilities altogether. The Campaign for Peace in Vietnam was formally constituted with an elected general committee and executive officers. Within three months, it had 615 members. The organisation was established and sustained through countless hours of volunteer labour.

But it was not easy. The Campaign for Peace in Vietnam initially struggled. As is typical with many voluntary organisations, whatever the focus, financial difficulties were always to the fore. Short of funds, needing new members and scrounging around for basic office equipment were universal problems. For example, one newsletter pleaded, 'Does anyone have a typewriter which could be lent to the Campaign for use in the office? The need is urgent!'[6] In their second newsletter, typed and roneoed off by volunteers, the first item was the lack of money. Although the Campaign really wanted a paid full-time administrative assistant, they could not yet afford one and therefore relied on unpaid volunteers to staff the office, which they argued, curtailed their activities. The newsletter continued:

> To give members some idea of the costs of publicity; we
> have spent some $1,250 on eighteen newspaper and journal
> advertisements since the Campaign began at the end of July;
> each large advertisement in the daily press costs us about $200;
> to mail all those on our mailing list (for instance to send out
> this NEWSLETTER) costs us about $125 in stamps alone;
> we have spent a small fortune in envelopes, paper etc; the fee
> for hiring a hall for a public meeting is around $60; week by
> week we mail items of literature to new members as they join
> and a note of thanks to those who contribute to our finances;
> our printing bill is large and growing (each CPV brochure, for
> instance, costs 4 cents).[7]

What they really wanted was regular monthly financial commitments from members – if they averaged $2 per month from each member, the organisation would be comfortable. 'If we average three dollars we shall be in clover – for instance, we shall be able to advertise on television'.[8] From now on, the membership was told, the success of the Campaign depended on the 'enthusiasm of its membership. 'Talk to your friends. Organise small meetings in your own homes of people who are interested, but not yet members. The Campaign will provide speakers.' Under the direction of the Committee of Publicists led by Dr Neal Blewett, members prepared pamphlets and trained door-knockers, as well as fundraised for the fledgling protest group. They had letter-writing panels, sold Christmas cards, badges and posters, organised conferences and film screenings to raise awareness of their cause and to raise money to keep the organisation afloat. The Campaign for Peace in Vietnam became the largest voluntary organisation of its type in South Australia.

Margaret Eliot, who was involved in the anti-war movement, felt that women often did the 'shit work' as she termed it; that is, all the stereotypical, less glamorous but essential parts of volunteer work. While the men were generally the 'leaders' the women were in the back room. As Margaret later recalled:

> I still couldn't understand why I'd end up typing the minutes
> ... the stencils on the Gestetner, and how come men couldn't
> type ... there wasn't a man I knew that could type. And so the
> magazines were put out on Gestetner, the stencils had to be
> typed, and women invariably did that, they invariably did the
> shit work, that was my experience.[9]

This was a common theme. Bev Symons, who was involved in the Association for International Cooperation and Development (AICD), felt the same way. Elected as a delegate to a conference, she hardly saw anything of it:

> The first couple of days I was stuck in the office all the time:
> Roeoing [sic], as we called it then, before photocopies. And we
> had to use the Gestetner ... So I'm churning out endless copies
> ... and I just worked hours and hours ... into the night – me
> and others – in the back room as it were.[10]

There were other voluntary protest organisations. Some, for example, Women for Peace, were religious based; others, like the working class organisation, Union of Australian Women, worked to improve the status of women in Australia. Money was raised by selling badges, stickers and posters, as well as running cake stalls and fetes. It produced and distributed leaflets, organised mail campaigns to politicians, and supported conscientious objectors and drafted resisters. Its members also were involved in the formation of Save Our Sons (SOS), perhaps one of the best-known anti-war groups of the Vietnam era.

Save Our Sons (SOS)

The idea for SOS came from Mrs Joyce Golgerth, a housewife from Pennant Hills in north-western Sydney, who with a young son of eligible age, watched the unveiling of the *National Service Act* throughout 1964 with increasing horror. In October, with the implementation of the legislation imminent, and strongly opposed to the idea of conscription for overseas service in peacetime (let alone war), Joyce began to contact other mothers of boys eligible for conscription.[11] SOS was officially formed in Sydney on 13 May 1965 at a meeting attended by nine women and convened by Joyce and Noreen Hewitt. SOS was a non-party, non-political, non-sectarian organisation formed by a group of suburban housewives and mothers, some of whom had twenty-year-old sons, who were opposed to the *National Service Act*. Its aims were simply to protest at the concept of conscription, particularly as eighteen-year-old youths could be conscripted but could not vote. Their objectives were to seek to repeal or amend the *Act*, including serving overseas and withdrawing the severe penalties for infringement of the *Act*. They maintained they were patriotic women speaking out not only for their 'own sons but also for those boys possibly less able to speak for themselves who are being forced into the army against their wishes'.[12] Their first public event was the following week in Canberra at a three hour Silent Vigil for Peace organised by bishops and clergy of various denominations. On Sunday 30 May, SOS marched under their own banner as part of a peace group demonstration.

Within six months, SOS had 300 members across New South Wales and branches in Brisbane (formed 30 June by Mrs Wilma Ward with fifty-six members), Newcastle (convened by Mrs Isobel McArthur and Mrs Cullen on 5 August), and Melbourne (convened on 18 August by Mrs

Jean McLean with fifty-six supporters). SOS attracted women from across the political spectrum and all walks of life. As Ceci Cairns related:

> because it was organised by women, it meant many people who normally would have found it difficult and threatening to participate in a political organization were involved. These women were a tremendous force because they were motivated by feelings of total revulsion at the war.[13]

On Wednesday 30 June 1965, SOS staged the first all-day vigil outside the Marrickville Army Barracks where the first intake of twenty-year-old conscripts was processed, and then followed the group to Central Railway Station where the conscripts were despatched to camp.[14] SOS returned to Marrickville for every conscript intake day until conscription was abolished. This activity became a popular form of public protest for SOS in all states. The issue was highly contentious and increasingly acrimonious. According to a Morgan Gallop poll held in November 1967, conscription by a televised ballot based on birthdays was supported by 65 per cent of the population, but only 37 per cent believed that the men should be sent to the Vietnam War.

Throughout the war, SOS was a thorn in the side of authorities largely because its membership base was outside the general parameters of the traditional anti-war protester. SOS members were essentially ordinary Australian women and mothers, a vast majority of them housewives, who were well versed in volunteering and knew how to establish and run a voluntary organisation. There were many very capable women attracted to SOS and they devoted years of their lives to the cause. Generally, SOS volunteers devoted a couple of hours each week to typing, organising, driving or demonstrating. They knew what was required to organise and mobilise, to get volunteers engaged.

Adele Pert, the very active Secretary of the New South Wales SOS, was in her late forties and living with her family in Ryde, Sydney, when her daughter's boyfriend left an SOS pamphlet lying around. With strong anti-war beliefs but not politically minded, she rang up and went to an SOS meeting. After that, Adele became a tireless volunteer for the organisation. She wrote letters to Australian Prime Ministers Harold Holt and

John Gorton, the United States Government and Army, and to the trade union movement (which was very supportive of SOS and the anti-war movement generally). She targeted marginal seats during elections; wrote letters to both government and opposition members of parliament; and answered correspondence from those wishing to join the organisation or asking to begin their own group. She facilitated the dissemination of information about SOS's actions and plans and she kept in touch with the other branches across the nation.

SOS was very careful not to ostracise either the conscripts and soldiers or the families of soldiers. When news of the first conscript death was announced, SOS members laid a wreath at the Cenotaph in Martin Place, Sydney in his memory. The mothers were very sympathetic to the plight of the parents of the boys 'so tragically killed'.[15] But they could not escape the politics of the highly volatile situation. Their notoriety brought accusations that SOS was created by the Communist Party of Australia, an idea Joyce Golgerth and the other women strongly refuted.[16] Although some of their members were from the Communist Party that did not matter to SOS. 'It was just a get together of people who were so much opposed to conscription. We worked as a team', Adele Pert said later, 'It was one of the few organisations who didn't have any differences because we were so united on what we were doing'.[17] Unbeknown to them, ASIO was watching the women from SOS – taping their telephone conversations, monitoring their meetings and observing their demonstrations. They would have been horrified. Like many voluntary organisations formed for a specific purpose, SOS was wound up at the end of the war, when Gough Whitlam was elected Prime Minister in December 1972 and conscription was abolished.

Australia–Vietnam connections

Australians were also involved in establishing organisations to assist Vietnamese civilians affected by war, as well as providing a way to support Vietnamese refugees arriving in Australia for resettlement. One such group was the Australian/Vietnamese Association of Victoria. On 8 November 1965, this association held its first general meeting, attended by about 100 people. The aims were specifically non-political – to foster and promote friendship, understanding and good relations between the peoples of Australia and Vietnam, and included the provision that one of the vice-presidents be of Vietnamese background. The organisation planned to arrange exchanges of information, speakers, hospitality, and to promote aid projects. The treasurer and publicity officer, Tony Carden, was a surgeon and had spent time working in Vietnam as part of an Australian Surgical Team.[18] The medical teams were created in response to a call from the Australian government to recruit experienced Australian nurses and doctors to assist in the Vietnamese civilian hospitals. The first team travelled to Vietnam in October 1964. Over the following eight years, hundreds of Australian doctors and nurses travelled to Vietnam, to work at the Long Xuyen Hospital in the Mekong Delta, or the civilian hospitals in Bien Hoa and Vung Tau. The conditions were primitive, the hospitals lacked suitably qualified staff and were chronically overcrowded with sometimes two or three patients in one hospital bed, many of them suffering from gunshot wounds, napalm burns, head injuries and fractures. Relatives of the sick lived in the hospital, camping next to the patients.

Because of the association with the medical teams, the Vietnamese/Australian Association of Victoria developed a connection with Bien Hoa Hospital. In 1970, the Association raised $200 to fund a scholarship to assist a student undertaking nursing training at the hospital. At the same time, nurses from the Camden District Hospital in New South Wales raised $146, and with matching funding to the value of $200 donated by Australian Embassy staff in Saigon, a second nursing scholarship was established at Bien Hoa. The two scholarship winners, Miss Luu Thi Tuyet Dung and Miss Tran Thi Ngoc, were presented with their awards on 2 September 1970 by the Australian Ambassador Mr Harry. Miss Dung, eighteen, migrated from North Vietnam with her family in 1954. When she started her nursing course in April 1970, she was consistently near the top of her class, and was described as an alert and attentive student, who demonstrated skilful nursing ability. On accepting her award, Miss Dung wrote:

> I attended nursing school because, first, I can help my parents
> to bring up my seven younger brothers and sisters. Moreover,

my parents are very old. The second reason is that I hope to reduce the suffering of patients, though I know my contribution to society is very tiny. I am very grateful to the Australian Vietnamese Society.[19]

Miss Ngoc came first in her course and remained at Bien Hoa Hospital where she was appointed as an assistant nurse in the operating theatre.[20] Miss Dung, who came second left the hospital to rejoin her family in Gia Dinh where she worked at the local hospital. During 1970–71, over $2000 was raised by the Society and it was decided to spend the funds on more nursing scholarships and to purchase badly needed equipment at Bien Hoa Hospital.

Australians also travelled to Vietnam to volunteer their services for a range of voluntary organisations. Jenny Leak, a nurse from South Australia, originally spent six months there as part of a medical surgical team, and returned to become involved in the education of poor, orphaned and refugee children. 'In Vietnam, education is not free', she told the *Women's Weekly* in an interview. 'Parents care about their children, but even when both work seven days a week the cost of food is so high that many families have only enough money to survive from day to day'.[21] So in 1968, she founded the non-profit interdenominational Vietnam Christian School Program, where Australian families sponsored the education of a Vietnamese child. Margaret Moses, from South Australia, went to Saigon in March 1971 to join her friend Rosemary Taylor who ran an extensive western adoption program and orphanages for abandoned or orphaned children. Rosemary later said:

> Nothing in my previous experience or reading had prepared me for this. I was coming into contact with hundreds of newborn babies; the fully Vietnamese and the mixed-race; the legitimate and the illegitimate! ... To give them caring parents was the first step.[22]

With her excellent French and good organisational skills, Margaret was an immediate asset to her friend. Later, during Operation Babylift that preceded the fall of Saigon in April 1975, Margaret and fellow South Australian nurse, Lee Makk, were killed when an American plane crashed on take-off, killing seventy-eight children and their escorts.

Volunteers for overseas

Not only did the Vietnam War see the 'radicalisation' of the Australian way of volunteering and the emergence of a range of activist volunteers, but the moving frontier – that relationship between governments and the voluntary sector – also further developed. It was during the 1960s that Commonwealth government assistance for international voluntary aid organisations was introduced. Indeed, the beginning of the Vietnam War instigated much of the discussion in regards to the role of voluntary organisations and overseas aid. Government subsidies affected the roles played by volunteers in assisting 'third world' and developing countries. Along with the Colombo Plan, initiated in 1950 to assist with Australia's engagement in the region including the sponsoring of Asian students to study in Australia, the Federal government also began supporting the Volunteer Graduate Scheme, a program established in 1952 to provide young volunteer graduates from Australian universities with posts in Indonesia and elsewhere.[23]

The Federal government's policy on overseas aid in the post-war period increasingly saw a place for the involvement of voluntary organisations. In November 1965, Paul Hasluck, the Minister for External Affairs, announced the government's policy towards the voluntary sector, reflecting this revised position. In a speech entitled 'Respective Roles of Government, United Nations and Non-Government Agencies and Opportunities for Co-operation in Overseas Aid Activities', he said:

> The government regards voluntary aid as a useful part of
> Australian overseas activity … perhaps the first task we need
> to attempt is to distinguish the sort of work that voluntary
> agencies do best; the sort of work that governments can do
> best; and the sort of work in which they need to combine their
> efforts.[24]

In Hasluck's terms this new relationship was about co-operation, which meant 'consultation, a sharing of information or exchange of advice, the avoidance of duplication' as well as providing financial subsidies. This policy was received favourably by the press with editorials in support of the government's decision to provide financial assistance to programs like the Overseas Service Bureau's Australian Volunteers Abroad, because these types of voluntary organisations could act 'where and when governments cannot, and can maintain links when government policy necessitates a cooling of official relations ... most of all they make the process of aid-giving more personal'.[25]

Herb Feith, the pioneer founder of the Graduate Volunteer Scheme (later renamed Australian Volunteers Abroad and now called Australian Volunteers International) was a young post-graduate university student in the early 1950s, passionate about engaging with and fostering good relations with our near neighbour Indonesia through volunteering. Pre-dating the British Voluntary Service Overseas (1958) and the American Peace Corps (1961), Feith argued that 'through the decades the value and importance of volunteering has not changed. Volunteering is symbolic of human solidarity, of human equality'.[26]

The formation of the Australian Council for Overseas Aid (ACOA) in April 1965 also confirmed this new era of co-operation between governments and international volunteer aid societies. Membership of the ACOA included all major voluntary organisations interested in overseas aid (with the exception of the Australian Red Cross), many of whom were involved in assisting Vietnam. Included were Community Aid Abroad, the Overseas Service Bureau, Australian Council of Churches, Australian-Asian Association of Victoria, Catholic Overseas Relief, Lutheran World Federation, Lions International Australia, YWCA, YMCA, Freedom from Hunger and Apex. The purpose of the Council, which was well funded by the Commonwealth, was to provide co-operation and assistance between voluntary organisations interested in overseas aid and to provide an avenue for dialogue between Commonwealth and state governments, the United Nations and overseas governments. The Council saw itself as a peak body representing its members and providing a viewpoint on various questions to do with overseas aid and migration issues. It also hoped to keep the issue of overseas aid in the public domain. The Australian government, on the other hand, was also keen to develop closer ties with these organisations, especially in regards to the role they could play in providing general overseas aid. In early 1966, the Federal government funded an ACOA conference in Canberra to create a forum where officials from the Department of Immigration and External Affairs and ACOA could undertake an 'interchange of ideas between officials and voluntary leaders'.[27]

However, this new era of co-operation raised questions about Commonwealth financial assistance to voluntary aid organisations. On 20 June 1966, a senior public servant in the Prime Minister's Department wrote to the Prime Minister, Harold Holt, concerned that the government was receiving an increasing number of funding requests from a range of voluntary organisations to provide aid abroad, especially to Vietnam. The organisations included For Those Who Have Less, the Australian Freedom from Hunger Campaign, the Australian Committee for UNICEF, Community Aid Abroad, the Australian Council of Churches, the Australian Council of Aid to Refugees, and Aid for India Campaign. They were seeking government financial assistance for a range of items including freight costs and fares. At this point there was no official policy, no rules or criteria regarding grants to voluntary organisations providing overseas aid. Grants were awarded or rejected on an ad hoc basis by different ministers – either the Prime Minister, the Treasurer, Billy McMahon or Minister for External Affairs, Paul Hasluck, depending on whom the organisations targeted. Something needed to be done to streamline the process. Although the financial assistance requested by these organisations was generally not large, it was felt that if proper policies were not implemented, the effect would be voluntary organisations 'determining the direction and form of a significant part of Australia's aid expenditure'.[28]

Billy McMahon, as Treasurer, always fiscally tight and conservative, reflected the traditional view that voluntary organisations represented the 'voluntary efforts of private citizens' and that apart from the Australian Volunteers Abroad Scheme, the best and most 'practicable policy' was to 'insist that voluntary aid schemes undertaken by private organisations in Australia should be self-financing'.[29] No doubt the contentious nature of Australia's increasing involvement in the Vietnam War played a part and propelled much of the discussion in regards to the role of voluntary organisations and overseas aid. It took until 1970, when policy determined that all funding requests were to come under the Department of External Affairs portfolio.

Despite the complexities of the new relationship between the Commonwealth government and voluntary aid organisations, and the increasingly divisive views on the Vietnam War, Australians continued to volunteer abroad and donate generously to these organisations. By 1967, nine Australian voluntary organisations were operating in South Vietnam providing assistance to civilians displaced by the war, the sick, the aged and the maimed. Over $200 000 was raised from Australians and dozens of Australian volunteers were working in the country.[30]

Pushing the boundaries

During the 1960s, the expansion of volunteering and the shifting frontier was evident in other areas of Australian life. In literature, for example, the momentum continued with the development of federally based national organisational bodies. The Children's Book Council consolidated, and continued to be run by a dedicated group of volunteers passionate about children and children's literature. The Council received very little in the way of sponsorship and funding from any level of government. Up until 1966, the Children's Book of the Year Awards were funded by the Council itself, and were more symbolic than monetary, following on the tradition of the first winner in 1945 who received a gardenia from the Botanical Gardens. Financial support began in 1966, when the Federal government provided an annual grant of $500 from the Commonwealth Literary Fund to recognise the role played by the Children's Book Council.

In the area of heritage, local history and environment, the National Trust, based on the British example, expanded. It was originally formed in 1945 in New South Wales by Annie Wyatt, a career volunteer and activist. She founded the Ku-ring-gai Tree Lovers' Civic League in the 1920s, which took the lead in creating the Balls Head Reserve at North Sydney. She was also involved in the Prisoners' Aid Association, the United Association of Women and the Australian Red Cross. But it is the preservation of heritage and conservation for which she is best known. Her motto was that heritage and the environment were held 'on trust for the nation' and 'that we might learn from the past'.[31] The National Trust was built up entirely on volunteer labour, receiving its first state government grant for

$1000 in July 1959.[32] In 1960 it acquired parliamentary sanction through the NSW *National Trust Act*, with the following objectives:

> To acquire, protect and preserve for the benefit of the public, lands and buildings of beauty or of national, historical, scientific, architectural or cultural interest; to safeguard natural features and scenic landscape and conserve wildlife; and to encourage and promote public appreciation, knowledge and enjoyment of these things.[33]

Similarly keen to protect buildings and heritage, local history groups were formed by volunteers passionate about their history. From 1935, affiliate organisations began to join with the New South Wales Royal Australian Historical Society but it was in the 1950s and 1960s that the movement really took off. Nineteen historical societies were formed in the 1950s and ninety-six societies in the 1960s. Most of these were local historical societies but there were also groups such as the Society of Australian Genealogists and the History Teachers' Association of New South Wales.[34]

My grandmother, Nancy Nivison, and my parents were involved in this 'associational impulse' with the establishment of the Walcha District Historical Society in 1962. Purchasing land and an old slab cottage in Walcha, the whole town contributed to the project. As well as spending hours on painstaking historical research, solicitors, carpenters, painters, electricians, labourers and local women volunteered their skills and expertise to bring the project to fruition, often carrying out their volunteering on the weekends and after hours. The opening of the Pioneer Cottage in May 1963 was a huge event for the small country town, with over 2000 people in attendance. Official guests included a Councillor of the National Trust of Australia, Miss Rachel Roxburgh, who said that Walcha was leading the way in preserving old buildings. The project, she said, was a:

> classic achievement of forethought, unselfish enterprise and a gratifying dedication to a wonderful accomplishment which could well be emulated in many other cities and much larger towns in Australia.[35]

During the 1960s, volunteering in the environment movement also increased at a local level at a time when these matters were not on the public agenda. The publication of Rachel Carson's *Silent Spring* in America in 1962 led to the beginnings of a nascent environment movement in Australia. As usual, it was volunteers at the grassroots level who identified a need and gathered other like-minded individuals together to form associations to, in this case, protect our environment. Annie Wyatt and the Tree Lovers' Civic League, for example, were already active planting trees, distributing seed, organising school competitions and lobbying local and state governments.

The National Parks Association was formed in 1957 in New South Wales after the Hunter-Manning and Central Region National Parks Associations decided to form a state-based group. Led by environmental volunteer luminaries such as Paddy Pallin, Allen Strom, Rod Earp and Myles Dunphy, this voluntary organisation grew in size and influence. It successfully lobbied the New South Wales government to form the National Parks and Wildlife Service (through the *National Parks and Wildlife Act 1965*). Through this sustained political pressure, twelve existing national parks were protected, including the Blue Mountains, Kosciuszko and Royal National Parks. Another major voluntary organisation, the Australian Conservation Foundation, was founded in 1966 by well-known CSIRO entomologist Francis Radcliffe, and conservation volunteers, after a two-year gestation, that included a national conference in Canberra in August 1964 that laid the foundations for this important national environmental organisation.

Little Athletics, sport and volunteering

In the post-war period, one of the main innovations in sport was the development of organised sport for children. Sport has long been an integral part of Australian culture and identity, almost all of it centred around volunteers and a range of voluntary associations and clubs like the YMCA, YWCA, National Fitness Council, Scouts and Guides, as well as specific sporting bodies associated with athletics, football, hockey, tennis and cricket to name a few. The Pony Club movement, modelled on the British example and begun in the aftermath of World War II, was an early example of organised sport for children. Another, which is uniquely Australian, is Little Athletics. Trevor Billingham, from Geelong in Victoria, a high school physical education teacher and middle distance runner of some note, realised there were few opportunities for primary school aged children to compete in athletics events. In the early 1960s, the Victorian Amateur Athletics Association expanded and athletics in Geelong received a boost with the construction of the Landy athletics field in mid-1962. But there was nothing for younger children, who were turned away from athletics events. So Trevor and a group of locals got together and in October 1964 created an informal athletics program on Saturday mornings. Modelled on 'international track and field' events, but adapted for children, the program was called Little Athletics.[36]

The idea took off and Little Athletics Clubs mushroomed across Australia, with many towns and suburbs establishing their own community club. In December 1968, the Randwick Botany Little Athletics Centre was the first club established in New South Wales. Soon there were clubs in Hornsby, Sutherland, Eastern Suburbs, Manly, Deniliquin and the Murrumbidgee, and in 1970, following the Victorian example, the New South Wales state association was formed. The concept spread to other states, and within a few years Little Athletics developed into a national organisation. It became an Australian institution, closely linked to Australia's unique culture of sport, the outdoors, good weather and good health. The program runs over the Australian summer, beginning in mid-October, and continues until March. The season includes a regular weekly program, invitational meetings, state relay championships, state and national championships. The scheme largely relies on the active engagement of parents and carers, and these volunteers are integral to the successful management and operation of each club. When Trevor Billingham died in 2005, former Australian running champion, Ron Clarke, said, 'A lot of us have ideas and a few of us have dreams and visions. But very few have that capability to take that dream and vision and bring it to a reality'.[37]

As the Little Athletics example demonstrates, a feature of volunteering and the voluntary sector is the ability of an individual or individuals to identify a need in the community and to act upon that need. Generally, it involves bringing together other like-minded people to establish a group that works towards specific goals. These examples are found in any area of society and are generally only later either funded by government subsidies or taken over by a government program. At that point, the voluntary origins and the roles played by volunteers are lost. The Asthma Foundation's Children's Swimming Program in New South Wales is a good example of this.

The Asthma Foundation and the Children's Swimming Program

Australia has the unenviable reputation of having one of the highest incidences of asthma in the world. Because of this, Australia is one of the leading countries for research into asthma, and each year the government spends millions of dollars on asthma research and asthma prevention. Yet few remember its humble beginnings in the 1960s when a couple of mothers, passionate to find out why their children were suffering, set out to find a cure. None of it would have been possible without the volunteers who became the bedrock of the Asthma Foundation and Asthma Society. As Babette Smith, the Foundation historian wrote:

> They [volunteers] ranged from professional and businessmen with an ethic of community service to an army of women from a range of backgrounds and interests who recognised the distress asthma caused and were committed to solving it.[38]

The origins of the Asthma Foundation concern two Australian mothers of asthmatic children who were frustrated at receiving little assistance from the medical establishment. The view of the medical world in the late 1950s and early 1960s was that asthma and allergies in children were essentially psychosomatic in nature and associated with overly protective mothers. The treatment for asthma was rudimentary and there was little medical research or indeed medical interest in the life-threatening disease. The two mothers, Leila Schmidt and Mickie Halliday, were incensed by their treatment at the hands of the medical establishment.

They received little interest from doctors who viewed asthma as an illness not a disease. Mickie's daughter Catherine was severely allergic with what was known as 'strangulation asthma', and had survived numerous attacks with adrenaline injections. Married to a Macquarie Street dentist, Mickie was known in Sydney society circles and was actively involved in volunteering for the Penguin Club (a self-help group established to assist women in dealing with the 'public' world) where she learned the skills of public speaking and chairing meetings – two essential tools for volunteer leaders. Leila Schmidt worked as a secretary and had typing skills, also essential attributes for any voluntary organisation. Although quite different in style, they were passionate crusaders with determination and commitment.

The two women decided to find a cure for asthma – by inaugurating a Foundation that would raise money to fund research. In 1961, along with Dr Claire Isbister, a medical practitioner, paediatrician and mother of a severely asthmatic child, the women began to plan. The following year, the New South Wales Asthma Foundation was founded. 'We opened the doors and the world rushed in', said Mickie.[39] A hugely successful door-knock appeal was launched in August 1962, raising over £250 000. Thousands of women volunteered their services to the new organisation, and within a short space of time the Foundation became very much part of the society circles of Sydney. Many volunteers had a direct link to asthma such as Brodie Mullan, from Vaucluse, whose twenty-one-year-old son died from an asthma attack not long after she joined the Foundation. Brodie made tea and stuffed envelopes – the tried and true activities of a volunteer. She went on to start the Vaucluse Auxiliary, one of the most prolific fundraising groups.[40] As was common for voluntary organisations at the time, the Foundation established a Women's Committee to concentrate on fundraising. Famous aviatrix, Nancy Bird Walton, was patron, and a series of auxiliaries in metropolitan and rural New South Wales were established.

In 1962, an Asthma Society was formed under directorship of Leila Schmidt, and was renamed the Asthma Welfare Society two years later. With its own journal, *The Asthma Welfarer,* edited by Dr Claire Isbister, it reported on the distribution of funds of the Foundation's research program, news of the society, and informed and educated the parents and children about asthma. The journal was non-profit making, its editorial staff and contributors all volunteered their services, with expenses covered by advertising.[41]

In 1964, another innovation was the establishment of a swimming program to assist young children cope with the physically debilitative nature of asthma. Once again, the key protagonists were the original founders. Because of breathing difficulties associated with asthma, asthmatic children generally avoided sport or were often excluded from school sporting activities. Many could not swim and were a very unfit and unhealthy group of children overall.[42] In the days before Ventolin, there were few drugs available to treat asthma.[43] As Claire Isbister said, we 'knew that most asthmatic children could not swim, hated putting their faces in the water and feared drowning. We decided that they must need special teaching'.[44]

After meeting Anne Melrose, a professional swimming coach and the sister of former Olympic swimmer and asthma sufferer, Jon Henricks, they decided to establish a swimming program, one of the first of its kind in the world. Swimming in warm indoor pools with one-on-one supervised lessons could enhance an asthmatic child's quality of life by providing both a specific method of breathing through exercise, and most importantly by providing a happy and safe swimming environment. Along with two thoracic physiotherapists and three specialist clinicians, a unique asthmatic swimming method was developed, with a specific exercise program and individualised tuition. They decided to use 'mature women volunteers' rather than paid swimming instructors because it was believed that professional swim coaches were too rigorous and unsuited to this specialist group who needed the nurturing qualities of trained female volunteers. Groups of volunteer swimming instructors were recruited and trained by Anne. These self-titled 'Monday Mums' included Gloria Guthrie and Pat Hutcherson, who both ended up working as volunteer swimming instructors for forty years.[45]

The Children's Asthma Swimming Program formally began at Frank O'Neill's indoor heated pool at Pymble in April 1964.[46] Within two years, over seventy-two volunteer instructors were working in eight heated municipal and private pools across the suburbs of Sydney, and by 1968 over 750 children had attended the swimming program. With control devolved to the local level, swimming sub-committees were established to organise volunteer coaches and asthmatic children in each area.[47] The success of the program was due to the organisation of the volunteer scheme and the dedication of its fully trained women volunteers.

Social welfare volunteering

In social welfare, a traditional area for volunteers and volunteering, the 1960s was both a time of continuity and change. Despite the increasing numbers of women in the paid workforce, there was still a large cohort of willing and able women available to undertake a range of volunteer tasks. This silent army of unpaid workers helped to make the voluntary sector an integral component of social welfare delivery in Australia. As John Lawrence, Professor of Social Work at UNSW, argued, the voluntary sector was not 'a subject of peripheral interest', but rather one 'of central importance to our way of life'.[48]

The moving frontier

There were significant changes in the relationship between the voluntary sector and governments especially in the application of state welfare provisions after World War II. As shown in chapter 4, the Commonwealth government began to fund voluntary organisations involved in the provision of social welfare through a range of subsidies. In 1954, for example, legislation was enacted to make voluntary organisations eligible for aged care subsidies. Then came home nursing in 1956 and marriage guidance in 1960. Other areas where the Commonwealth pushed the frontier forward, was in the administration of additional grants to the states (then distributed to voluntary organisations), including free milk for primary school children (1950), the development of emergency housekeeping (1951) and blood transfusion services of the Australian Red Cross (1953).[49] This made up for lost revenue through increased taxation, as it was argued by some that those who once supported voluntary action now only did so through their taxes, and that 'giving' had diminished as a result.[50]

With these changes, the voluntary sector actively sought more co-operation between it and all levels of government. Although the sector was robust – with churches and myriad social welfare groups operating at local, state and national level, the so-called 'welfare gadflies' – community organisations such as Rotary, Lions, Apex and Quota, and new peak bodies like the Australian Council of Social Service (ACOSS) formed in 1956 – there was a view that more could be done. At the heart of it was the question of the relationship between the voluntary sector and the state. As the frontier moved, the voluntary sector sought reassurance as to its role and function. Although a junior partner, the sector sought clarification. Do 'we [the voluntary sector]' asked the Anglican Coadjutor Bishop of Melbourne, Geoffrey Sambell, 'exist for the State or for the right of voluntary action: or to serve the needs of people?'[51] It was a valid question. Secondly, the government had to be continually reminded of the advantages offered by the voluntary sector, which included the pioneering of new services, experimentation and research, community planning and consultation.

In 1966, in recognition of this changing environment, ACOSS organised the first major national conference to examine the state of social welfare and voluntary organisations in Australia. The conference attracted social welfare groups keen to discuss the issue of increased Commonwealth subsidies to deliver specific services, or what became known as the mixed economy of welfare. A key aspect to emerge from the conference was a recognition that the government and the voluntary sector needed to have shared aims, which benefited both parties. The relationship between the voluntary sector and governments in Australia was mercurial. The voluntary sector wanted more dialogue with governments, more guidance and inclusion in broad discussions regarding social welfare policy. The sector recognised and accepted the increased statutory action but was increasingly unsure of where the 'moving frontier' lay, and what their roles should be.

Marriage guidance counselling

The experience of marriage guidance counselling is a good example of the difficulties in this relationship. On the one hand, the voluntary sector appreciated government funding and liked the idea of working alongside government in an important area of social policy. The connections gave the voluntary sector added legitimacy and recognition. But with the funding came new guidelines and benchmarks that concerned some groups.

Innovation has always been a hallmark of the voluntary sector. One of its strengths has been the ability to identify a need and do something about it quickly by pioneering a new range of services. The voluntary sector long identified the need for marriage guidance and/or family assistance for a range of relationship problems affecting Australian families. The marriage guidance movement began in Britain in 1943, where centres offered assistance with marriage problems, marriage preparation and family life education for young people. The counsellors, all fully trained volunteers, completed a forty-eight lecture course, sat a series of tests set by a National Selection Board, and served a year's probation. 'The real strength of the movement', stated Western Australian broadcaster, Catherine King, in an ABC radio talk, 'lay in the devotion and integrity of the officers, the committee members, counsellors and other workers who gave so much voluntary service and of so high a quality'.[52]

In Australia, organisations (like the Family Welfare Bureau) established both during and after World War II, addressed the area of marriage guidance. The National Marriage Guidance Council of Australia, representing all state groups, was founded in 1953, and by 1960 was under the patronage of the Governor-General's wife, Lady Slim. In the late 1950s, as part of the *Matrimonial Causes Act 1959*, the Commonwealth government sought to provide subsidies to selected marriage guidance organisations. The *Act* enabled voluntary organisations to apply to the Attorney General's Department for approval, and to receive Commonwealth funding.

To explain the scheme, voluntary organisations were invited by the Attorney General, Garfield Barwick, to attend a conference in February 1960. Those invited included the National Marriage Guidance Council of Australia, the National Catholic Welfare Committee, the Australian Red Cross Welfare Services, Brotherhood of St Laurence (Melbourne), the Citizens' Welfare Service (Melbourne), the Family Welfare Bureau and St Andrews' Cathedral Marriage Guidance Centre, both from Sydney.[53] To be administered by the Attorney General's Department, the scheme was seen by the government as 'an interesting experiment in social action'.[54] Although this was a new area of responsibility for the Commonwealth government, the *Act* merely formalised what many voluntary organisations were already doing.

By 1966, there were twenty approved marriage guidance organisations across Australia, with thirty-six counselling centres. Seven were non-denominational marriage guidance councils, and some, such as the Catholic Family Welfare Bureau, were specifically religious based. The voluntary organisations received both Federal and state funding subsidies ranging from £400 to £10 000. In 1966, there were twenty-four full-time and twenty-six part-time salaried staff and 356 part-time volunteer counsellors.[55] According to Les Harvey, a bureaucrat from the Attorney General's Department charged with implementing the scheme, the caseload for the 1964/65 financial year included general assistance with 7500 marriages, 2500 marriage counselling interviews and almost 3000 'pre-marital' interviews.[56]

From the government's perspective, the scheme provided a quality service at minimal cost. But the service could only be delivered because of the extensive use of volunteer counsellors. The question of national standards and procedures, and the selection and training of marriage guidance counsellors was a problem for both the Attorney General's Department and the voluntary organisations. There was an acute shortage of professionally trained social workers, especially in rural and regional Australia, which fuelled debates between paid and unpaid workers, between professionals and amateur 'do-gooders'. The voluntary organisations could not do without the 'traditional volunteer' or 'lay' counsellors but most also wanted to display a level of professionalism which meant employing fully qualified social workers. The challenge lay in establishing uniform national guidelines across different voluntary organisations, many of whom were well established and had been undertaking marriage guidance counselling for years. As the Reverend Coughlan, Director of the New South Wales Marriage Guidance Council, noted in 1962, there were differences of opinion between the various marriage guidance organisations in reconciling views between social workers and 'lay' counsellors, as well as differences with 'their restrictions, primary loyalties, geographical coverage and the degree of their democracy in organization and control'.[57]

One view on how to address the acute shortage of social workers was to use 'one of our greatest resources' as volunteer counsellors:

> That group of intelligent married women who around the age of 40 are tapering off the job of child raising, and are ready for a new challenge. These women, with their broad life experience and their interest in human relationships, are a gold mine of relatively unused talent. [58]

Many of the volunteer caseworkers worked, in an unpaid capacity, between three and twelve hours per week. They completed extensive training ranging from fifteen months to two years, covering topics such as sociology, psychology, physiology, anatomy, law, psychopathology, ethics, counselling techniques and practical skills. But the Commonwealth government did not fund training and recruitment, and voluntary organisations had to subsidise it out of their own scant resources, or ask the volunteers to pay for their own training.[59] There was a real cost to professionalisation.

This was a moot point with the sector. With Commonwealth funding came new benchmarks that not all organisations either agreed with or wanted. Furthermore, even if they agreed with the notions of professionalisation and full training of volunteer counsellors (in this instance), the Commonwealth refused to fund the essential training and recruitment. So, while the offer to work side by side with government was a good one, it compromised the independence of voluntary organisations and their volunteers and placed new pressures on organisations and volunteers alike. It was a double-edged sword. This pattern was to be repeated again and again in the following decades and profoundly affected volunteering and the voluntary sector in Australia.

The Family Welfare Bureau

One organisation involved in marriage guidance counselling that experienced increasing difficulties through the 1960s was the Family Welfare Bureau. In 1961, it was forced to move from 58 Martin Place, Sydney when the building was sold to the Bank of New South Wales. The social workers and clerical staff moved to 169 Albion Street, Surry Hills taking over a peppercorn rental from the Anti-TB Association, while the Handcraft service and shop remained at Martin Place. There was also a shakeup in the organisation with the retirement of long-time Chairperson Mrs CJ Pope due to ill health (she died two years later). May Pillinger, the Director of the Bureau since the war years, resigned in October 1960 but she continued to be involved through the auxiliaries or branches as they became known. Other changes saw a number of new branches formed in the suburbs to assist with fundraising, including Killara, Lane Cove, French's Forest, Parramatta and Northern Districts. In 1966, Lady Cutler, wife of the incoming Governor of New South Wales, became patron of the Bureau, which excited those who viewed this type of patronage in the voluntary sphere as a sign of success.

The Bureau became more closely involved with the Commonwealth government through its subsidy arrangements, and funding for marriage guidance began in 1962. Although the Bureau continued to receive funding from the New South Wales government through the Department of Child Welfare and Social Service, the Commonwealth government's marriage guidance subsidy of $6500 (by 1966) became increasingly relied upon as a key source of funding. Donations, subscriptions, fundraising and trusts provided the bulk of the Bureau's income, but the reliance on Commonwealth government funding was a significant shift. This supports the broad argument of a changing relationship between the voluntary sector and the state in the 1960s. Although state government funding to the Bureau remained static, the Commonwealth provided key grants through the Attorney General's Department and the Immigration Department (for assisting newly arrived migrants).

As a result, one can observe a discernable shift in the role played by the Family Welfare Bureau as it repositioned itself to focus on family and marital counselling services. This was because of the funding provided by the Commonwealth government and the Bureau's enhanced status as one of the government designated voluntary organisations offering marriage guidance counselling. The importance of the volunteer, strongly evident from the 1940s, diminished during the 1960s as the concept of the professional and paid social worker took over. The Bureau's focus became casework, and it employed four-year university trained social workers to undertake the work of its professional counselling services.[60] Other voluntary organisations carrying out similar services in Sydney at the time – the Australian Red Cross, the Catholic Welfare Bureau and Caritas Psychiatric Centre – all underwent this process of enhancing their 'professional competence', due largely to the new opportunities brought by increased government funding.

During the 1960s, the client base of the Family Welfare Bureau also changed. Many of the families referred to the Bureau were from the expanding outer suburbs of Sydney, including Liverpool and Blacktown; and the Bureau recognised the need to have a physical presence in the western suburbs. Issues of lack of suitable accommodation, lack of access to employment, alcohol abuse, behavioural and psychiatric problems were all problems that led to the breakdown of family relationships. The question of the social, economic and emotional issues concerned with fatherless families, either through desertion or death, was an increasing problem for clients of the Bureau. These families particularly suffered the 'social ostracism which the community imposed on a widow or deserted wife and her children'.[61]

By 1967–68, with a branch office at Parramatta, the Bureau employed two full-time and three part-time social workers and four administrative staff members. It also continued a longstanding practice undertaken since the 1940s, of providing social work student placements for students from both the University of Sydney and UNSW. Volunteers were still an integral part of the organisation but were increasingly in the background. This was despite the fact that the auxiliaries in the suburbs raising the bulk of the funds were entirely run by volunteers. The Bureau also continued to be managed by a volunteer executive committee, a volunteer bookkeeper, and eight volunteers worked in the office operating the switchboard, typing and filing.[62]

Aged care and Meals on Wheels

The iconic voluntary organisation, Meals on Wheels, has its roots in the 1950s and is another example of the slow and subtle shift in the relationship between the Commonwealth and voluntary sector. Modelled on a British idea, the Australian version was first brought to Australia by Mrs Nancy Dobson, the honorary secretary of the Ladies Auxiliary from the South Melbourne Council.[63] But it was in South Australia where the scheme was most developed due largely to the dynamic and untiring efforts of Doris Taylor. Although confined to a wheelchair since child-hood, Doris did not let her disability dissuade her from actively partici-pating in society. A member of the Labor party, it is said that she was responsible for encouraging Don Dunstan (later South Australian Labor Premier) to enter parliament. Involved in a range of volunteering and advocacy work, Doris Taylor's main legacy was the organisation Meals on Wheels, which she founded in 1953 in South Australia, with its first kitchen opening in Port Adelaide the following year. By 1967, Meals on Wheels had twenty-one kitchens delivering hot meals and providing other services to the elderly and incapacitated around the state.[64]

The development of Meals on Wheels was ad hoc and varied from state to state. By the late 1960s, some state governments assisted with funding, but others did not. Doris Taylor successfully lobbied the South Australian government and received generous assistance. In Victoria, the State Department of Health subsidised the activity through local munici-pal government and Senior Citizens' Clubs, while in Western Australia, the League of Home Help for Sick and Aged Inc and a couple of local government councils provided funding subsidies. In Tasmania, hospital kitchens provided the meals, with delivery organised by two voluntary organisations. In New South Wales, a Meals on Wheels service was begun by the Sydney City Council in 1957, with no state government subsidy at all. Although hospital kitchens were sometimes available to prepare meals, the program was largely left to local government, service clubs and community groups to fund and manage.[65] Neither was there state govern-ment support in Queensland where the fledging service struggled to survive. The concept was most well developed in South Australia, Victo-ria, Tasmania and New South Wales, with the remaining states almost devoid of services outside metropolitan areas.[66]

The possibility of a Commonwealth subsidy to Meals on Wheels to address the lack of uniformity across the nation emerged from Common-wealth and state discussions as part of the Australian Health Ministers'

Conferences in 1967 and 1968. Part of the Commonwealth's response was to create a new state/Federal funding agreement for home and nursing care for the aged; these initiatives included home nursing, a housekeeping service, home help and other specialist services.[67] The package was largely aimed at relieving demand for aged care accommodation in public hospitals and nursing homes, as well as encouraging the elderly to stay in their own homes.

In December 1969, a Cabinet submission from the Minister for Social Services, WC Wentworth, argued that voluntary organisations providing Meals on Wheels services should be allocated a $1 subsidy for every ten meals served. Although he noted that 'the valuable service rendered by many voluntary organisations throughout Australia providing meals to aged and invalid persons in their homes' was widely recognised, it was hoped that the proposed Commonwealth assistance would encourage the extension of the program and help keep the elderly in their own homes.[68] Most importantly, through the *Delivered Meals Subsidy Act 1970*, the Commonwealth subsidy to Meals on Wheels encouraged a more equitable system nationwide. It allowed voluntary organisations already delivering meals on wheels to expand and new ones to be created in states like Queensland, where there was effectively no program.

Commonwealth financial support for Meals on Wheels can be seen as part of the broader changes underway in aged care in the late 1960s. It is also symbolic of the shifting relationship between state and Federal governments in this area. The original Home Nursing Subsidy Scheme, introduced by the Commonwealth government in 1957, promoted the expansion and development of aged care homes to ease pressure on public hospitals, through funded initiatives such as home nursing services, housekeeper and home-help services, home visiting, senior citizens' centres and other services. All this is well known. But the impact these funding decisions had on the voluntary sector and the volunteers who largely staffed and ran Meals on Wheels is less well understood. The Commonwealth subsidy from 1970 was the 'shot in the arm' required to not only motivate Australians to volunteer their labour to undertake an invaluable social service but also proved that the task was an important one. Providing regular meals to the most vulnerable citizens, in their own home, with dignity, was now recognised by the Commonwealth government as important and the volunteers who made the service happen were also acknowledged. Doris Taylor, the public face of Meals on Wheels in South Australia, who created a model for all to follow, would have been pleased.

Conclusion

In terms of the development of an Australian way of volunteering, the 1960s was an exciting decade of new ideas, new initiatives and new directions. Volunteering became highly political with the controversy surrounding the Vietnam War leading to many Australians becoming activists for the first time in the anti-war movement. Volunteering also expanded as Australians became active in a diverse range of areas, including sport, heritage and the environment. Volunteering became more engaged, more complex and more multifaceted. In traditional areas of volunteering, such as social welfare, some voluntary organisations became increasingly reliant on government funding. Issues of professionalisation and standardisation began to have an impact on voluntary organisations for the first time. Likewise, the relationship between governments and volunteers developed further, with the 'moving frontier' shifting with the times. But the seismic social and political changes that were so much a part of the 1970s were about to be unleashed and their effects would also have an impact on the Australian way of volunteering.

PART III
BECOMING VISIBLE
1970–2008

Jillian Oppenheimer:
A new generation of volunteer

My mother's earliest memories of volunteering come from World War II when, as a young girl, she played the 'victim' of a mustard gas air raid. Armed with a label that said 'mustard gas, broken arm and leg – unable to walk' pinned to her coat, she was left at the war memorial gates at the top of dusty Derby Street in Walcha to await rescue. As part of the emergency responses and air raid precautions, the Red Cross, VAs and Volunteer Defence Corps (VDC) organisations from the small rural town were practising in case of disaster, bombing or invasion, all very real threats in the dark days of 1942. Owing to petrol rationing, air raid precautions were generally held on Sunday mornings at the hospital and showground, so locals could combine their church going and wartime volunteering. As was typical of many of her generation, my mother was a member of the Junior Red Cross and spent many hours swaddled in bandages on one limb or another and knitting socks for the war effort.

Jillian was one of the few young women of her generation to do the Leaving Certificate and attend university, obtaining a BA from the University of Sydney in 1953. She also travelled overseas including a period of study at the Sorbonne in Paris. But as was common with many young women in the 1950s, she fell in love and married, and after marriage came children and a life taken up with domestic duties. Returning to Walcha with her husband to live, Jillian's one intellectual outlet was to supervise her three children as they studied through correspondence school in their primary years.

Although Jillian supported her mother in a range of local voluntary organisations such as the horticultural societies, beautification committee and historical society, she branched out and became involved in more novel volunteer organisations, many of them associated with children such as the Walcha Pony Club. This was a relatively new phenomenon – parents becoming directly involved in their children's extracurricular activities, especially in the areas of sport and recreation.

During the 1970s, when Jillian's children were teenagers, she returned to university to complete an honours and masters degree at the University of New England in Armidale, a large educational town 60 kilometres away. This move began a change of focus, away from Walcha, her children and local issues, and she became closely involved in a number of areas that were to dominate her volunteering for years to come. The 1970s also brought significant change for my mother, as she took up a paid job at the university to support her family after a difficult and protracted divorce. She also became aware of the pressing issues of environment and heritage. Growing up on the land, Jillian had always been committed to preserving the environment, including tracts of bushland, and dealing with the all too familiar spectacle of drought. Brought up by her father who always said that 'we must leave the land in a better condition than when we received it', she and others on the northern tablelands were increasingly concerned about 'dieback', an insidious disease that was killing the eucalyptus forests of New England. My mother was always vitally interested in Australian history, heritage and the preservation of historic buildings. It was these two areas of heritage and environmental conservation in particular, that galvanised her attention from the 1970s onwards. Jillian took up the gauntlet and spent much of her spare time volunteering for these causes. Although she continued to support the areas pioneered by her mother, especially when Nancy died in 1973, Jillian forged her own path in other organisations.

Jillian became passionately involved with environmental issues especially the National Parks Association of New South Wales. Awareness of the issue of protecting wilderness areas, particularly old-growth forests that were being cut down to be made into wood chips, was growing in the 1960s and became popularised in the 1970s. This coincided with one of our famous family holidays, involving a camping trip to Tasmania. With the Cortina station wagon piled full of tents, sleeping bags and other camping equipment, we set off from Pyrmont Wharf in Sydney on the Sydney–Tasmania car ferry. As well as appreciating historic Port Arthur, we spent time driving around the woodchip mills of Tasmania and being shocked by the clear-felled forests and denuded lunar-like wasteland of Queenstown on the west coast.

Jillian helped to form the Walcha Branch of the National Parks Association of New South Wales in 1975 with a group of concerned locals, including John and Margot Fleming who were worried about the degradation and general environmental changes on their rural property. By establishing a branch of an authentic and influential grassroots environmental organisation, they hoped to attract experts to the Walcha area to provide themselves with expertise to manage the different facets of environmental conservation, both for current and future genera-tions. The branch also hoped to develop national parks in the falls area to the east of Walcha, not only to preserve and conserve but also to attract tourists to the region. The branch existed for nine years, closing its doors in June 1983 after helping to create the Oxley Wild Rivers National Park.

My mother also became involved in the Armidale Branch of the National Trust (NSW) and, in an effort to push heritage issues in regional and rural areas, she helped form the New England Regional Committee that extended its influence from Tamworth in the south to Tenterfield in the north; and from Walcha and Armidale in the east to Narrabri, Inverell and Moree in the west. From this time on, the National Trust became one of Jillian's key volunteering interests, working and lobbying to secure Saumarez Homestead for the National Trust, chairing and participating on a range of committees. For almost forty years she has volunteered for that organisation, including five years as a council member, and then ten years as Vice President of the Board of the National Trust (NSW) from 1991 to 2001.

Jillian continues to spend at least 20 hours per week volunteering at Saumarez and sitting on the National Trust Conservation Committee and other bodies. Every Tuesday morning, you will find her in the Walcha Local Heritage Centre, attached to the local library, running the centre, answering enquiries, and helping the random 'drop ins' searching for their Walcha forebears. Although she was recognised for her volunteer work with an Order of Australia in 1999 and also a New South Wales government Heritage Volunteer Award in 2003, it hardly seems enough for all the hours she has spent volunteering over her lifetime. And she is not yet done!

6 Pushing the boundaries

With almost fanatical zeal we tried to SAVE THE BUSH
spending so much time and energy trying to convince people that
it should be saved … and like most missionaries trying to convert,
encountered much opposition … many friendships were lost in the
hot arguments that arose. [1]

Monica Sheehan

The 1970s heralded the beginning and end of many things in Australia – it was the end of that most unpopular war in Vietnam, and the beginning of the second wave feminist movement when the baby boomers came of age. The decade saw Labor hopes raised and dashed, with the election, after twenty-three years in the political wilderness, of the Whitlam government in 1972 and its controversial dismissal in 1975. The 1970s saw a social revolution in gender equality, Indigenous rights, migration policies, and the development of a counter-culture and sexual revolution. It was also a time of high inflation, high unemployment, huge fluctuations in oil prices called oil shocks and political instability. Once again, Australians were influenced by events overseas such as the civil rights protests and the Vietnam moratoriums in America, the May 1968 riots and general strikes in France.

By the 1970s, Australians were, largely, affluent, highly mobile, well travelled and consumers of a wide range of services. A McNair Anderson gallup poll conducted in 1974 highlighted the diversity of Australians, across both ethnic and state borders.[2] The poll found that many households had two incomes, indicating a high disposable income. Thirty-three per cent of women were employed, either full- or part-time, with 67 per cent not employed. Fifty-nine per cent of Australians aged thirteen and over were interested in music compared with 54 per cent in sport. Fifty-eight per cent enjoyed reading books and almost one in two Australian women read the *Australian Women's Weekly*. Ninety-six per cent of Australians had a television and the top television programs included *Number 96* and *Division 4*. People over thirteen spent on average 19 hours and 14 minutes watching television each week. Over 70 per cent approved of daylight saving, which was legislated in 1974–75 by all state governments, with the exception of Queensland. Unfortunately, but not unsurprisingly, this new way of creating a 'thumb-nail sketch of some characteristics and attitudes of Australians' by using 'large-scale house-to-house sample surveys'[3] did not include volunteering.

In terms of political advocacy and volunteering, the 1970s started with a bang with the Vietnam moratorium campaigns of 1970 and 1971. The anti-war movement in Australia was reasonably sophisticated by this stage, having worked since the mid-1960s to end the increasingly unpopular war. Modelled on the American moratoriums, the rallies attracted hundreds of thousands of people and were some of the largest public demonstrations ever seen in Australia. The moratorium campaign, with the motto 'Stop, Pause, Think.' gave the anti-war movement a new lease of life. New groups, such as the Vietnam Moratorium Campaign, Western Australia, were formed around the organisation of the mass demonstrations. With a strong religious and trade union base, the committee requested volunteers for 'typing, distributing of literature, wrapping *Moratorium News*, public speaking' and arranging discussion groups.[4] By April 1971, they had 115 members, with the Premier of Western Australia, JT Tonkin MLA, as their patron.

The first moratorium, held on 8 May 1970, drew over 150 000 protesters to the streets. The Campaign for Peace in Vietnam was the largest anti-

Vietnam War voluntary organisation in South Australia. Thousands of volunteer hours were devoted to the production and distribution of moratorium materials, including posters, stickers, badges and leaflets letterboxed to every household in Adelaide. From April 1970, Australian troops were gradually withdrawn from Vietnam. But Save our Sons (SOS) and other anti-war organisation volunteers continued to pressure the Liberal government of Billy McMahon until the election of the Whitlam Labor government in December 1972, when conscription was abolished and the final hundred or so troops withdrawn. After almost eight years of continual hard work, SOS felt 'joy and relief' that it was now behind them. At a meeting in April 1973, it was moved and accepted that SOS be wound up. As Adele Pert recalled, they did not have a big celebration; it was more:

> 'goodo – that's done, we've done a good job'. And we just
> packed up our records ... we had a meeting and we decided
> 'Well we've completed what we set out to do – which was [end]
> conscription' and we packed up all our records and sent them
> down to Canberra to the National Library.[5]

So how did the Australian way of volunteering handle the changes in this controversial and difficult decade? If World War II was a high point for volunteering, then the 1970s was another. This decade witnessed a distinct period of increased voluntary action. Over 30 per cent of voluntary organisations in existence today have their origins in the 1970s.[6] The increase was largely due to increased citizen participation, government recognition and financial assistance. Governments for the first time took a direct interest in volunteering. Social policies of the Whitlam government, especially programs such as the Australian Assistance Plan (AAP), resulted in a fundamental shift in the shape and configuration of volunteering and voluntary action in Australia. The expansion of the 'moving frontier' and the relationship that developed between volunteering and governments saw further consolidation.

The 1970s also witnessed the spawning or expansion of new volunteering activities, especially in the environment, heritage and advocacy in social welfare areas such as women's refuges and resident action groups. There was increasing discontent over the rate of development in the major cities (especially Sydney) that led to the foundation of voluntary groups such as the Battlers for Kelly's Bush and the expansion of nascent organisations such as the Australian Conservation Foundation. My mother's involvement in the National Parks Association and her assistance in forming the Walcha branch in 1975 is but one example, but her actions and those of her fellow volunteers in the Walcha branch were replicated across Australia. Volunteering as a form of active citizenship symbolised the period, much of it propelled by and centred on women's new found freedoms and the second wave feminist movement.

However, as will be revealed in this chapter, this 'volunteering impulse' was not uniform. Some traditional areas began to feel the effects of declining volunteer numbers. Changes in women's expectations, the breaking down of barriers to full participation in the workforce and a general shift in social and cultural perceptions contributed to an increasing shortage of volunteers in some areas such as surf lifesaving and the traditional social welfare organisations. At the same time, a move was made to enlist senior members of society (who were healthier, retiring earlier and living longer) to make up for the corresponding shortfall of traditional volunteers; that is, women of child-bearing age, who were increasingly moving into paid work and were not available to volunteer as they had traditionally done. These changes made the 1970s a dynamic period for the moving frontier and the Australian way of volunteering.

This transformation will be shown through a number of case studies from the areas of social welfare, the environment, political activism, health and sport, including the Battlers for Kelly's Bush and the beginnings of the green bans, and surf lifesaving, a quintessential icon of Australian volunteering that struggled to remain relevant in the 1970s. I will also give a brief analysis of the Australian Assistance Plan (AAP), a short-lived social policy initiative of the Whitlam era, to reveal the influence and impact of governments on Australian volunteering.

Volunteerism as a broader concept

From the beginning of the decade, commentators noted an increased awareness of volunteering and 'voluntarism as a broader concept', espe-

cially the increase in self-help groups and the development of societies concerned with social and environmental change.[7] One of the first
research projects on volunteers in Australia was undertaken in 1971 by
the Victorian Council of Social Service (VCOSS), under the directorship
of Marie Coleman and Professor Ronald Henderson from the University
of Melbourne's Institute of Applied Economic and Social Research. The
project sought to find out who volunteered in Victorian welfare agencies,
and what kind of jobs they did. The 400 or so agencies and organisations
that responded to the survey, reported that over 68 per cent of volunteers
were women. There were few men or women volunteers under the age
of twenty, and unlike today, few volunteers over the age of sixty. Many
volunteers had minimal job classifications or task definition, few were
given training, and the organisation of volunteers was limited.[8]

Associated with this evolving interest in volunteering as a 'concept',
was the beginning of organised volunteer centres, and what we now know
as the peak body, Volunteering Australia, and its state-based centres. Once
again it was the initiative of an individual, in this case Mrs Rose Miller,
who was organising volunteers to assist mentally handicapped children at
the Grosvenor Hospital in Summer Hill, Sydney. She realised that there
were people who wanted to volunteer but were not interested in her particular 'mothering' work. So, influenced by the bureau models established
in countries such as the United Kingdom, Canada and Hong Kong, Rose
organised a booth in the Sydney Town Hall during Old People's Week
in October 1972. Supported by the New South Wales Council on the
Ageing, Rose organised a series of interviews with potential volunteers.
Eighty-two people were interviewed, and sixty-three volunteers were
referred to twenty-five organisations, including the Australian Red Cross,
hospital auxiliaries and community groups.[9]

After the success of this preliminary project, the Department of Social
Services was approached with a view to establishing a Bureau for Volun-
teers. One year later, in November 1973, with financial support from the
Commonwealth government's Social Welfare Commission, a Volunteer
Bureau was established within the headquarters of the New South Wales
Council on the Ageing. Opening its doors in February 1974 for three
days per week, and run by Rose Miller, the 'primary aim was to match

volunteers with jobs'.[10] The Bureau also wanted to provide 'maximum satisfaction for both volunteer and agency' in terms of time available to volunteer, location and availability of transport, and agency requirements, as well as assisting those of retirement age to consider volunteering.[11] A range of volunteers was attracted to the Bureau through an advertising campaign. The majority were aged between twenty-five and fifty-five, confirming the stereotype of volunteers as married women 'within the general child-rearing age group'.[12] Only 9 per cent of the volunteers recruited by the Bureau during this pilot project were of retirement age. Meals on Wheels was particularly popular as a destination for the volunteers, and it welcomed the new source of assistance. 'We can always use volunteers', they claimed.[13] The new volunteers included a young man who offered the use of his truck during his lunch hour to deliver city Meals on Wheels, and a retired doctor and his wife who volunteered with Meals on Wheels together.[14]

This pilot project confirmed Henderson's research that only a small percentage of volunteers were retired. This compares with today when a large proportion of volunteers are also from that cohort. The idea of volunteering as the natural domain for the retiree or older Australian is a relatively recent phenomenon. It is linked to the increasing female participation in the paid workforce as well as the overall ageing of the population, lower mortality rates and increasing life expectancy (with the exception of Indigenous Australians who have a much lower life expectancy). From the 1970s, better health outcomes meant that Australians were living longer. The annual average life expectancy for a woman increased from seventy years at the end of World War II to 78.3 years in 1980.[15]

Promoting volunteering 'as an ideal' in the 1970s was, therefore, quite new. The assumption that there was a pool of volunteers who could fill volunteer vacancies through placement similar to 'any commercial employment agency' was not without controversy.[16] Michael Horsburgh, a researcher from the University of Sydney, was commissioned by the Social Welfare Commission to evaluate Rose Miller's Volunteer Bureau pilot program between September and October 1974. His report was highly critical. He believed that the Bureau was established on false pretences (that volunteering could be treated like paid work) and that it failed because only about 50 per cent of potential volunteers were success-fully placed. However, the New South Wales Council on the Ageing was committed to supporting the Bureau and in 1975, Heather Buck was appointed as a salaried Executive Officer.

The idea that the Volunteer Bureau could act as a referral and screen-ing centre for both volunteers and agencies, and assist with better train-ing and supervision, became the model for other states. Over the next few years, the fledgling New South Wales Bureau, through disasters such as Darwin's Cyclone Tracy in 1974, developed procedures, policies and practices, and soon became an integral part of Australian volunteering. Joy Noble was one of the people responsible for the establishment of a Volunteer Centre in South Australia in 1982, but her interest in volun-teering began a decade earlier when she was employed with the South Australian Community Welfare Department to initiate the 'radical' idea of volunteer community aides as part of the new *Community Welfare Act 1972*. Although not 'overenthusiastic about the idea' in the beginning, she was one of the first bureaucrats to develop a real interest in volunteer-ing. As she later wrote:

> I found that the volunteers enhanced the efforts of paid
> workers, and as their confidence increased, some questioned
> existing perceptions and practice. They were like a breath of
> fresh air.[17]

The rise of the eco-warriors

An area that began to attract increasing numbers of volunteers in the 1970s was environment and heritage. People worked tirelessly in their own communities, trying to protect and raise awareness of the fragility of our environment and preserving old buildings at risk of demolition. Over the past forty years, there have been a number of defining events in the environmental movement in Australia. These include the damming of the Gordon-Franklin River in Tasmania, a proposal put forward by the Tasma-nian Hydro-Electric Commission that would have flooded a pristine area of wilderness, and the green bans. In all the major capital cities during the

1970s, small groups of Australians formed themselves into groups to fight and save their communities from what they saw as crude over-development and rampant destruction of heritage buildings and precious open spaces. Inner city resident action groups and neighbourhood centres were formed in Woolloomooloo, Waterloo and The Rocks, all largely working class areas of inner Sydney. Nita McRae, a leader of The Rocks Resident Action Group argued that it was a long standing community that was being threatened by development. As she said:

> They've been through a lot, but it still hasn't broken them up.
> They still have the same churches, schools, play areas, pubs, dart
> teams, pension centres. One half of the area is related to the
> other half. It's all interconnected ... that's a community![18]

Many of the volunteers involved in the urban community movements saw themselves as progressive, enlightened community-minded people who cared about the urban environment, about trees and parks and open spaces and who were politically active. They probably did not identify themselves as volunteers, but rather as agitators, activists or agents for social change. But they were certainly volunteers. The Battlers for Kelly's Bush is but one of many examples of this environment activism that captures the flavour and passion of the 1970s.

Battlers for Kelly's Bush

In the salubrious waterfront suburb of Hunters Hill in Sydney in 1971, trade unionists came together with a group of middle-class housewives, called the Battlers for Kelly's Bush, to save a piece of bushland from development. This movement was no different to others begun in a small way, with concerned citizens – volunteers – from all walks of life coming together to agitate and push for reform. Some, like the National Trust, developed into national organisations, others like the Battlers existed for as long as was necessary to save the bush.

The Battlers for Kelly's Bush was a small voluntary organisation formed by thirteen women in September 1970 in suburban Sydney. Kelly's Bush was 12 acres (4.9 ha) of natural bushland – the largest remaining piece of bushland hugging the Parramatta River on the foreshores of Sydney

Harbour that included a range of native vegetation and Aboriginal rock carvings. The Sydney Smelting Company occupied a waterfront section of land, with the rest of the block, largely natural bushland, nominated as 'open space' by the County Council of Cumberland. For over seventy years, it was used by local residents as a place to walk and for children to play. In the 1950s, the Hunter's Hill Council bought the top 7 acres (2.8 ha) for a park. In 1967, the smelting works moved to Alexandria, an inner industrial suburb of Sydney and an option on the land was given to AV Jennings, a property developer, for high-density housing.

The thirteen local women, many of them friends, lived in the vicinity of Kelly's Bush, and came together to form the Battlers for Kelly's Bush. When I sat down in the Mitchell Library in Sydney to examine the contents of three slightly untidy, musty boxes of files, I was reminded once again of Anne Bourdillon's observation about volunteers with a 'new enthusiasm' creating societies, as mentioned in chapter 2. In the boxes I found a small green Ancol exercise book – the minute book – the holy bible for voluntary organisations revealing the genesis of the group, how it was nurtured and developed, and the ideas behind it.[19] Led by Mrs Elizabeth (Betty) James and Mrs Kathleen Lehany, the women met informally a few times in private homes to voice their concerns about the future of Kelly's Bush. Determined to do more, they then organised a public meeting. The first entry in this little green exercise book, written with blue biro in the neat hand of the elected secretary, Mrs Kathleen Lehany, concerned the recording of this first public meeting held at the Parish Hall in Hunters Hill on Sunday 27 September 1970 at 8.30 pm, where the committee to be called 'Battlers for Kelly's Bush' was formed. Its initial aims (which soon changed, because the government was not interested in saving the bush) were to raise funds to help the state government buy Kelly's Bush to prevent development by AV Jennings.[20] Mrs Betty James was elected president, and the committee consisted of Mrs Majorie Fitzgerald, Miss Margaret Stobo, Mrs Mary Farrell, Mrs Miriam Hamilton, Mrs Kathleen Chubb, Mrs Judy Taplin, Mrs Jo Bell, Mrs Monica Sheehan, Mrs Trudi Kallir (representing the Ryde Hunters Hill Flora and Fauna Protection Society), and Mrs Mary Campbell (representing the National Trust). The treasurer, who was elected at a later date, was Mrs Dawson, and Dr Joan Croll joined the Battlers

Committee the following week. As with all public meetings, there was lengthy discussion about strategies and politics, with the meeting finally closing at 11 pm. The Battlers for Kelly's Bush was duly registered as a charity through the Chief Secretary's Department and a Commonwealth Bank account was opened in the name of Kelly's Bush Fund.

The women volunteers, 'quite aggressive and non-genteel women Battlers' according to Joan Croll had varying motives for committing themselves to the new organisation.[21] Miriam Hamilton later said her primary concern 'was the importance of open space as the lungs of Sydney' and her boys playing in Kelly's Bush also influenced her.[22] Monica Sheehan believed that 'children's fingers would have accused us' if they had not acted.[23] And Trudi Kallir joined because Betty James asked her to help 'preserve a remnant green bushland along the Parramatta River' and their daughters were in the same Brownie group – another voluntary organisation.[24] The Battlers' approach was simple. They contacted a range of groups to ask for support and donations. Their children were asked to keep Kelly's Bush clean and to report any rubbish dumpers (one of the claims of the pro-developer lobby was that the bush was a dumping ground and not worth saving). The media was contacted and a campaign was launched, accompanied by letter writing and submissions to a range of politicians including the Premier Robert Askin, local government officials, and Sir AV Jennings, the proposed property developer.

The Battlers held fundraisers, called 'Boil-the-Billy' down in Kelly's Bush that were very well organised. Miss Stobo was in charge of tea, the information desk was manned on roster, hot water was organised, tours were scheduled, and a two page information sheet was prepared for distribution. A brochure detailing the history was sold for 20 cents and included a forward by high profile Hunters Hill resident, author Kylie Tennant. In it she said:

> The beaches are being ploughed up, the hills chewed out to
> make roads and the prospect of a gibbering concrete jungle
> advances. So that the struggle to preserve this place to unspoilt
> land becomes more significant. It is a confrontation of values.
> Kelly's Bush is a symbol of our lost land. Take away Kelly's Bush
> and you take away one more assurance that in man is left a

possibility for the future. The unborn Australian will ask for his birthright and be handed a piece of concrete.[25]

The group made continual representations to government, networked with other conservation groups such as the Wildlife Preservation Society of Australia, the National Trust, Hunters Hill Trust, the Civic Design Society, the Institute of Architects, and Save the Lane Cove Valley Committee, stimulated interest with local school children through an essay writing competition attracting over 200 entries, held public meetings at which over 400 people attended, and created an intensive media campaign to alert the public to what was happening at Kelly's Bush and other suburban bushland areas. Despite all this, the Minister for Local Government, Mr Morton, signed documents to re-zone the land for residential development on 3 June 1971.

What happened next was to create history. At their wits' end, and with the bulldozers scheduled to begin demolition of the bush (Premier Askin even telephoned Betty James to inform her when the bulldozers would arrive), the Battlers for Kelly's Bush – those thirteen middle-class housewives from Hunters Hill – were approached by Bob Pringle from the Builders' Labourers Federation (BLF) with the offer of assistance, after seeing a television interview. The Trades and Labour Council signalled their support, and together with Jack Mundey and the BLF, the unions placed a black ban on the site; that is, unions in the BLF would not work. This effectively stopped the development. This action soon became known as a green ban, a world first. [26]

The women, the Battlers, formed an organisation because they cared about the destruction of their environment and bushland. As volunteers, they became activists and lobbyists and, along with the trade union movement, managed to block the developers and politicians. However, the experience created enormous tensions for the women, their families, and neighbours. As Monica Sheehan's quote at the beginning of the chapter reveals, it was very controversial. The women were accused of being communists, in bed with unionists, and some were vilified. 'One long-standing friend even made a door-knock seeking signatures to present to council as a protest against saving the bush' wrote one Battler later. It was an extremely divisive period. Although the development was stymied with the green ban in place, it took until 1983, when Neville Wran, as the New South Wales Labor Premier, announced that the government would purchase Kelly's Bush. It took the Battlers and their supporters thirteen years, but once the business was completed and the job done, the organisation folded. The last entry in the old musty Ancol minute book in March 1983 signalled the end of the organisation.

The Australian Assistance Plan

During the 1970s, the relationship between governments and the voluntary sector – the 'moving frontier' – shifted, propelled by the election of the Whitlam government in December 1972. The Australian way of volunteering was transformed, assisted by government policies and funding subsidies that both increased awareness of and encouraged the broad expansion of volunteering.

The Australian Assistance Plan (AAP) played a key role. Although a controversial and short-lived program of social welfare reform, Whitlam described the AAP as a 'pioneering experiment in community involvement', with its 'essential purpose' of seeking out areas of need 'based on regions, on regional communities', with its work and planning 'done by genuinely independent, genuinely community based groups of concerned citizens who know the special needs of the community of which they are a part'.[27] The AAP involved the Commonwealth government directly funding local community endeavours. Rather than funding social welfare through the traditional method of grants to the states, in this program the Commonwealth government effectively side-stepped the states and directed funding at a local community level through a system of regional development councils. We are quite familiar with this type of funding arrangement in the twenty-first century, but in the 1970s it was largely unheard of and considered by many to be an example of encroaching Federal powers in our highly 'territorial' system of federalism.[28] The AAP was 'a vehicle for developing a community soul',[29] as well as 'an experiment in democracy' because it was not introduced by directives or legislation but by 'discussion papers, progress reports, encouragement, financial assistance and advice'.[30]

The AAP was based on a program established in Geelong, Victoria where the Geelong Community Chest and Victorian Council of Social Service developed a 'co-operative social planning' model, including all three levels of government and the local community.[31] Similar ideas were being implemented in South Australia under the dynamic leadership of Premier Don Dunstan, and the *Community Welfare Act 1972*. Typical of much of the history of Australian volunteering, programs were influenced by developments overseas. In this case, the American community movement and Community Action Program of the 1960s, the 'War on Poverty' initiatives, the British Community Development Project of 1971 and the 1966 Canadian Assistance Plan (from whence, presumably, the name came).

The creation of the AAP was the first attempt by a Commonwealth government to not only include voluntary organisations as part of its social policy but to acknowledge their importance in the delivery of a wide range of social welfare services within communities. The AAP was 'about voluntary agencies, their service delivery patterns, their decision-making structures'.[32] Voluntary organisations would no longer be taken for granted. As Bill Hayden, Minister for Social Security, stated in March 1973, 'the Assistance Plan ... will aim to give greater recognition to the volunteer principle as a means of securing grass roots involvement'.[33] This emphasis on community involvement, citizen participation, and self-help projects helped to transform community grassroots politics and the voluntary sector in Australia.

The central feature of the AAP was the creation of Regional Councils for Social Development (RCSD). Formally constituted and run by volunteer management committees, with newly created positions of social planners and community development officers (funded by the Commonwealth), the RCSDs were to function as a 'cooperative forum for statutory and voluntary agencies and community groups'.[34] Six pilot projects were to be established to test out the ideas of the AAP. Following the implementation of this 'action research program', others would be encouraged 'to seek an involvement in the planning and development of social welfare programmes affecting their community'.[35] However, local communities found the chance of acquiring federal money for local initiatives too good to miss, and questions arose as to why certain regions were getting pilot funding and not others. By November 1973, the pilot program had ballooned from six to thirty-five regional areas, covering inner and outer metropolitan areas, city and country, working and middle class, in order to 'enable the widest possible information to be analysed and evaluated'.[36]

The AAP included administration grants of $20 000 per annum for three years, capitation grants to undertake community welfare activities of $2 per head of population per annum; and funds of up to $12 000 per annum to employ community development officers to help in the planning process.[37] With this type of Commonwealth money now available, the response was instant. Across the country, volunteers formed new organisations or revitalised others. The types of programs eligible for funding under the AAP included family and child-care, adolescent services, aged pension care, and community health and welfare centres.[38]

The Nunawading North Neighbourhood Project in Melbourne, for example, received AAP funding to establish a neighbourhood centre to provide a community workshop, community kitchen, food co-operative, and migrant conversation group. In Wagga Wagga, NSW, the Community Action Group received funding for its operating costs. This voluntary organisation ran an emergency housekeeping service, an information centre and trained volunteers. The Victorian St Albans East Latchkey Kids Project's funding went towards equipment, administration and cleaning costs for an after-school program, and the Marrickville Women's Refuge Collective in Sydney received funding to establish and maintain a women's hostel for homeless women and children.[39]

The new channel of federal funding stimulated local communities by supporting existing organisations, and in some cases helped to establish others. A range of self-help organisations in areas such as child-care, after-school care programs, disability services, migrant needs, women's refuges and community health centres benefited directly. It was almost like the heady days of World War II when thousands of organisations were formed. In the early 1970s, as long as there was the energy and capacity in the community and the idea was a good one, the projects were funded through the AAP. Many local communities built community centres through AAP funding. For example, in Kogarah in south-west Sydney, the Kogarah Community Aid and Information Centre was established with funding for equipment and running costs. The Bunbury Apex Club Community Resource Centre in Western Australia provided essential services to six voluntary organisations – Marriage Guidance, Citizens' Advice Bureau, the Good Neighbour Council, Samaritans, Task Force and Legal Advice.

In other areas it was simply that local meeting places needed a makeover, such as the RSL Hall in Hillston, a small town in remote western New South Wales, which needed long overdue renovation, equipment and facilities. The Macclesfield Residents and Ratepayers Association also requested money to renovate their local hall, used regularly by the community. Then there were completely new initiatives such as the community access AM radio station in south-west Sydney which received funding to establish and maintain the radio station (as long as a broadcasting licence was forthcoming). Children's facilities featured prominently too. The Playgroup Association of New South Wales, St George Group received funding to establish a resource and administrative centre and the Apex Club in Williamstown, near Newcastle, received funds towards the establishment and equipping of an adventure playground. Environmental groups also featured, such as the Blackburn and District Tree Preservation Society in Victoria, which received funding to publish a booklet encouraging residents to improve the environment, providing information on waste disposal, pesticides and fuel conservation. The Keep Australia Beautiful Junior Council in Glenmore, Victoria also received funding to establish and maintain the organisation. The Huon Area Tourist Council in Tasmania received money to establish and assist a working committee for publicity and organisation. And the St Paul's Community Youth Task Force in Victoria gained funds to organise young volunteers to do various jobs for the aged in the community.[40]

The Federal government increased funding grants to the voluntary sector from $44.6 million in 1973–74 to $131 million in 1975–76.[41] This significant increase in government funding had a flow-on effect not only on volunteers and their organisations but also on government perceptions of the sector. Governments realised they had very little information about the sector, including the size and extent of volunteering, which had never been counted, nor any value imputed for volunteers working in the areas of marriage guidance, Meals on Wheels, and the myriad of community bodies contributing to social development such as the Australian Red Cross, CWA, YMCA, YWCA and so on.[42] The AAP was challenged, unsuccessfully, by several conservative state governments in the High Court in regard to Commonwealth powers, so it was not surprising that the AAP was disbanded in 1976 by the incoming Fraser government. There was also considerable debate among contemporary commentators as to what participation and community engagement actually involved. 'The rhetoric of empowering disadvantaged communities to take some control of their destinies' was hotly contested.[43] Carol Pateman, who was quoted extensively during the AAP era, examined the 'place of "participation" in a modern, viable theory of democracy'.[44] To American sociologist Rolf Dahrendorf, 'participation [was] about citizenship and citizenship as a social process', a means of getting every individual to exercise their own social rights and obligations in society.[45] However, many believed that there was little to indicate a move towards a genuine citizen participation movement through programs and initiatives of the AAP.[46] The conclusion was that these ideas of popular participation on a local level were unrealistic and unachievable.[47]

But it is often with hindsight that broader patterns can be discerned. As Adam Graycar, a sociologist involved with the AAP, stated in 1979, the idea of citizen involvement in community planning and citizen empowerment, combined with the development of a range of self-help projects did create a new generation of 'active community politics' that transformed volunteering and the voluntary sector.[48] The impact of the AAP on volunteers and communities was long lasting. It got people talking about community engagement and community development and enabled many to become involved in a variety of causes, many of which continued to be funded by state governments.

The Mountain District Co-operative was one example, when a group of about fifty women in the Dandenong Ranges on the eastern outskirts of Melbourne established the Co-op to help women at home with young children become involved in community life. A new suburb of largely lower middle class and upper working classes, it was well placed to receive government funding. Initially receiving a $12 655 grant from the Department of Tourism and Recreation Innovation Program to get established, the Mountain District Co-op received further funding from the International Women's Year National Advisory Committee. The Co-op established a shop, run by volunteers, selling women's handcrafts. They ran an arts and craft class with child-care provided, a playgroup, a women's drop-in centre, a monthly newsletter, and personal development classes for 'house bound' women and married couples. The government funding enabled them to employ two part-time workers, an administrator and community worker.[49]

International Women's Year and Miriwinni CWA

The Whitlam philosophy of providing federal funding to grassroots voluntary organisations continued through one-off events such as International Women's Year in 1975. Controversy surrounded the program, whereby $2 million was allocated to women's organisations during the year. Some believed that this was 'a contemptible misuse of public money' and that funds would be directed to a 'radical fringe'.[50] But this was not the case with most of the funds allocated on a competitive basis to organisations such as the CWA and YWCA. For example, the Miriwinni branch of the CWA in northern Queensland received funding to erect a fence around their hall. With a train line at the rear of the hall and a road at the front, mothers from the sugar cane country did not feel safe attending meetings and functions knowing that their children were in danger from either trains or cars. What was needed was a fence. The honorary secretary, Mrs Dulcie Menzel, a widow and mother of five with fourteen grandchildren, was the key organiser of the application. After watching a television interview with Miss Elizabeth Reid, the Prime Minister's special adviser on women's issues, Dulcie decided to write an application for funding.[51] She presented a persuasive argument when, in her hand-written application, she wrote that women around Miriwinni were disadvantaged: with no job opportunities, no adult education, no recreation centre, child minding or pre-school. 'We claim', she argued 'the women of our community have been pushed into a category which can be labelled "second class citizen"'.[52] Furthermore, she stated that although their organisation had 'no technical skills', they did 'have the grit determination and the guts to get the job done'.[53]

Miriwinni was at the centre of a small farming district on the Bruce Highway, 80 kilometres south of Cairns. It had a hotel, post office, grocery store, service station, sawmill, CWA Hall and a few houses. Many of the women were housewives and mothers and also worked alongside their husbands in the sugar cane fields surrounding the town and district. The CWA Hall was dreary and in need of a coat of paint but it urgently required a fence. 'We would not wish any of our drabness on your beautiful Canberra but we would be very happy if you would enable us to have a little bit of Canberra style in Miriwinni', Dulcie Menzel wrote to Elizabeth Reid in September 1974.[54] Despite, or perhaps because of, the differences between Dulcie's world and that of heady Canberra in the 1970s, Reid approved the application.

This small branch of the CWA in Far North Queensland with its sixteen members provides us with a wonderful microcosm of life for some women in remote areas of Australia in the 1970s, and what volunteer organisations such as the CWA were doing. Dulcie described in her application how they held discussion groups about issues relating to women in society; women came in to teach handicrafts – Mrs Vi Stroud taught basket making, bark pictures, jewellery; Mrs Jean Edwards taught knitting and Mrs Jan Tuttle, crochet. Saturday afternoon was for the younger set, and girls from the district attended classes free of charge. They were also going to begin a Health Watchers Clinic 'as a good diet makes for a trim figure as well as good health', and had written to the Heart Foundation for brochures and information on the prevention of heart disease. First aid lectures were provided by the local ambulance superintendent, Mr Bert Good, on a range of topics including snakebites, and subjects for future talks included sea stingers and their treatment; 'causes of gastroenteritis in Aboriginal children and the part we can play in helping to prevent it'; first aid for burns; and plans to get the Innisfail baby health clinic sister to attend a meeting and to invite Aboriginal and Torres Strait Islander mothers.[55]

Miriwinni CWA branch members always provided refreshments to 'guests at their own expense'. They worked:

> constantly to make articles for sale at fetes, cent stalls and street stalls to raise money for hall improvements. We have ceiled and lined the building painted it and installed fans bought tables chairs and crockery, an urn to boil water, curtains tablecloths etc and each individual member pays for all material used in articles made and sold. We have made contributions to Disaster Fund Appeals such as the Darwin one. Last year we made a contribution to a family left destitute when their home and belongings were destroyed by fire. We do want to help raise status of women in our district to do this we believe we must make our centre attractive and safe for the children so mothers can relax.[56]

Recreational volunteers

International Women's Year and the broader AAP experiences revealed that if the right government funding opportunities were provided, there were plenty of ordinary people at the grassroots who could make communities come alive. Despite the experimental nature of the AAP and its sense of urgency as programs were rushed into being, the flow of Commonwealth funding through these initiatives stimulated the voluntary sector and volunteering through the 1970s and beyond.

This can be seen in other areas including 'recreational' voluntary organisations such as golf, bowling, tennis, swimming and football clubs. A survey of recreational volunteers was carried out in the mid-1970s in the towns of Liverpool, Campbelltown, Tamworth and Inverell in New South Wales to ascertain what the attitudes were to volunteering in local sporting clubs and associations. Sixty-three per cent of the respondents were men, three-quarters of whom were married and aged between twenty-five and forty-four years of age.[57] About one-third of the volunteers (35 per cent) volunteered for only one organisation; about 33 per cent volunteered at two organisations, and about 32 per cent volunteered at more than two organisations. Over half said they volunteered between one and six hours per week; 13 per cent between 11 and 20 hours per week and 5 per cent over 20 hours per week.[58] The reasons why they volunteered were similar to those given in later surveys – 'I enjoy helping others'; 'This activity or sport needs support'; 'I enjoy meeting other people'; or 'It is a constructive way of filling in my leisure time'.[59]

Few of the volunteers received any training, yet one-quarter were involved in training and instructing others at the particular clubs. Although many volunteers expressed an interest in receiving training, the organisations either could not afford it or did not have the structures in place to train volunteers. Some of the country organisations expressed problems with training, as large distances were a real concern for volunteers from the bush. It was also found that volunteers from Scouts and Guides organisations were more highly organised and trained, but this was probably a reflection of dealing with children and the types of activities undertaken. When asked what government could do to help support volunteering, at least two-thirds of volunteers said they believed that providing subsidies for equipment and facilities was most important, followed by financial assistance.[60] Some volunteers suggested that government involvement would mean bureaucratic red tape that would stifle the groups, but the general view was that 'the main role for government in the club and association system of recreation' was 'a behind-the-scenes supportive role rather than direct involvement or control of recreation'.[61]

By the 1970s, it was acknowledged that Australia had 'developed a fine voluntary leadership system in the sport and recreation areas', but in order to move forward 'the ... system should be supplemented by the use of professionals and semi-professionals in both the administration and the instruction areas'.[62] In a report by Professor John Bloomfield commissioned by the new Minister of State for Tourism and Recreation, FE Stewart, it was argued that although in the 1970s, clubs and associations still remained the cornerstone of Australian sport and recreation, there was a belief that 'the army of volunteers' was gradually dwindling and there were fewer people available to volunteer. Whether this was true or not, it was believed that the government should assist or 'act as a catalyst' through funding opportunities.[63]

In recognising the role that volunteer organisations played, as well as being confronted with rising levels of obesity and the 'poor state of the nation's health', a Department of Tourism and Recreation was created, along with an Australian Institute of Sport.[64] Based on the idea that Australians would have more leisure time due to shorter working hours, earlier retirement and increasing longevity, people needed to have access to a range of activities that could be provided through community recreation centres. Reminiscent of Lloyd Ross, the National Fitness Council and the post–World War II era, this ideal, it was argued, should be fostered at the local government level. The centre could not be 'just a physical facility placed in a centralised location in a community but should be the focal point for the functioning of the majority of recreation programs in the local community'.[65]

With financial assistance from Commonwealth grants and subsidies, the community centre would provide facilities and programs for local schools, church youth clubs, choirs, dramatic art societies, senior citizen associations, Scouts and Guides, Little Athletics clubs, the YMCA and YWCA, and others. Many of these small volunteer sporting and recreational organisations could now apply for funding from different Federal government departments such as the AAP, the Department of Tourism and Recreation and the new Ministry for the Arts. The Whitlam government completely overhauled the way the Commonwealth involved itself with community groups and volunteers in a range of areas. The result was a cultural renaissance of performance arts, dance, fine arts and crafts, and dramatic art at the national, state and local community level. For example, a revamped Australia Council (built on an earlier Australian Council for the Arts) was created under statute in 1975 with a series of boards that included Literature, Dance, Performing Arts, Music and the Aboriginal and Torres Strait Islander Arts Board. Many voluntary organisations gained access to financial grants for the first time. For example, the Literature Board of the Australia Council first funded the Children's Book Council in 1973 when they received a grant of $5000.[66]

There was also a significant shift in other areas of society where, with government support and financial assistance, volunteers in the creative arts, literature and the law could flourish. Community legal centres were established across Australia in the early 1970s. They soon became an integral part of the legal system, sitting between private legal firms and state Legal Aid Commissions, jointly funded by both state and Federal governments. Operating with minimal paid staff, the community legal centres always relied extensively on volunteers, mostly trained lawyers, to undertake pro bono work. The centres were 'radical and innovative' reflecting the mood of the 1970s 'because they combined direct services with an emphasis on law reform and social change, community work and community education'.[67]

Surf lifesaving

If some volunteers were getting a new lease on life in the 1970s, others were finding it very tough going. Surf lifesaving had considerable difficulty attracting younger members and surf lifesaving historian, Sean Brawley, described the decade as 'the darkest period in the history of surf lifesaving in Australia'.[68] Surf lifesaving volunteers represent many of the quintessential features of Australian culture and identity. The Life Saving Clubs, established across the nation at all the major beaches in the first decade of the twentieth century – when ocean bathing became popular and daytime bathing restrictions were lifted – came to epitomise the Australian way of volunteering. Amateur swimming associations formed their own surf lifesaving clubs as there were real safety concerns for swimmers, with both state and local governments seemingly unable to act. Although there is a huge debate as to which surf club – Bondi or Bronte – was formed first, the 'surf safety issue' was 'resolved by the community itself'.[69] Australians largely rejected British lifesaving methods and the clubs developed their own equipment and procedures, including the surf reel, the cornerstone of lifesaver safety and rescue, to meet the Australian surf environment.

However, by the 1970s, surf lifesaving represented an 'old' Australia, largely white, Anglo-Saxon and male. Clubs that were predicated on volunteers and fundraising were not attracting the younger generations, and as one member gloomily predicted, 'the age of the volunteer was over'.[70] Bondi's experience was symptomatic of a general malaise:

> Today's young men of Bondi are also different in outlook
> from earlier generations. Most of them feel no desire and no

responsibility to join the Bondi Surf Lifesaving Club. Against the old lifesaver tradition of discipline (and often quite remarkable heroism), they represent a new cult devoted to pure enjoyment and physical skills, the pursuit of the perfect wave, and essentially, every man for himself.[71]

Other problems concerned spiralling costs for volunteers and their surf lifesaving clubs. This affected all volunteer organisations, but particularly groups that required insurance and regular equipment replacement. In 1973, the Bondi Club's expenditure was $7000. By 1977, this had risen to $12 000 and the following season to $20 500. Inflation saw club savings undermined, with insurance payments, for example, escalating by 500 per cent in 1978. Combined with the tired and run-down Bondi beachfront, endless debates as to how to remedy the 'environment' and development of the suburb affected the surf lifesaving club. Poor morale and dwindling numbers of members put increasing pressure on those ageing volunteers still active in the club.

One of the ways to arrest the declining membership was to open surf lifesaving up to women. They were only ever involved in surf lifesaving auxiliaries (the bedrock of the fundraising), and on the periphery. Many did participate unofficially in surf lifesaving activities; for example, in 1923 with the Tweed Heads and Coolangatta SLSC, Edie Kieft was arguably the first Australian woman to qualify for the Surf Bronze Medallion but she did not receive the medal because she was a woman.[72] Although there were ongoing debates through the post-war period about allowing women to participate in competitions and march-pasts, little was done to address this increasingly divisive issue. From 1975, the peak body, Surf Lifesaving Australia, ordered its clubs to think about including women and in 1979, it announced that 'female active membership of the movement' would begin in 1979–80. This finally occurred the following summer.[73]

Winding up

Some voluntary organisations were unable to cope with the seismic shifts and closed their doors. The Family Welfare Bureau, for example, system-atically moved away from their volunteer roots during the 1960s in an effort to 'professionalise' but still could not successfully navigate their way through the changed environment. This paradox increasingly challenged the voluntary sector through the 1970s. As it became more visible to governments (the willingness of the Social Welfare Commission to fund the pilot Volunteer Bureau for example) and received more funding support (for example, marriage guidance funding as discussed in chapter 5), the most traditional areas of volunteerism especially in social welfare became more vulnerable. Shortages of trained staff, raised expectations about standards, accountability, legal requirements and increasing professionalisation, placed considerable stress on both the voluntary sector and its volunteers. Added to this was an increasing diversity and choice in terms of where to volunteer, with a range of new groups and organisations starting up, that caused more problems.

Towards the end of the 1960s, the Family Welfare Bureau began to decentralise as their client base shifted to the outer suburbs and clients resisted travelling to the city centre. Branches were established in Parramatta and Manly Warringah. Commonwealth subsidies increased from $12 896 in 1971 to $24 252 in 1974. In 1971–72, 85 per cent of their caseload concerned marital, pre-marital, family and immigration issues, with community work of the Residents Group at Waterloo, the Endeavour Club and South Sydney Action Group comprising 12 per cent.[74] Rising costs, an almost dysfunctional head office (due to a series of disastrous appointments), retiring volunteers, and a changing social welfare landscape, with the focus of problems shifting from the 'individual' to needs 'within a community setting', made life very difficult for the Bureau. 'It could well be that small voluntary agencies have outlived their usefulness and … if we become too dependent on Government subsidies we will inevitably forfeit much, if not all our independence' bemoaned the president.[75] Within a year, the Executive Committee decided to call it a day. The Family Welfare Bureau closed its doors and handed its assets over to the Smith Family. Speaking at the 28th and last Annual General Meeting of the Family Welfare Bureau on 18 September 1974, the Patron, Lady Cutler, lamented the 'sad and sorry state of affairs that the Bureau [had] been forced to close because of lack of finance'. She went on, 'Unfortunately it is not always realised by some government departments what a valuable contribution is being made by voluntary agencies towards strengthening and helping family unity'.[76]

Remaining relevant: voluntary aids and the Australian Red Cross

A feature of volunteering over time is its ability to identify a need or problem in the community and to act upon it. Innovation and immediacy are two key ingredients. It involves a couple of individuals actively seeking to remedy the problem in question by bringing together other like-minded people to establish a group that works towards a specific set of goals. Once those goals are met, the volunteers pack up and go home. Some organisations, such as Surf Lifesaving, struggled on hoping for better times and others, like the Family Welfare Bureau, closed their doors. The Red Cross VAs reinvented themselves to stay relevant.

The 1970s was a period of readjustment and restructure for the Red Cross, one of Australia's largest and best-known non-profit organisations. These changes can be clearly seen within its VA program. Firstly, there was a name change – from VA to Voluntary Aid Service Corps (VASC) – but this did not address the major concern, of the recruitment and retention of members. The Red Cross, like many other traditional volunteer-based organisations, was suffering from a slow decline in volunteer numbers because of the increasing opportunities for married women entering the paid workforce and competition from other organisations. Women who may, in the past, have become VAs were now either too busy or not interested in undertaking volunteer work in their spare time. Married women were now heading into the workforce as barriers to employment disappeared and social expectations changed. Secondly, as already mentioned, the 1970s saw a growth in a range of volunteer organisations that directly affected traditional organisations such as the Red Cross and Surf Lifesaving. Volunteers had more choice with the types of organisations in which they could participate. This, in turn, created more competition for older, established organisations.

The challenge during the 1970s was to remain relevant. In the VASC's case, it turned to training. Red Cross First Aid Certificate courses were developed and run for the general public as well as for a range of voluntary organisations including Scouts and Guides, Duke of Edinburgh Scheme, and the Bushfire Volunteer Fire Brigade. A wide and diverse clientele was attracted to this service, including teachers, pharmacists, lifesavers and university medical students. From this, the Sydney Mobile VASC was formed, consisting of both men and women aged between seventeen and twenty-five, who provided a highly trained, fully equipped team of volunteers ready to offer emergency assistance. Members were trained in basic search and rescue techniques, disaster nursing, welfare, registration and tracing and advanced driving techniques. This team provided first aid services to sporting events such as the 1975 National Surf Championships.[77]

Training for three-year home nursing certificates included emergency casualty care, oral resuscitation and 'health in the home', and were carried out with the assistance of trained nursing sisters. Emergency care kits for motorists, approved by the Roads Safety Council, and assembled by VAs, were also sold. In New South Wales, the VASC Training Section began to charge for its courses and it became very successful. By 1984, it had raised nearly $46 000 for the Red Cross.[78] VAs also continued their unpaid work in rural and suburban hospitals and blood banks as they had always done: staffing canteens, hospital visiting and providing reading materials. Due to ongoing staff shortages and lack of adequate financial support, blood bank services in rural communities were heavily reliant on volunteers who worked in the sterilising supply departments and mobile units. VAs continued to volunteer in ex-service and general geriatric civilian facilities at the various Red Cross homes. They offered their services to other community-based organisations including Community Aid Bureaux and Meals on Wheels, where they provided both personnel and transport.

Migrants and refugees

The escalating crisis in Indo-China in April and May 1975, with the fall of Saigon and the Khmer Rouge taking control of Cambodia, created a refugee crisis and a new set of problems for governments and the voluntary sector alike. VAs became contact workers for the Good Neighbour

Council, assisting recently arrived migrants and helping with the increasing number of refugees arriving from Indo-China. Some refugees were flown in to Mascot airport where VAs met each plane, and accompanied the refugees to the various migrant hostels. Although many traditional social welfare organisations, like the Red Cross and churches, responded as always to the crisis, new volunteer organisations were formed in response to the government's initial refusal to accept any refugees. For example, the Adelaide-based Indo-China Refugee Association (ICRA) was established in 1975 by a group including Don and Mary Whitelum and Don Simpson. They worked to support the intake of Indo-Chinese refugees, to assist with their resettlement and to change public opinion. The first group of refugees arrived in Adelaide in April 1976, and ICRA set to work finding jobs, accommodation and generally helping with language and cultural difficulties. The ICRA 'became known for "getting things done"' and soon more refugees were resettled in Adelaide.[79] From April 1976, the ICRA expanded its advocacy work especially focusing on educating Australians and changing public opinion towards the arrival of the 'boat people'.

The 1970s witnessed changing government policy towards migration and the move from assimilation to integration and then to multiculturalism. These policy shifts affected migrant groups and the volunteers who worked with them. Reflecting changing views of the migrant experience on Australian society, and embracing 'ethnic concentrations' and 'enclaves', the term 'ethnic groups' was changed to 'national groups' and a National Groups Liaison Unit was established within the Department of Immigration. This unit surveyed the national groups in an attempt to not only find the extent of the voluntary organisations but also to discover what kinds of assistance they provided and to whom. Over 2000 groups were identified, and 905 were deemed appropriate to research in more detail. Overall, the survey concluded that apart from the large, well-established ethnic groups, including the Italians, Germans and Jewish ones that received Grant-in-Aid funding, many migrant volunteer groups were not delivering adequate services to their client base due to lack of funds and their volunteer nature.[80]

The traditional voluntary organisation, the Good Neighbour Councils, first established in 1950 by the Department of Immigration, had by the 1970s become totally reliant on government funding and were seen as increasingly irrelevant. By April 1973, its eight state councils employed seventy-four full-time staff and despite re-organising their agendas, it was believed that the Councils could 'no longer claim to be significant community educators paving the way for multicultural social development'. By 1978, believing that it was 'inconsistent with the multicultural nature of Australian society', the government cut funding and the Councils folded.[81]

The disaster years

From the late 1960s to 1974, Australia experienced a series of natural disasters, including floods, earthquakes and bushfires, as well as disasters caused by human error, such as the collapse of the Melbourne West Gate Bridge in 1970. The statutory emergency services and voluntary organisations were reformed and, in June 1974, the Commonwealth government's Natural Disasters Organisation was created. Voluntary organisations were also involved in the major national emergency of the 1970s, Cyclone Tracy, which had a significant impact on disaster volunteering in Australia. The cyclone hit Darwin on Christmas Eve 1974, leaving 45 000 Darwin residents homeless, over sixty people dead and hundreds injured. There was a complete breakdown of facilities, with no electricity, water or sewerage, and over $500 million damage. It was Australia's worst national disaster. Along with the Federal government's National Disaster Organisation, led by General Alan Stretton, the military and RAAF, the Red Cross, Salvation Army and other voluntary organisations mobilised hundreds of volunteers across the country. The Secretary General of the Red Cross, Leon Stubbings, organised blood supplies, co-ordinated the voluntary relief supplies, the registration processes for evacuees and an enquiry information centre for concerned relatives.[82] Red Cross Relief Teams were sent to Darwin to assist with the evacuation of over 25 000 people, including families, children, the sick and elderly. As they were flown south, volunteers met the evacuees, acted as escorts and provided a range of services and provisions.[83]

Across Australia, people responded overwhelmingly to the disaster as appeals to assist those affected by the cyclone were launched. The larger charities such as the Salvation Army and Red Cross were inundated with offers of assistance and financial donations. Spectators at the Boxing Day test at the Melbourne Cricket Ground donated $1300 into a tarpaulin carried around during the lunch break, and Channel Nine TV organised a national telethon on New Year's Eve that raised over three million dollars. All donations to public funds were given tax deductions that certainly enhanced the positive response.[84]

In the aftermath of Cyclone Tracy there was considerable discussion about the lack of preparedness and warnings by local authorities, and how to prepare in the future for a range of natural disasters such as floods, bushfires and cyclones.[85] There was significant emphasis on research, education, training, and organisation of disaster responses. With the formation of the Commonwealth Natural Disasters Organisation, the focus shifted from 'civil defence' to 'counter-disaster orientation'.[86] State and territorial governments delegated ministerial responsibility for emergency services for the first time, as well as enacting a range of emergency services and disaster management Acts. The importance of self-help and the mobilisation of local community resources were also noted. 'Trained volunteers can complement the local police, fire services and medical services' but 'whatever the population size and material resources of a community, the available human resources need to be coordinated into a viable operational system'.[87]

Conclusion

In terms of the development of an Australian way of volunteering, there is little doubt that the 1970s was a period of upheaval and change. While some areas of volunteering expanded and thrived, others clung to the hope that the failing interest of Australians in volunteering was only transitory, that the decline in particular types of volunteering would be arrested and reversed. Federal governments became involved in funding local voluntary organisations at unprecedented levels and the first forays into volunteering research were undertaken in an effort to understand the concept of volunteering and to quantify and qualify it. The profile of the volunteer also began to shift as the traditional cohort of volunteers, women from child-bearing age to middle years, entered the paid workforce in greater numbers. Changing demographics, early retirement schemes and better health care meant that older Australians could now become the doyens of the volunteering sector. All of these shifting patterns are clearly discernable in this decade of change.

In many ways, the 1970s was a watershed. For, while the direction of volunteering shifted in interesting and exciting ways (especially in the area of the environment and activism), the increasing drive towards the professionalisation of volunteering, through measurements, surveys and research, and for volunteers and their organisations to be treated more like paid workers in terms of recruitment and training, was just around the corner. The relationship between governments and volunteering was about to become much more complicated.

7 Swimming against the stream

In recent years economics has dominated everything that we do. Everything has its price, everyone has their price, so volunteers are swimming against the stream ... in the past the concept of volunteering has been too soft and too nice. It must have enough guts to challenge attitudes which are not conducive to building community.[1]

Bill Armstrong

The Australian way of volunteering continued to evolve through the last decades of the twentieth century. As described in this book, volunteering developed in new areas as social, political and cultural needs changed. The 1980s and 1990s were years of continuity and expansion, but there were also significant changes in the relationship between governments and volunteers. The complexity of the relationship, the shift in the moving frontier, especially in terms of the new economic philosophies referred to by Bill Armstrong above, all had an enormous impact on the voluntary sector, volunteers and volunteering. Governments had always interacted with the voluntary sector, and the relationship was an integral factor contributing to the development of the Australian way of volunteering, but circumstances changed dramatically in the 1980s.

As outlined in the previous chapter, Australian governments became 'aware' of volunteering in the 1970s and began to implement policies that included volunteers, albeit on a small scale. The effect of these policies, especially in terms of increased Federal government funding, assisted in the diversification of volunteering into new areas. However, in the 1980s, volunteering and the voluntary sector were 'discovered' again by Australian governments, mirroring developments overseas, particularly in the United Kingdom and Canada. Mark Lyons has argued that the sector was 'invented', just as the business sector was invented in the 1960s.[2] The voluntary sector was given a name – the third sector – and it was referred to as a 'loose and baggy monster', a term coined by British researchers Jeremy Kendall and Martin Knapp, because the third sector covered such a wide range of organisations, activities, motivations and ideologies.[3] No longer could our society be broken up into the simple binary of governments and markets. There was a whole new world of associational activity, hitherto never sufficiently acknowledged or understood, underpinned by volunteering, and called the third sector.

Through this 'discovery', governments began to acknowledge and push volunteering as an activity in which all good Australian citizens should participate. Governments increased funding, but at the same time they also began to measure volunteering, to quantify and qualify it. Just as airline passengers became 'customers' and welfare recipients became 'clients', so too did volunteering become commodified, driven by 'outcomes'. It became an activity to be counted, assessed and evaluated. Because of the rapid changes, it was feared that volunteering might simply become a source of cheap labour, rather than an integral aspect of a flourishing democracy. 'Falling into that trap', argued Robert Fitzgerald, 'could be the death of volunteering'.[4]

This chapter focuses on these special challenges and the corresponding impact on the Australian way of volunteering. These challenges came largely from the movement in some advanced western democracies, including Australia, labelled 'economic rationalism', a term coined by Australian sociologist Michael Pusey.[5] There were further challenges stemming from wider social change. As the competition for volunteers intensified, and with an ageing population, volunteering as an activity for older people and retirees became a prominent issue. Although some areas struggled to cope within the increasingly regulated environment, others saw new opportunities, especially in the case of environmental, sport and emergency services volunteering. As has always been the case, the expansion was uneven reflecting the complex nature of the Australian way of volunteering.

Economic rationalism and volunteering

A major factor affecting volunteering and the voluntary (or third) sector at the end of the twentieth century was the sweeping influence of neo-liberalism, a new economic theory, which re-examined and re-positioned the roles and functions of governments and markets. Some western countries, especially the United States of America under Ronald Reagan and the United Kingdom under Margaret Thatcher and John Major, took up the new economic reforms and developed a framework that asserted the supremacy of the private sector economy over governments for most, if not all, services. Governments, it was claimed, were bloated and inefficient, and essentially failed because they did not follow the market principle of allowing the market to determine the best way to produce and distribute goods and services. If everything were given a price and commodified, then the 'free' market would produce the best outcome. To create this mythical free market, tariffs and subsidies were reduced or removed in many sectors of the economy, and widespread economic disruption and unemployment resulted. These ideas galvanised those in power, from governments to the boardroom.

The argument that the market always knows best led to the conclusion that governments should sell off or 'privatise' many of the enterprises they had created or acquired. In other areas government activities were restructured or 'corporatised' to resemble private companies that charged fees, treated the people they served as customers or clients and their staff as 'human resources'. The policies and rhetoric of the 'New Right' concluded that the general public paid too much of their income in taxation and part of economic rationalism involved cuts in personal income tax and an increase in the socially regressive taxation on goods and services (GST).

The triumph of economic rationalism was even more apparent after 1989, with the fall of the Berlin Wall and the collapse of the Soviet Union.

In Australia, the cry for lower taxes and reduced government emerged through the press and political forces in the Whitlam period, when the Federal government increased spending on education, health and the community sector. But it was in the 1980s that the newly elected Hawke Labor government implemented the agenda through floating the Australian dollar, selling off the Commonwealth Bank, attempting to introduce a GST and curtailing the trade union movement through the Accord. It could be argued, however, that the impact of the changes was softened by having a Labor government in charge. This all changed in 1996, with the election of the Howard coalition government that pushed economic rationalism much further, with increased corporatisation, reduced health and education spending, regular income tax cuts, introduction of the GST and an attack on workplace conditions and the unions.

In countries like Britain and America, where the voluntary sector was more developed and the relationship with governments more sophisticated, it was argued that governments could withdraw from a range of services or redirect their efforts because the voluntary sector, communities and volunteers did it better. British Prime Minister Margaret Thatcher, a great proponent of neo-liberalism, believed that volunteers were 'at the heart of all our social welfare provision'. [6] Across the Atlantic, American President Ronald Reagan advocated the downsizing of government and the mobilising of the private sector, 'to bring thousands of Americans into a volunteer effort to help solve many of America's social problems'.[7] Policy makers looked to the voluntary sector to assist governments in repositioning and redefining the parameters of the relationship, and to cut government spending. In 1982, Timothy Raison, the British Home Office minister responsible for the Voluntary Service Unit stated that volunteering was:

> a natural extension of the normal and creative urge to help one's
> family, friends and neighbourhood. In our fragmented society,
> where our lives are all affected by changes ... many people find
> in volunteering a purpose and a commitment that gives wider
> meaning to their lives. They give up their time, their skills,

their money – sometimes all three – to help others and to make the community in which they live a better place. We believe that volunteers and the voluntary groups to which they belong deserve all our encouragement and support.[8]

However, many were deeply concerned about the new directions and the role volunteering was playing as part of the government's programs. Was it simply a way for governments to downsize and shift their responsibilities, largely predicated on the goodwill and unpaid labour of their citizens? These 'reforms' continued until the mid-1990s when in Britain, Tony Blair led his 'new Labour party' back to power after eighteen years in opposition. Support of the voluntary sector, voluntary action and volunteering became one of the defining characteristics of the Blair government. 'We recognise that voluntary action … is part of the expression of citizenship' argued a Labour report in 1992.[9] Influenced by sociologist and former director of the London School of Economics, Anthony Giddens, this 'third way' offered a new direction through the process of social democratic renewal.[10] Determined to create a new statutory-voluntary relationship, two main features were the use of partnerships and collaboration, as well as the development of a series of compacts to construct a middle path between old Labour's focus on state control and the Conservatives' reliance on markets. Central to this was the compact, introduced in 1998, which provided a structure and basis for the future, 'predicated on the belief that the independence of the voluntary sector was crucial to its healthy functioning'.[11]

The effects of economic rationalism on volunteering

So how did these changes in government policies and perceptions affect volunteering and the voluntary sector? In the area of social welfare particularly, voluntary organisations increasingly became an arm of government through the development of new social policies such as mutual obligation, funding and contracting that increasingly resulted in community-based organisations being involved in competitive tendering and the delivery of an increasing range of services.[12] The expectation of operating within defined business models placed further stress on volunteers. Many of these organisations, especially the traditional ones, relied on volunteers both as workers and to keep costs down. It was a continual struggle to adapt to the rapidly changing environment. The 'moves towards privatisation and marketisation' ran counter to 'notions of altruism and freely given time', the pillars of volunteering.[13]

The other major shift was in the competition for government grants, whereby voluntary organisations were now expected to tender to provide services rather than simply apply for and receive government grants and subsidies. This new and radical approach to funding directly affected organisations as they tried to cut costs in order to remain 'competitive'. Volunteers increasingly became a 'resource' or commodity, and the added pressure from this new regulatory environment and market model of funding created significant stress. These were uncharted waters.

The reforms brought inevitable changes to business practices as volunteers were now expected to provide business plans and deliver 'targeted outcomes'. These shifting government demands are captured starkly in an exchange of correspondence in 1995 between the Chair of the Australian Non-English Speaking Background Women's Association (ANESBWA) and the Assistant Secretary, Equity and Community Relations Branch, Office of Multicultural Affairs. The language and assumptions underpinning the new relationship – such as outcomes, goals, strategies, and performance indicators – are clearly evident. In order to receive funding, government guidelines required non-government organisations to present three-year business plans with corporate and annual work plans. ANESBWA had forwarded a draft plan that was clearly, in the view of the bureaucrat, not up to scratch. In a letter dated 28 April, the Assistant Secretary wrote:

> the funding agreement between our organisations is to
> fund outcomes, not activities … we believe that these issues
> should generally be issues that are on the Government's
> agenda, rather than outside it, to improve the likelihood of
> an effective Government response … we believe too that your
> plan should identify the short, medium and long term goals
> ANESBWA wants to achieve, and that each objective should be
> accompanied by a strategy to achieve it, details of the necessary

action and resources required to accomplish this, and a list of identified outcomes, and performance indicators, within the intended timeframe.[14]

This was not received well by ANESBWA. In response, the Chair, Irene Pnevmatikos, hit back at the idea of the organisation working only towards issues on the government agenda and stated that ANESBWA's first priority was to its membership and constituency. Furthermore, she believed that their role was to identify issues and bring them to the attention of governments 'in a dynamic fashion rather than on ANESBWA being required to change its agenda in order to receive funding'. Irene continued:

> As a peak national organisation ... one of our strengths is our community based structure which is able to reach grassroots women and translate their issues into policy implications and options for government and other relevant organisations.[15]

This exchange was not an isolated case. It reflects not only the changing dynamics of the relationship between governments and voluntary organisations but also the outcomes-based, competitive environment within which organisations were now forced to operate. The full story of ANESBWA is described later in this chapter.

As has been shown throughout this book, the pattern of Australian governments funding voluntary organisations to deliver a range of social services developed slowly. A feature of the Australian way of volunteering is this relationship between voluntary organisations and governments. But up until the 1980s, Australian governments were largely pragmatic in their use of the voluntary sector, never developing a coherent philosophy or understanding, but using the sector when it suited. From the 1980s, however, the frontier shifted considerably, and the result was a blurring of the boundaries between non-profit, for-profit and governments. With the relationship now visible, governments were pressed to provide clear policy on the sector and its volunteer workforce.

Other social and technological changes

During the 1980s and 1990s, Australian society underwent significant changes, as writers such as Paul Kelly, Hugh Mackay, and Clive Hamilton have explained.[16] Volunteering was affected through a combination of more (and then less) leisure time, technological advances, better educational opportunities, as well as increasing demands for flexibility and diversity. Changes in workplace culture and paid work patterns, as well as early retirement, revealed a pool of people who wanted to use their skills and experience in positive ways in the community. Generally fit, healthy and energetic, these men and women, the 'retirees' became sought-after volunteers. Increasing youth employment and higher education goals also led people to volunteer to enhance their skills in the hope that this would lead them into paid work. Women were also entering the paid workforce in larger numbers and married women were staying in the paid workforce, which influenced volunteering, especially in school communities and the 'traditional' volunteering roles.

Changing social values and views in regards to the deinstitutionalisation of the disabled with the International Year of the Disabled Persons in 1981 and the Richmond Report of 1983 fundamentally recast the range of self-help and welfare organisations as volunteers sought to assist the re-integration of these vulnerable groups into the community. The period of the enactment of the *Commonwealth Disability Services Act 1986* was especially problematic, as volunteers and their organisations responded to increasingly complex delivery systems by employing professional management structures and processes (borrowed from the business world), yet continuing largely to rely on volunteers. In 1991, the Commonwealth/State Disability Agreement saw many disability issues devolved to the states, which again witnessed the beginning of a cycle of contracting, tendering for supplying services, benchmarking, and increased bureaucratic reporting requirements.

The 'discovery' of volunteering and the beginnings of a research culture

Did economic rationalism and this radical shift in Australian government policies and practices lead to the 'discovery' and corresponding research interest in volunteering in the 1980s and 1990s? Or was the timing accidental? Many contemporaries believed it was not accidental but as I argued in chapter 6, there was a nascent interest in the previous decade, with a couple of research projects completed. It was certainly recognised by the 1980s that there was little research on volunteers in Australia and that this omission was a problem as the new welfare regimes placed a 'great deal of emphasis on the real and potential contribution of volunteers'.[17] But it was also feared that the new interest in volunteers was driven by governments hoping to reduce costs and replace paid staff with volunteers. Statements by the then Minister for Social Security, Senator Fred Chaney in May 1982, arguing that the increasing dependence on state provisions represented a decline in both personal and family responsibilities, and that more volunteer activities and family obligations would 'diminish dependence on government' did little to allay these fears.[18]

The 1980s and 1990s saw an increasing interest from academics, research centres and women's groups on researching Australian volunteering.[19] Those concerned with social welfare volunteering were most prominent. Early examples include Adam Graycar and Jill Hardwick from the Social Welfare Research Centre at the University of NSW, who produced a working paper based on a survey undertaken in the early 1980s. It focused on an analysis of 37 000 non-government welfare organisations to provide a series of classifications and descriptions of the sector. They collected valuable data on volunteers and determined that at a conservative estimate, between 7 and 13 per cent of Australians over the age of fifteen (or 10 per cent of the population) were involved in some form of social welfare volunteer work worth about $1.5 billion or 1.1 per cent of GDP.[20]

In 1983, a co-operative project with the National Women's Advisory Council and the National Council of Women was undertaken because the volunteer work of women and their contribution was largely unrecognised in 'official statistics and planning'.[21] The study was based on female volunteers who worked for one or more of the 570 voluntary organisations affiliated to the National Council of Women. These included hospital auxiliaries, mothers' clubs and schools, community welfare such as St Vincent de Paul and the Australian Red Cross, self-help organisations such as Lifeline; church-based groups and development organisations such as the YWCA and Girl Guides. The volunteers, 40 per cent of whom were aged between fifty-one and sixty-five, did between two and fifteen hours volunteering per week. They spent time fundraising, working on stalls and in school tuckshops, attending meetings, visiting the sick and elderly, as well as providing secretarial and accounting help. Two-thirds of the sample was not in the paid workforce.[22] This cohort, as presented in the pilot survey, represented older volunteers who were particularly active in church-based and community welfare groups. The involvement of women, especially mothers in school-based volunteering, through parents and citizens' associations (P&Cs), in uniform shops and tuckshops was also noted in the study. One woman responded that she volunteered because the services were integral to community wellbeing, especially in the bush. 'It is a *community service* in the truest sense', she said. Another commented that volunteers did not want 'recognition or publicity. They have clubbed together in different organisations or are on their own to do something that can help someone else'.[23]

In 1988, one of the first Australian books on volunteer management was published. Margaret Curtis and Joy Noble set out to explode a few myths concerning volunteering in Australia that were, the authors believed, as intransigent as they were incorrect. The myths were that young Australians did not volunteer (the authors found that 13.2 per cent were aged between fifteen and twenty-five, with almost 61 per cent under forty-five); that most volunteers were women (the study found that 54 per cent were women and 46 per cent were men); and that most volunteers were not in the paid workforce (46 per cent were in workforce).[24] This study revealed that volunteering as an activity, and volunteers themselves, had changed. The authors concluded that volunteers were more diverse, more highly skilled, and more adaptable than previously thought. These shifts required new policies, new volunteer programs, and new positions such as volunteer managers. Then in 1991, Joy Noble published *Volunteering: A Current Perspective*, again one of the first full length books published in Australia concerned with the 'human resource management' of volunteering. In its opening pages Noble pleaded for volunteering to be taken seriously as a subject for study, to recognise the 'extent and nature of volunteer effort' to try and debate what were the accepted boundaries for volunteering, 'both now and in the future'.[25]

One of the most highly regarded academic studies of the period was completed by sociologist Cora Baldock. She attempted to analyse the resurgence of the voluntary sector and volunteering in reaction to the privatisation ideology and the withdrawal of government services 'as an economic and political strategy', as well as a 'means of returning responsibility and freedom to the individual and the "community"'.[26] This tension, she argued, between volunteering 'as low-cost welfare provision, and volunteerism as a means of self-development and growth for individual volunteers' was at the heart of many discussions as well as the increasing reliance on government funding for survival.[27] Baldock's study on social welfare volunteers in Western Australia was published as *Volunteers in Welfare* in 1990. The project selected volunteers from forty-two voluntary organisations, self-help and social action groups and statutory authorities in that state. Baldock concluded that volunteers, particularly in the welfare sector, were predominantly women, from an older age group, a substantial minority were not married, most were European or Australian by birth, and many worked in paid employment.[28] However, they were not exclusively from the middle classes, either when classified by their partner's occupation or by their own work definition. Many women undertook volunteer work to escape the domestic sphere, reflecting the historical antecedents that women's volunteer work assisted them to move from the private domestic sphere and into the public domain. Dame Beryl Beaurepaire, a doyen of Melbourne philanthropic circles and one of the founders of the Liberal party in the 1940s, reflected a common view when she stated that her prime motive for 'charity work' as she called it was to get out of the house.[29] Altruism or feelings of social concern and responsibility for others was another reason people volunteered as well as motives of social interaction, using and developing skills for the paid workforce and personal growth.[30]

Australian academics were encouraged by these early studies and influenced by overseas developments especially in Britain, by researchers such as Justin Davis Smith, Nick Deakin, and American Robert Putnam. They formed academic organisations such as Australian and New Zealand Third Sector Research with academics Mark Lyons and Jenny Onyx leading the embryonic field.[31] Journals such as *Third Sector Review* and the *Australian Journal on Volunteering* were also launched, providing a forum for the publication of specific research on Australian volunteering.

Government studies

After an initial spurt in the 1970s especially during the Whitlam years, governments took surprisingly little interest in collecting data on volunteering. In 1982, the ABS undertook surveys in Victoria and Queensland, and New South Wales and South Australia in 1986 and 1988 respectively.[32] The South Australian statistics revealed there were 92 100 volunteers in sport and 50 400 in health and welfare. This was broken down further in terms of gender with 56 per cent of those volunteers in sport being men and 44 per cent women. But in the welfare category it was quite different, with 70 per cent women and 30 per cent men. In sport, almost half were between thirty and forty-four years old; almost three-quarters were in paid employment and two-fifths were married with children. In terms of welfare, the volunteer profile was quite different. The vast majority were from the forty-five to sixty years age group, one-third were in paid employment and over half were married with no children under fifteen. The main volunteering tasks in sport were coaching and umpiring, committee work, administration, serving, fundraising and maintenance. Again, the jobs in welfare were subtly different: administration, transport, serving, teaching and committee work.[33]

At a national level, it was not until the early 1990s that the ABS began to focus on volunteering, with two 1992 reports: *Unpaid Work and the Australian Economy* and *How Australians Use their Time*, and a 1993 survey on sport.[34] It was the Australian Federal government's 1991 *Lavarch Report*, an inquiry into women's lives in Australia, with a particular focus on the effectiveness of the *Sex Discrimination Act 1984*, that propelled a call for detailed research on women's volunteering. It was acknowledged that women carried out a significant proportion of volunteer work in the community, for which there was insufficient recognition, reflecting the low status of volunteering generally.[35] The committee recommended that the ABS include volunteer and domestic labour in its statistics, to help 'record the interdependence of the market and domestic economies'.[36] The ABS countered that this would be inconsistent with international standards (as originally pointed out by Marilyn Waring and discussed in chapter 1), so the committee then recommended that the ABS carry out supplementary reports.

In June 1995, the ABS conducted its first detailed study on national volunteering trends as part of its Monthly Population Survey. For the first time in Australia, there was a comprehensive analysis of who was volunteering and where, across the nation. Surveying people over fifteen, and based on the previous twelve months, the ABS adopted the international classifications of non-profit organisations and defined a volunteer as 'someone who willingly gave unpaid help in the form of time, service or skills, through an organisation or group'.[37] It was found that 19 per cent of Australians carried out volunteer work within the previous twelve months, estimated to be 433.9 million hours. People living outside the metropolitan area were more likely to pursue volunteer work than those living in capital cities. New South Wales had the lowest volunteer rate, of 15 per cent, compared with the ACT, at 26 per cent. The breakdown of the organisational categories and percentage of volunteers (volunteers could work in more than one field) was:

Sport/recreation/hobby – 31.4%
Emergency services – 4.9%
Welfare/community – 29.7%
Business/professional/union – 3.3%
Education/training/youth development – 25.3%
Religious – 17.7%
Law/justice/political – 1.7% Arts/culture – 4.1%
Health – 6.9%
Foreign/international – 0.8%
Environmental/animal welfare – 3.7%[38]

Although this 1995 ABS report did not attempt to put a monetary value on volunteer work, in 1992, the value of unpaid volunteer labour in Australia was estimated to be over $18 billion.[39]

This ABS report was followed by a lengthy inquiry of the Industry Commission, whose Report into Charitable Organisations was tabled in Federal parliament in September 1995. Over 450 submissions were received by the inquiry and over 150 organisations and individuals presented evidence to the commission during public hearings. Despite concerns as to why a government economic body was reporting on non-profit community services organisations, ACOSS President Robert Fitzgerald felt that such information was useful in determining the 'size and scope of the community sector' in Australia.[40] The commission made a number of recommendations to recognise the role and needs of volunteers who work in community social welfare organisations, especially in resourcing the 'training, supervision and insurance of volunteers'.[41] The report estimated that about 1.3 million Australians gave '95 million hours annually as volunteers through community service welfare organisations', which was 'equivalent to about 50 000 persons working a forty-hour week'.[42] Overall, volunteering was worth $42 billion a year to the Australian economy.[43]

The professionalisation of volunteering

Other problems affecting volunteers and volunteering in the 1980s and 1990s concerned the professionalisation of volunteering and the changing environment within which volunteers worked. Tighter legislative frameworks and workplace reforms, especially in the areas of occupational health and safety, insurance, compensation and risk evaluation all affected volunteers. As Australian society became more litigious, the environment for volunteering became more complex and restrictive. Not only did volunteers have to negotiate the new landscape of training, job specifications and time sheets, they also had to adapt to changing practices and expectations. 'It's difficult to get our ladies who've been making sandwiches for 50 years to wear latex gloves and all that sort of stuff, but that's what you've got to do', reported one volunteer manager.[44]

One of the ways to address these issues was for volunteers to organise themselves more formally. The establishment of the New South Wales Volunteer Centre in the 1970s led to other states following suit, including South Australia and Queensland in 1982 and Western Australia in 1988. A key figure in New South Wales was Margaret Bell, who went on to become involved in volunteering internationally with her election, in 1988, as President of the International Association of Volunteer Effort. In 1993, the state-based volunteer centres established the Australian Council for Volunteering (ACV), with Margaret Bell elected inaugural President. The ACV brought together two peak volunteering organisations, the Australian Association of Volunteering and the National Association of Volunteer Referral Agencies, under the one umbrella. After sustained lobbying, federal funding was secured the following year to assist in the administration of both the state-based volunteer centres and the national peak body, which in 1997 changed its name to Volunteering Australia.

Because of government policies and rapid changes to the sector, Volunteering Australia put together a series of principles and definitions concerning the practice of volunteering. The eleven principles included the basic tenets of volunteering – that it was undertaken of one's own free will and was not to be used as a way of receiving government allowances or pensions; that volunteering was not a substitute for paid work and should not be used to replace paid workers; that it only occurred in the not-for-profit sector, and that it was always unpaid.[45]

These principles highlighted a growing concern that volunteering was being 'misused' by some, especially in terms of public policy initiatives. Federal governments, through programs such as the Community Volunteer Program, the 1997 Voluntary Work Initiative or, from January 1998, the inclusion of volunteering within mutual obligation arrangements, fundamentally recast the role and function of volunteering. Recipients of welfare payments were being effectively coerced into volunteering in return for a range of social security benefits. Including volunteering within an 'obligatory program that had as its basis the capacity to penalise unemployed people for non-participation' was not to be condoned, argued the peak body.[46] There were also concerns about using the terminology of 'volunteering' at all for community service orders, work experience, emergency work during industrial disputes and work for the dole programs – none of which fell under the formal definition of volunteering. These examples were all of unpaid work but were not volunteering because the labour was not freely volunteered.

Another concern was the perception, real or otherwise, that volunteering was in decline. Certainly in some areas such as social welfare and the service clubs particularly, traditional organisations were suffering. Membership numbers in the branches of the Australian Red Cross and Country Women's Association, for example, both historically important organisations, were falling. Some women's groups, such as Quota and Zonta were never very large but they managed to remain stable and in some cases grow. But the traditional, well established, originally male-only service organisations, the 'welfare gadflies' as John Lawrence described them in the 1960s, such as Apex, Lions and Rotary, were in free-fall.[47] Each organisation had a slightly different focus but all were involved in community and welfare development in towns and suburbs across Australia. Both Rotary and Lions, established in Australia in 1921 and 1947 respectively, were imported from the United States. Apex was an Australian idea, formed in the early 1930s, and based on the membership of men between the ages of eighteen and forty. With the group's symbol of a triangle, representing citizenship, fellowship and service, it was founded to:

> make the ideal of service the basic command, a means of
> forming friendships, to promote understanding and citizenship
> and lend our neighbours a hand … to organise and attack
> problems which could not be overcome by individuals.[48]

Apex was involved in a range of important national projects, including many related to specific medical areas such as the Royal Flying Doctor Service, multiple sclerosis, sudden infant death syndrome, as well as other organisations such as the Association of Civilian Widows. However, by the late 1990s, Apex was suffering a real decline in membership, from a peak of 17 655 in 1978 to around 5500 in 1999, despite allowing for male, female and mixed clubs from 1998.[49]

Lions clubs were also declining, from a peak of 35 000 in the mid-

1980s to 29 500 in 1998, and Rotary was facing similar problems. While the impact on communities, especially in rural and regional Australia, was easily identified, the reasons for the declining membership were less clear. Lack of interest from younger Australians and a seeming inability 'to encourage young people into community service' were given as reasons for the decline.[50] People were working harder with less spare time to devote to their community and to attend meetings; and job insecurity, family commitments and financial pressures all played a part. The knock-on effects of economic rationalism, with the closure of a range of government services and businesses in rural areas such as banks, post offices and general infrastructure, crippled local communities. The decline of the service clubs and general community engagement, an integral aspect of Australian society, was a consequence of these economic reforms.

Surf lifesaving

Many sporting areas such as surf lifesaving were not immune to these seismic changes. Surf lifesaving entered the 1980s in considerable trouble but the inclusion of women and the Nippers (children aged seven to thirteen, a concept begun by parents in the 1960s as a separate club) under the umbrella of the senior clubs, helped to reinvigorate the organisation. Events such as the 1988 Bicentenary and the emergence of a new Australian nationalism, often characterised by Australian beach culture and the surf lifesaver, helped to propel the volunteer organisation forward. Having the former Dee Why lifesaver and Governor-General, Sir William Deane describe surf lifesaving as a 'showcase of selfless service' only enhanced the image. In 1994, it was estimated that the actual cost of running voluntary patrols was about $20 million per year. In 1999, the national peak body, Surf Life Saving Australia, stated it had a total membership of 97 927, with an active patrol membership of 22 061 and over 38 000 Nippers.[51]

But it was in the area of corporate sponsorship where surf lifesaving was particularly affected. The development of this type of funding was a double-edged sword. While on the one hand, the 'hyper commercialisation' of some sport, including the surf lifesaving movement, helped to alleviate perennial funding problems, it also transformed the activity of surf lifesaving into a marketable commodity, especially through its iron-man competitions, a derivative of American competition imported to Australia in the 1960s. By the end of the 1980s, assisted by Gold Coast ironman champion Grant Kenny, the Kellogg's cereal 'Nutri Grain', and the film *Coolangatta Gold*, the ironman competitions developed into a professional activity with athletes, nominally surf lifesavers, earning significant sponsorship money. This was at odds with the spirit of the volunteer organisation and a split developed between those volunteers who wanted to remain true to the movement's original values and those who, it was argued 'had become preoccupied with issues of "money, spon-sorship and competition"'.[52] Two reports undertaken in the early 1990s found that the surf lifesaving movement was 'undervaluing the services of its volunteers' as well as evidence of a high level of burnout, with volunteer lifesavers disheartened by the professional competition, who were walking away from the organisation.[53] Another problem that further alienated the volunteer base was the increasing 'professionalism' of the administration. Common to many sporting volunteer organisations was the perception that paid staff in administrative positions were necessary. Barry Kerr, in an early 1990s study stated that he believed this tension was common when 'the move to "professionalism"' was seen as 'threatening'.[54]

From the 1970s there were increasing numbers of paid lifeguards (an American term) employed at major beaches around Australia. Changes to public liability laws found lifesaving clubs open to prosecution and vulner-able, so some local governments introduced paid lifeguards to compensate for the new laws. At the famous Bondi club, for example, Waverley coun-cil began investing more in paid staff than volunteers, who were criticised for their work and patrolling duties. As lifesaving historian Sean Brawley stated, 'council needed certainty in this new public liability environment and council employees were seen as more reliable than volunteer lifesav-ers'.[55] The creation of the Australian Beach Inspector Lifeguard Associa-tion and the Australian Professional Ocean Lifeguard Association in the 1990s added to the tensions between professional and amateur, paid and unpaid worker. Towards the end of the century, the surf lifesaving move-ment was still struggling and some gloomily predicted that the volunteer surf lifesaver was an 'endangered species'.[56]

NSW Asthma Children's Swimming Program

One volunteer organisation, the NSW Asthma Children's Swimming Program, started the 1980s strongly but largely due to organisational changes at head office did not ultimately survive. First mentioned in chapter 4, this organisation was started in the early 1960s by a group of dedicated volunteers, all mothers who had asthmatic children. A key figure was Colleen Wardell, who began volunteering as a swimming instructor in 1965 and continued her involvement as the volunteer co-ordinator for twenty years from 1983 to her resignation in 2003. Colleen estimated that she spent about fifty hours each week on her administrative duties, all in a voluntary capacity. She received no wage, although all her expenses, including travel, telephone, postage and stationery were paid.[57]

During Colleen's period at the helm, the program grew from strength to strength reflecting her commitment, energy and organisational abilities. From small beginnings in one pool with twenty children, by 1988 there were swimming classes operating in thirteen suburban pools and fourteen country towns including Tamworth, Wagga Wagga, Port Macquarie and the ACT.[58] The program peaked in 1994, with 1476 children receiving individual one-on-one swimming tuition in thirty-six pools.[59] For about one-third of the children, the swimming program was free. For the rest, parents paid the full cost of each session or a portion of the costs, depending on their financial circumstances. Costs were kept down through the in-kind support of pool operators (largely local councils and hospitals) who donated the pools free of charge. And, of course, the swimming instructors were volunteers, all fully trained in the asthmatic swimming program's teaching format and in asthmatic first aid as well as current resuscitation methods, updated every twelve months. Colleen Wardell worked closely with Dr Claire Isbister, undertaking research and co-authoring a number of papers promoting the program and the medical and scientific benefits of swimming for asthmatic children, published in prestigious medical journals such as the *Medical Journal of Australia*. Colleen also championed the scheme overseas and assisted in establishing similar programs in Argentina, Brazil, Taiwan and the United States.

Over thirty years, about 25 000 children were taught by 2000 swimming volunteers, including national swimmers and Olympic champions.[60] Co-founder and original co-ordinator, Leila Schmidt, paid tribute to the volunteers when she said:

> We can never be grateful enough to them – travelling often very
> long distances, putting our children before their own home
> and families with such regularity … no words are adequate to
> express my personal appreciation of their efforts.[61]

In 1999, it was estimated that if the volunteer swimming teachers were paid the standard hourly rate, the wages bill would be almost $500 000. This unique volunteer program continued to run with no government subsidy or financial assistance until 2005 when, after Colleen's resignation, the program was handed over to the New South Wales Department of Sport and Recreation and incorporated into their Austswim program.

Changing directions

The question of changing directions, the professionalisation of voluntary non-profit organisations and its effects on volunteers were highly emotive issues during the 1980s and 1990s. Many grappled with these problems. The questions of relations between volunteers, paid staff, management and board members, the risk of taking volunteers for granted or changing management style and direction were fraught. In some cases volunteers simply walked away, but other disputes went public. In 1995, when Save the Children Fund closed its Opportunity Shop at Crows Nest in Sydney's northern suburbs on the pretext of changing business plans and fundraising policy (all part of the professionalisation process), the volunteers were incensed. Run by a group of over fifty volunteers, the shop sold bric-a-brac, and second-hand goods and clothing. 'It might be an ugly little shop but … there are so many old and lonely people in this area. Many would come in and browse for an hour, just to meet people … I know it is our job to raise money, not talk to people, but it meant we were part of the community', said one volunteer. They were also particularly angry about the way management publicly described the shop and its volunteers as 'old ladies', and its attitude that the organisation 'was not in the business of providing a place for them [volunteers] to go twice a week ... the shops were not viable and were taking up resources at head office'.[62] As volunteer Sheila Etherington wrote:

> As one who has helped at Crows Nest as long as [the shop] has been open, I can definitely state I know not one volunteer who was there for something to do. We are all busy people who wanted to help the world's children, the innocent victims of war and other disasters, and at the same time help local people.[63]

Older volunteers

It was this sort of attitude that was behind the formation of the Older Women's Network, a self-help and advocacy group established in 1988 to provide a voice for women aged over fifty. This cohort gave much to society; they generally lived longer than men, yet they rarely received sufficient acknowledgement for their contribution. As Noreen Hewett explained, 'a partnership is needed, combining grassroots experience, commitment, qualifications and professionalism. Through peer support, women who are trained can pass on their knowledge to others'.[64]

The tension between taking older volunteers for granted, ageism and the perceived need for organisations to professionalise and use modern business methods, as seen in the Save the Children Fund op-shop example above, was further complicated by other developments. As discussed earlier in this book, the contemporary assumption that volunteering is the 'workplace' or 'playground' for older members of our society is a relatively recent phenomenon. It was in the 1980s and particularly the 1990s that both organisations and governments began to see older people as a cohort of potential volunteers. With significant demographic changes, an ageing population, with the baby boomers approaching retirement age, and with better health outcomes, the 'social dimensions of ageing' and the role that volunteering could play became a key issue.[65] An ABS Family Survey, published in 1992, confirmed the substantial contribution older Australians made to the community through their informal assistance to family members including child-care, crisis support and home maintenance. The challenges brought by the 'greying' of Australia and the supposed economic and social burden that this would place on future generations became an increased focus of interest.

Researchers began to concentrate on this important group. So did the Consultative Committee on Ageing, a group advising the New South Wales government, who ran a series of workshops in 1995 to look at the contribution of older people. Their report, *Volunteering and Older People*, concluded that despite assumptions to the contrary, more older Australians volunteered or gave care than received it; and that volunteering enhanced the ageing process through providing social interaction, a sense of achievement and belonging, and by keeping active. However, the report also concluded that better government support and infrastructure was required, as well as better communication and networking between governments and the voluntary sector itself. Finally, the long-held view that volunteering was in decline was not upheld but rather that the volunteer environment was 'complex', with new challenges arising such as increased competition for volunteers, a decline in loyalty to particular organisations (mirroring the changing landscape in paid employment) and changing expectations in regards to the type of volunteering undertaken.[66]

Volunteering and diversity

Was volunteering in Australia culture specific? Was it essentially white and British? As mentioned earlier, research by Baldock, the ABS and others carried out during the 1980s and 1990s indicated that volunteering was largely undertaken by the Australian born and those of Anglo-Saxon descent. Migrants, those born outside of Australia and Aboriginals and Torres Strait Islanders, did not feature largely in the statistics. However, I believe the analysis was flawed and the ways of measuring volunteering not adequate or sophisticated enough to pick up the range of culturally specific volunteer patterns. As I argued in chapter 5, migrants were very adept at forming volunteer organisations, especially self-help groups at the migrant hostels as soon as they arrived in Australia, or once they had established themselves in the community. Migrants volunteered through church-based organisations, sporting and arts groups, and ethnic community radio and television stations. Malgorzata Mascibroda, for example, first became involved in volunteering at age fifteen, when she worked on a Polish radio program on 5EBI-FM in South Australia.[67] She is but one example of many thousands who used volunteering as a way of engaging with the Australian community.

From the 1970s, non-English speaking background (NESB) groups developed a voice and became very active in advocating their position in the wider community. One of the largest and most active peak bodies during this period was the Federation of Ethnic Communities Councils of Australia (FECCA). In 1986, FECCA prepared a report on the key issues affecting women of non-English speaking background, who comprised 20 per cent of all Australian women.[68] In a submission to the 1995 Industry Commission charities inquiry, the New South Wales body, the Ethnic Communities Council of NSW stated that the reasons NESB people did not appear in traditional volunteer areas or did not use specific services in mainstream organisations were complex. Issues of inclusiveness, in terms of cultural diversity and cultural practices, language problems and lack of interpreter services, as well as the position of women within many cultural groups, were identified as areas of concern and reasons why migrant groups were under-represented in the statistics.[69]

In March 1982, about 300 immigrant and refugee women from across Australia met in Sydney at a 'Speakout' to discuss a range of issues, including marginalisation, health problems, wage exploitation and sexual harassment. A working party was formed and for two years, volunteers worked with little resources to establish the Immigrant Women's Speakout Association until, in 1984, government funding was obtained. New South Wales state politician Franca Arena was very supportive, as were a range of non-government organisations, including the Australian Council of Churches and FECCA. The creation of the Association of Non-English Speaking Background Women of Australia or ANESBWA was another attempt by women to address some of the problems of NESB women. Major NESB organisations and migrant bodies were male dominated and it was argued that women needed their own voice. Formed in 1986 as a 'national policy, information, advocacy and community development organisation', its objects were 'to act as an independent advocate for NESB women at a national level, committed to the goals of achieving cultural, social, economic, educational and sexual equality for NESB women'.[70] It was an organisation formed by NESB women for NESB women, and was concerned about the needs of first-, second- and third-generation women who faced multiple disadvantage largely due to poverty, isolation, lack of English language skills, and lack of culturally sensitive and linguistically appropriate programs and services.

One of the founders of ANESBWA and its first chair, Matina Mottee, was a driving force behind the organisation. Born in Tasmania in 1931 of Greek immigrant parents, and the eldest of six children, Matina spent her life raising her four children and helping women from non-English backgrounds deal with bureaucracies, including hospitals, doctors and lawyers, through translating and interpreting, all in an unpaid capacity. Once her children were grown up, and at age fifty, she attempted to join the paid workforce – but with no formal qualifications, it took three years to get a job in follow-up work with immigrant women in women's refuges, and as co-ordinator of the NSW Immigrant Women's Resource Centre in Lidcombe.[71] Established in 1986, ANESBWA was run in a totally volunteer capacity by Matina and her committee, with no paid staff and no permanent office until an operational grant of $10 000 was secured from the Office of the Status of Women in 1989. This followed a grant from the Office of Multicultural Affairs in 1988 to research and write a policy options paper on 'Issues for women in multicultural Australia' and to run a series of leadership workshops. By 1995, ANESBWA had grown considerably. With an annual budget of around $200 000, the vast majority of funding came from a range of government grants, and the major expenditure was on wages. With operational funding from the Office of the Status of Women and the Department of Immigration and Multicultural Affairs, a number of paid staff ran the office, produced a regular newsletter, as well as funded research reports on topics such as domestic violence and the effects of enterprise agreements on migrant women.[72]

In 1996, the incoming Howard Liberal/National government decided to streamline or 'mainstream' a range of policies, which meant the scaling down of specialist women's policy units and programs, and the withdrawal of funding. It was argued that complex social and economic issues of concern to migrant women required formal interagency co-operation and partnership with the community.[73] This action could also be interpreted as merely an excuse to save money. Either way the impact on a range of volunteer organisations, including ANESBWA, was immediate. The organisation lost 75 per cent of its funding, including the monies for its national co-ordinator. After ten years, ANESBWA was back to where it started in 1986, with little funding, and volunteers carrying out the advocacy, policy and research work of the organisation.

Volunteering is also part of Indigenous culture, although formal volunteering itself is not an Aboriginal and Torres Strait Islander concept – rather, extended families undertake to care for and look after each other in a largely informal way. An attempt to collate the volunteering activities of Aboriginal and Torres Strait Islanders was made in 1994 during a national survey, where it was stated that about 27 per cent of Indigenous people aged over fifteen volunteered their time, and that 41 per cent did at least six hours per week. Their volunteering constituted hunting, fishing and gathering bush food (11 per cent); community work and sport (9 per cent); committee work (8 per cent); and working at school or with youth groups (6 per cent).[74] As Sol Encel stated, 'when culturally appropriate definitions are used, Aboriginal and Torres Strait Islander people have a very high rate of participation in voluntary work'.[75] South Australian Shirley Peisley, an Aboriginal woman who has worked tirelessly for Aboriginal issues and received an Order of Australia in 2000 for services to the Indigenous community, put it well when she said:

> Volunteering is a topic that Aboriginal people know a lot about.
> It is something that we have had to learn to do, and to do well,
> in order to ensure that our people are given the opportunity to
> enjoy the same rights as other Australians.[76]

Green power

If some areas of volunteering were finding it very hard going during the 1980s and 1990s, others were blessed with new initiatives, new momentum and, most importantly, government involvement and financial support. The environment took centre stage during these decades, and Australian volunteers were at the forefront of unique ideas and organisations that were later transported to other parts of the world. Two examples of this, at the heart of the Australian way of volunteering, were Clean Up Australia and Landcare – one the vision of an individual, the other a collective approach. Round-the-world yachtsman, Ian Kiernan, formed the first Clean Up campaign in 1989. Concerned for the state of Sydney Harbour and the amount of plastic and rubbish in it, he described the genesis of the organisation as forming 'a committee of volunteers', raising 'some money' to begin work on that first event, 'Clean Up Sydney Harbour'.[77] Forty thousand volunteers turned out in January 1989 to remove over 5000 tonnes of waste. The idea was enthusiastically taken up across Australia, and governments then began to take an interest; for example, in dealing with sewage overflows into Sydney Harbour. Kiernan was later invited by the United Nations to establish Clean Up the World and by 2000, over 40 million volunteers from 120 countries were participating in a volunteer program that encouraged people to 'think globally and act locally'.[78]

Landcare is a quintessentially Australian volunteer initiative, supported and assisted by all governments, local, state and Federal, coming together to address a particularly urgent need – that of protecting, saving and redeeming our fragile Australian environment, ranging from the dry and desert landscapes of the interior to the tropical rainforests of northern Australia. The origins of Landcare lie with progressive farmers who were concerned about land degradation, soil erosion and eucalyptus die-back. From the 1960s, there were initiatives with local community organisations and governments working together with farmers, including Victoria's Soil Conservation Authority group conservation projects, the Potter Farmland Plan in the mid-1980s, the South Australian Soil Conservation Boards of the 1980s and Greening Australia from 1983.[79] The term 'landcare' was first used by farmer-based community groups wanting to 'tackle common issues of land degradation in a cooperative manner; share information and resources; and provide mutual support and encouragement'.[80] In 1986, in an attempt to thwart the major salinity problems of south-eastern Victoria, Joan Kirner, the then Minister for Conservation, Forests and Lands, along with Heather Mitchell from the Victorian Farmers' Federation, banded together to form autonomous community-based volunteer groups called Landcare. Within a year, thirty Landcare groups were formed, representing about 1000 farms.[81]

In 1989, this small state-based program became a national phenomenon when a 'decade of Landcare' was launched by Prime Minister Bob Hawke, in the hope of achieving sustainable management of Australia's natural resources by 2000. Involving Federal and state governments, with encouragement from Philip Toyne from the Australian Conservation Foundation and Rick Farley from the National Farmers Federation, Landcare is arguably one of the most successful examples of the partnership between governments and volunteers in the last fifty years. Australian government funding originated from a number of programs, including the National Soil Conservation Program (1983–92), the Natural Heritage Trust (1997–2008) and the National Action Plan for Salinity and Water Quality (2000–08). Fifty-six regional Catchment Management Authorities now oversee Landcare programs across Australia.

An important aspect of the Landcare initiative is the involvement of all Australians, from both rural and urban areas. As Barbara Hardy, a noted environmentalist from South Australia commented, 'farmers were beginning to understand the need for Landcare, but urban people needed to be convinced that some of their taxes should be spent in this way'.[82] Although $360 million was pledged over the ten years, the eventual funding exceeded this figure, with about $500 million allocated between 1995 and 2000 to Landcare groups, representing over 5000 groups and more than 120 000 volunteers for tree growing, salinity control and amendment of soil degradation.[83] Some groups also banded together to achieve regional outcomes, as in Armidale, in northern New South Wales, where an attempt was made to create bird corridors through the city to join rural corridors across the whole region. The Landcare groups vary in size, depending on location, and are overseen by a committee whose volunteers apply for project funding and tree planting. Many have a paid co-ordinator, funded by government, who facilitates and co-ordinates the group's activities, including training and development.

Landcare is also part of the international phenomenon of 'sustainable communities'.[84] Simon Schama argued in his book *Landscape and Memory* that observations and stories about landscape were handed down from one generation to another. In the telling and retelling of these stories over time, the precision of the landscape was lost, and myths and stories changed from generation to generation. This type of ecological conscious-ness can be created through environmental volunteer experiences, and through stories of the landscape, which are repeated over time and shared between volunteers.[85] A major theme to emerge from Margaret Gooch's study on environmental volunteers was that developing and maintaining an ecological identity was important in sustaining environmental volun-teer commitment. Her study suggested that volunteers responded to and identified with the physical location where their volunteering took place, and that this 'sense of place' could be cultivated to foster active volun-teer groups. Through the development of 'shared beliefs, interests and values', volunteers could build up an ecological awareness and identity that strongly motivated and sustained them. [86] Gooch defined a sense of place as something which:

> creates both a connection with the environment and with the
> people and local organizations who inhabit those places. It is
> not something that is acquired when you move into a new area
> or suburb, it has to be cultivated. Like culture, sense of place is
> changing and adaptive, not fixed.[87]

Since most of the Australian population lives in urban environments, the need was identified to create sustainable urban communities as well as rural initiatives. Bushcare, Dunecare, Watercare, Rivercare and Coast-care are all spin-offs of the original Landcare program. They involve a range of activities such as water quality monitoring, tree planting, weed-ing, mulching, watering and clean-up days. Beginning in Sydney, urban Bushcare programs were soon established in other capital cities, includ-ing Brisbane, Melbourne and Perth. In my local area, Balmain, a former industrial inner-city suburb of Sydney, hugging the harbour foreshore and once the home to the Colgate-Palmolive and Unilever factories, ship building and even coal mining, Bushcare groups have been established to care for the very small remnants of bushland in the area.[88]

Environmental volunteering has particularly benefited from the 'branding' of Landcare, with over 80 per cent of Australians recognising the name in 2000. It also has broad community support and has been very successful with marketing strategies involving celebrities, major Australian companies, and Landcare awards ceremonies. For example, from 1997–2000 over 40 000 volunteers planted 2.6 million trees and shrubs as part of Olympic Landcare.[89] Landcare has become a 'powerful discursive tool' to assist the groundswell of support that brought Australians together on the question of the environment and now climate change. It also attracted international interest because of its community basis 'as a working example of participatory sustainable development'.[90] However, despite the positive views that Landcare was participatory and inclusive and a real grassroots movement, there is clear evidence that it is also highly bureaucratic and too reliant on government funding. As Lockie pointed out, Landcare groups, far from being 'free of direct control', are actually highly institutionalised and held to account by a competitive grants scheme.[91] There was a certain tension in the boast of a recent Federal minister that Landcare is the 'most successful community based program ever implemented by an Australian government'.[92]

Emergency volunteers

Emergency volunteers, especially rural fire fighters and to a lesser extent, the State Emergency Services (SES) volunteers were largely quarantined from government funding cuts during the 1980s and 1990s but still experienced significant changes due to the professionalisation of volunteers. Although a 'repetitive feature of the Australian environment', the summers of the early 1980s were unusually severe fire seasons.[93] In Tasmania, South Australia and Victoria, bushfires were particularly destructive, but special mention must be made of the 1983 bushfires. Between 16 and 20 February, over 100 fires broke out across Victoria, from the Dandenong Ranges, the Great Ocean Road, the Otway Ranges and around Mount Macedon. Called the 'Ash Wednesday' fires, over 8000 people became homeless and forty-seven people died in fires causing damage costing upwards of $200 million.[94] In the small town of Cockatoo, almost all 307 buildings were destroyed and six people lost their lives; and in Upper Beaconsfield seventeen volunteer fire fighters lost their lives when a wind change trapped them. Across the border in South Australia, twenty-eight people lost their lives and more than 300 homes were destroyed. Over 16000 fire fighters were involved, including thousands of Country Fire Authority volunteers from Victoria and other states.

The National Disasters Organisation, the main Commonwealth body overseeing disaster management, created just before the Cyclone Tracy disaster of 1974, saw significant changes. Focusing on training, liaison and research, it was re-named Emergency Management Australia in 2001, and moved from the Department of Defence to the Attorney-General's Department. Provided with additional resources and funding, one of the briefs of the agency was to support the almost half a million volunteers involved in emergency services across Australia, from the Salvation Army, Australian Red Cross and St John Ambulance to rural fire brigades, State Emergency Services and volunteer coastal patrols.

However, questions of the use of emergency volunteers and their adequate resourcing and training continued when five volunteer fire fighters, including a seventeen-year-old high school volunteer, were trapped in their truck and died on 2 December 1998 at Linton, near Ballarat in central Victoria. Travelling in tandem with a paid Geelong fire crew, the volunteers were caught in a fireball as the wind changed direction. With empty water tanks (due to faulty readings, they had no idea how much water remained), they quickly succumbed to the flames. Questions over access to up-to-date equipment and training came to the fore as the community grappled with the deaths. At the time the Victorian Country Fire Authority (CFA) had over 67000 volunteers, but spent only $7.6 million on volunteer and brigade support, including a pitiful $1.5 million for training.[95] The problem of the under-resourced volunteer army was one that beset all state fire fighting authorities, especially in rural areas. Added to these problems was the general population decline in the bush, and a shrinking volunteer pool from which to draw. The Victorian CFA undertook research on why its volunteers left the organisation and found three major reasons. Firstly, people were mobile and moved around, generally exiting the bush. Secondly, many found it too hard to juggle both paid work, family and volunteering commitments; and thirdly, 18 per cent of volunteers said their reasons for leaving related to leadership and conflict issues within the organisation.[96] The changing nature of volunteer management, increasing regulations and controls on volunteers, a perceived lack of local autonomy, changing demographics and an overall decline in volunteer numbers all affected volunteer fire fighters.

Conclusion

The 1980s and 1990s saw enormous changes both in the ways Australians volunteered and in how governments reacted towards them. The changes were uneven depending on the field of volunteering. Not only was there growing competition between organisations for volunteers, but new government policies required volunteers and their organisations to be much more professional and businesslike in their operations and activities. The new government philosophy created an increasingly complex network of regulatory provisions that affected the volunteering environment. While some volunteers, especially in the traditional areas of social welfare, were managing to negotiate the constantly changing parameters within which they worked, the experiences of other volunteers particularly those in the environment arena were quite different. The Australian way of volunteering continued to evolve, especially with concepts like Landcare, a unique partnership of local grassroots volunteerism, government policy and funding.

It is also true to say that volunteering became visible both to governments and to the broad Australian society for the first time. Through research, there was a better understanding of who was volunteering and where that volunteering was happening. Volunteering was gendered, with women dominating in the social welfare areas and men in the sport and recreational fields. Older volunteers became an integral part of the landscape. Volunteering grew and expanded further into new areas such as the environment, ably assisted by increased government recognition and most importantly, funding. All in all, despite the upheavals, the Australian way of volunteering ended the twentieth century with an increased maturity and a certain level of optimism. Perhaps volunteering at last was counting for something.

8 Counting for something

> *We need to ensure that volunteering is constantly valued as an integral part of Australian society ... volunteering helps us to refocus on what is important: participation in society, a sense of altruism and a willingness to be responsible for others within our community.*[1]
>
> Robert Fitzgerald

Volunteering in Australia was propelled to the centre of our consciousness at the dawn of the new century. Two international events – the 2000 Sydney Olympic Games and the United Nations International Year of Volunteers in 2001 – had a significant impact on the shape and form of Australian volunteering. Not only did volunteers receive unprecedented media coverage and public acclaim but governments began a series of new initiatives. Led by South Australia, some governments began demonstrating a commitment to volunteering by establishing offices within government departments, designating specific Ministers for Volunteering, and designing policies and practices that recognised and assisted volunteering.

There was a corresponding and sustained interest from Australian academics and advocates from a wide variety of disciplines, including social sciences, business, tourism and sport studies to undertake research. Corporate engagement with volunteers and the voluntary sector increased through social enterprises and ideas of corporate social responsibility and sustainability. The number of philanthropic trusts also increased and with a boost in financial donations and 'giving', the concept of philanthropy was dragged out of the nineteenth and into the twenty-first century. Issues such as the protection of volunteers through regulation, the use of new technologies and the internet, the ageing of Australia, involving Australians from culturally and linguistically diverse backgrounds, and whether or not volunteering was indeed in decline, all contributed towards discussions on the value of volunteering and its role in contemporary Australian society. But events such as the destruction of the World Trade Centre in New York in 2001, the 'war on terror', and the complacency of incumbency of the Federal government, also affected Australian volunteering. The century began with high hopes but was much of it illusionary? Have the gains fallen short of the rhetoric and goodwill of the first couple of years of the new millennium?

The 2000 Sydney Olympic Games

Volunteering began the new century with the staging of the highly successful Sydney 2000 Olympic Games. Not only did Juan Antonio Samaranch, President of the International Olympic Committee, announce they were the 'best Olympic Games ever' but also that they had 'the most dedicated and wonderful volunteers ever'.[2] It was widely acknowledged that without the unpaid labour of approximately 60 000 volunteers (45 000 for the Olympics and 15 000 for the Paralympics), the Games could not have been staged. The volunteers, in their distinctive blue uniforms and akubra hats, were an invaluable labour force and the public face of the Olympic Games.

Considering the numbers involved, the organisation of the volunteers was a challenge. It was, arguably, the largest volunteer event management task undertaken in Australia since World War II. In May 1996, a Volunteer Services Program was established by the Sydney Organising Committee of the Olympic Games (SOCOG) for the recruitment, selection, training and management of volunteers. Before the process began, it was determined what specific jobs and roles would be contracted (that is, paid) and what jobs would be allocated to volunteers. The volunteers were then grouped into two categories: general and specialist volunteers. General volunteers were assigned to transport, spectator services and community information positions around the Olympic sites and in the Olympic village. Specialist volunteers had specific skills and included, for example, doctors, nurses, and those with sport and language expertise. According to Brendan Lynch, manager of the Volunteer Recruitment Program, there were, in the end '60 000 contractors, 60 000 volunteers and 3000 paid staff'.[3]

A nucleus of 500 volunteers, called the Pioneer Volunteers, was recruited between November 1996 and mid-1997. This group was used to test procedures and events and also assisted in the promotion of volunteering for the Games. Pooja Joshi, an Indian student enrolled in a Masters in Human Resources at UNSW, became interested in volunteering and was selected as one of the Pioneer Volunteers. As part of her volunteer training, she worked on the Sydney City to Surf run, assisted the sports competition managers and three or four times a week after university classes, assisted with databases and mail-outs.[4]

During October 1998, a series of community information sessions was held across Australia and a registration of interest form for either specialist or general volunteers was inserted in all major newspapers. Over 75 000 applications were received; 78 per cent of them from New South Wales, the host state. This was perhaps not surprising, as volunteers had to pay for their own transport, accommodation and associated costs. Twenty-four per cent of applicants were aged between eighteen and twenty-four years; 18 per cent for both aged twenty-five to thirty-four and forty-five to fifty-four-year-olds; and 22 per cent over fifty-five years. More women than men applied (53 per cent versus 47 per cent).[5] Apart from the Pioneer Volunteers, who undertook considerably more volunteering (approximately 3000 hours each across the three years), the volunteers were committed to working an eight-hour day for at least ten days during the Games. In 1999, a conservative estimate valued the total hours of volunteer contribution at over $109 million. This did not include the cost of uniforms (a basic incentive for volunteer participation) at $6 million.[6]

Another source of volunteer labour used in the actual recruitment process included hundreds of university students studying human resource management at various universities across the country. As part of their coursework, these students 'volunteered' to carry out the recruitment and selection of the Olympic volunteers. Volunteers were also used in other areas, such as the torch relay. Nominated by their local communities, 11 000 people participated in the relay, with many having to drive long distances to undertake their 'leg'. Australian communities rallied to support the relay with one rural community lining the torch path with tractors 'as a symbol of work, welcome and community'.[7] During the three-year program, a number of issues were raised concerning the management of volunteers, their expectations of the jobs available and adequate levels of communication. Approximately 4 per cent of volunteers did not turn up for work at all, and over the three years about 30 per cent of volunteers who first applied withdrew their application. The level of attrition was quite high but they were replaced with a steady stream of late applications so there was never a shortage of volunteers.[8]

The Sydney Olympics experience revealed to governments and bureaucrats not only the extent of volunteering in Australia but especially how volunteering could be used to contribute towards hosting other large international events. As Sandy Hollway, the Chief Executive Officer of SOCOG later admitted, 'it was not until taking this job ... that I realised the breadth of volunteering'.[9] It was no surprise that Australian Olympic volunteers were in demand for the 2004 Athens Olympics, and in January 2005, the Federal Treasurer Peter Costello announced funding worth $18.2 million to plan, recruit and train the 15 000 volunteers required to run the Melbourne Commonwealth Games the following year. This was another example of a high profile international event from which Australia would garner considerable public acclaim, predicated on the successful mobilisation of volunteers.

The United Nations International Year of Volunteers, 2001

After the ticker-tape parade was over and once the 2000 Olympic Games volunteer's uniforms were carefully laundered and put away, it was time to welcome the United Nations International Year of Volunteers (IYV). This idea was proclaimed by the General Assembly of the UN in November 1997, with the objectives 'of increased recognition, facilitation, networking and promotion of volunteering' across the world.[10] Building on the globalisation of volunteering and the early efforts of two peak bodies: the International Association for Volunteer Effort (IAVE), formed in 1970, and CIVICUS: the World Alliance for Citizen Participation, founded in 1994, the event was enthusiastically taken up, with over 120 countries establishing IYV committees.

The first event of IYV was the IAVE world conference, held in Amsterdam in February 2001, where the new Universal Declaration on Volunteering and the Global Agenda for Action to Strengthen Volunteering were launched.[11] This global agenda to focus on and strengthen volunteering targeted governments, business, education, the volunteer sector and the media. The declaration reflected the recognition that volunteering was 'the fundamental building block of civil society'. Volunteering was:

> an increasingly credible way to build and sustain the institutions
> of civil society, to help solve serious problems, to create
> healthier communities, and to empower people to lead more
> productive and fulfilling lives.[12]

The objectives of IYV included the recognition of the impact of volunteering by governments and the business sector through documenting, analysing and counting the contribution of volunteering. The promotion of volunteering was also advocated by encouraging people to volunteer, supporting the mobilisation and management of volunteering through appropriate practices, as well as ensuring that volunteering was inclusive of culture, race and religion.[13]

In Australia, the secretariat functions of IYV were funded by the Commonwealth government's Family and Community Services (FaCS) portfolio. Around $16 million was allocated to IYV, including $5.4 million to provide funding of up to $5000 to local communities for projects to celebrate IYV, $7 million for a Small Equipment Grants Program to assist over 2800 voluntary organisations purchase equipment for volunteer programs, and eight Practical Solutions Grants worth up to $25 000 for peak organisations.[14] In order to provide the community with a voice during the IYV, a National Community Council of Advice was formed in June 2000 by Volunteering Australia and Australian Volunteers International, the body representing the United Nations Volunteer Program in Australia. Speaking for ninety-four organisations across the breadth of the voluntary sector, including sport, community services, health, heritage, international aid, service clubs and youth, the council organised consultations around the country in order to draft an Australian national agenda 'to ensure a legacy for volunteers and volunteering beyond' 2001.[15]

A key achievement in the IYV was the publication of the second ABS report into volunteering. Published in June 2001, and using data collected in 2000 (not including the Olympics), it was found that the number of Australians aged over eighteen who were volunteering was 4 395 600 or 32 per cent of the population (up from 24 per cent in 1995). In 2000, volunteers contributed 704.1 million hours (up from 511.7 in 1995) but the median weekly hours of volunteering remained steady at 1.4 hours. Volunteers were more active in rural areas, with the highest volunteer rate occurring in Western Australia (outside Perth – 45 per cent) and lowest in Sydney (25 per cent). The nature of people's volunteer work was closely related to their type of paid work. Almost two-thirds worked for one organisation only; and a further 31 per cent worked for two or three groups. Twenty-six per cent of volunteers worked in the community/welfare sector, which was the largest area for volunteers, but coming a close second was sport and recreation.

Of particular interest was the rise in volunteer rates of both men and women in the fifty-five to sixty-four years age group, which was up from 24 per cent to 33 per cent. The call for younger Australians to volunteer appeared to be working, with an increase in the eighteen to twenty-four years age group, from 17 per cent in 1995 to 27 per cent in 2000. However, replicating the 1996 survey, the highest rate of volunteering occurred in the thirty-five to forty-four years age group. Volunteer rates overall were slightly higher for women (33 per cent) as compared with men (31 per cent) and this was regardless of family status, birthplace or labour force status.[16]

Government responses

Apart from the ABS survey and financial assistance directed to the IYV activities, government responses were mixed, lending credibility to Sandy Hollway's warning that the IYV could be 'just a puff of smoke'.[17] Although volunteering was now becoming 'visible', the field was largely devoid of public policy, and with limited exceptions, state and Federal governments reacted in a fragmented way. The Federal government, for example, talked about a 'social coalition' or partnership between governments, business, the non-profit sector and individuals, as part of its new social policy agenda, with volunteering an important component. In January 2000, Prime Minister John Howard stated that these policies were new initiatives 'to build a new social coalition … each contributing their own particular expertise and resources'.[18] Market liberalism, a hallmark of the 1990s in Australia, continued unabated into the new millennium, with mutual obligation programs such as work for the dole. The compulsory elements of these programs made many voluntary organisations very uneasy: to 'invest in such reluctant "volunteers"' threatened 'the essential heart of volunteering as a freely chosen gift of time to the community'.[19] The political emphasis on active citizenship and the role volunteering played in building social capital and civil society concerned many in the sector. Sceptics believed the rhetoric of building stronger communities through active volunteer engagement represented an untapped resource for governments who 'seized upon a discourse about social capital in order to legitimise changes in welfare policy'.[20] Although FaCS (later re-named to include Indigenous Affairs) was responsible for volunteering issues at a federal level, volunteering was rarely accorded serious representation at a ministerial or administrative level at any time during the Howard years. Volunteer programs were scattered across multiple departments, with no concise and uniting whole-of-government policy framework. It was piecemeal and prag-matic politics. The coalition government even went to the 2007 election without a policy on volunteering. This has led some of our key thinkers on the third sector and volunteering, such as Mark Lyons, to remain pessimistic. In 2006, he wrote that there was 'no political leader ... interested in the third sector', and that 'no Australian government has sought to develop a coherent policy toward the sector'.[21]

In terms of developing detailed volunteering policy, South Australia is, in my view, by far the most proactive and enlightened state govern-ment. In 1999, the South Australian government sponsored a Volun-teers Summit and Forum to identify key concerns and issues in regards to the needs of the volunteer sector and its relationship with govern-ment. Afterwards, Premier John Olson appointed the Hon. Iain Evans as the first Minister for Volunteering in South Australia, and indeed in Australia. The premier then directed each of his ministers to formulate a volunteers' policy within their relevant portfolios, including the use of volunteers and funding allocations. An Office for Volunteers, now based in the Department of Justice, was formed in 2001 to further formalise the relationship, and support and promote volunteering in that state. When Mike Rann won office in 2002, as well as being Premier, he took on the Minister for Volunteering position himself which enhanced the position of volunteering and confirmed its importance to the South Australian government. Similar to the 'social compact' created in the United King-dom, an alliance between the volunteer sector and the South Australian government was formulated. The aim of the 'alliance' was to formalise the state government's new policy towards volunteers and volunteering and to standardise and provide consistency across government depart-ments. In May 2003, a partnership agreement between the government and volunteer sector, Advancing the Community Together Partnership, to provide a 'roadmap' for future collaboration was announced. This mutual agreement was reviewed in 2005, and each year a report focus-ing on the partnership has been published and tabled in parliament. The South Australian initiatives were innovative and, in this new era of 'partnerships' between government and the volunteer sector, provide a good workable model for the rest of Australia. But, typical of Australian federalism, each state differs in its approach and timing, and with little leadership at the Federal level, the overall result has been mixed.

In 2002, after extensive community consultation through a Volunteering Reference Group, Western Australia introduced a minister with responsibilities for volunteers and a Volunteering Secretariat.[22] In May 2003, a partnership agreement was signed between the Tasmanian government and the volunteer sector. The two most populous states, Victoria and New South Wales, largely developed their volunteer policies through community portfolios, such as the current Department of Planning and Community Development in Victoria where there is no designated volunteers' minister. Recent debate and discussion has revolved around issues of social inclusion, which includes volunteering as part of community capacity building. But without the designated focus of a minister or Office for Volunteers, the impact on volunteering is muted. In New South Wales, the Carr Labor government produced a policy document, 'Promoting our Volunteers: Labor's Plan for Volunteering', in 1999 in which a compact similar to that in Britain was mooted, but the idea was dropped by the time the New South Wales Strategic Agenda for the IYV was published in 2001.[23] A 'Working Together' agreement was eventually in place by 2006 but it largely focused on non-government human services, not necessarily the broad areas covered by volunteering. In 2007, the Hon. Linda Burney became the first New South Wales Minister for Volunteering and an embryonic Office of Volunteering was established within the Department of Premier and Cabinet. While volunteering was included as part of a ten-year State Plan, there are, as yet, no specific detailed whole-of-government policies on volunteering. In Queensland, the first official government policy on volunteering, 'Engaging Queensland', was released in 2001. A detailed policy strategy concerning volunteers and how to respond to volunteering in the twenty-first century was published in 2007 and included the establishment of an Office for Volunteers within the Department of Communities, 'as a central point to provide leadership on identified volunteering issues'.[24] Three main goals included supporting volunteers and volunteering, building a stronger base for volunteering, and strengthening rural and regional communities. No specific Minister of Volunteers was appointed.

Protection of volunteers

The first years of the twenty-first century have been significant for Australian volunteering because of the changing attitudes towards volunteers and the consideration of the rights and protection of volunteer workers. Changes to legal liability, occupational health and safety, risk management, the protection of children and the aged, brought about new institutional environments for both volunteers and the organisations within which they work. But once again the journey continues to be a difficult one, with different state regulations ensuring that there is no uniformity of volunteer protection.

The major international events of the Olympics and IYV and the involvement of some governments to form compacts or agreements with the voluntary sector contributed to the discussions. In its 2001 *National Agenda on Volunteering*, Volunteering Australia and the Community Council of Advice called for governments to address the legal status of volunteers. The complexity of the delineation between paid and unpaid workers, the different state legislative approaches, and the recommendation that volunteer-based organisations provide public risk policies, personal accident insurance, professional indemnity insurance, directors' and officers' liability for its volunteers places enormous pressures on both voluntary organisations and volunteers.[25] The collapse of insurance companies such as HIH in 2001 and the escalating costs of insurance premiums only fuelled anxieties. The addition of GST payments and the position of volunteers within the new tax system also caused considerable unease.[26] All these problems raised the question of the protection of volunteers in the workplace. Unlike paid workers who are protected under a comprehensive system of Federal and state industrial laws built up over time, the Australian industrial relations system does not recognise volunteer work because there is no remuneration for work performed.[27] However, in today's workplaces, there is often little difference between a paid worker and a volunteer. This was clearly seen during the Sydney Olympics when volunteers and paid workers laboured side by side, carrying out the same or similar jobs. There are also inequalities between volunteers themselves. For example, in New South Wales, emergency service volunteers such as the State Emergency Services (SES) and volunteer fire fighters are covered under the State Emergency Service Amendment Bill 2005 (NSW).[28] The 'danger' volunteers are the only volunteers covered by workers compensation legislation under the *Workers Compensation (Bush Fire, Emergency and Rescue Services) Act 1987* (later updated January 2000). Other organisations providing emergency services, such as the Australian Red Cross, St John Ambulance and the Volunteer Rescue Association receive no specific protection under the Act.

The concern of volunteer civil liability particularly propelled the South Australian government, after consultation with the volunteer sector in 1999, to introduce the *Volunteers Protection Act 2001*. Based on federal American legislation (*Volunteer Protection Act 1997*), the South Australian laws were introduced to protect volunteers from 'incurring serious personal liability for damages and legal costs in proceedings for negligence'.[29] A volunteer accidentally spilling hot soup on an elderly person as he or she was delivering a meal was given as an example where the volunteer had no protection against potential litigation. It took the insurance crisis of 2001 to get the other governments to the table. Despite the fact that the Federal government deemed the issue one for the states to deal with, it did facilitate a forum, and with the publication of the *Review of the Law of Negligence* (or Ipp Report) in 2002, state governments enacted a range of legislation to cover volunteer liability. But as McGregor-Lowndes points out, there continues to be no uniformity of cover in Australia and although 'in all jurisdictions a volunteer is protected from civil liability ... this protection is subject to exceptions'.[30] These differences make it difficult for both volunteers and the volunteer organisations for which they work, especially those that operate nationally. The same issues apply to occupational health and safety laws, with no uniformity across the nation and volunteers treated on the whole very poorly. They are not treated as legitimate 'workers' or employees but rather as 'other persons' or 'visitors', for whom all organisations have a general duty of care. Consequently, volunteers continue to be undefined in the workplace and largely invisible.[31]

There was also confusion in regards to the regulation of charities and the non-profit sector. As Mark Lyons noted, 'laws covering incorporation of and fundraising by non-profit organisations are a confusing jumble' in Australia, and there is a real need for appropriate regulation and accountability measures.[32] The voluntary sector 'has a very fractured structure. Businesses quite clearly fall under ASIC regulations but there is a diversity of regulations both state and Federally that govern the not-for-profit sector and that makes it a bit of a nightmare' argued Sarah Lucas in the ABC Radio program *Background Briefing*.[33] In 2000, after sustained lobbying by the non-profit sector and the Democrats, the Federal government established an inquiry, 'to properly reflect the development of the third sector's role in a modern democracy'.[34] The Inquiry into the Definition of Charities and Related Organisations reported in August 2001. Despite its twenty-seven recommendations, including a broader definition of charities and the establishment of one regulator (such as the British Charities Commission), the Federal government accepted and implemented none. They simply put it into the too-hard basket and walked away.

In October 2002, the non-profit sector sought to re-ignite the stalled reforms with the creation of a national peak body, the National Roundtable of Nonprofit Organisations. Involving a range of national organisations in philanthropy, aged care, sport, the arts and advocacy, the Nonprofit Roundtable released an initial statement in May 2004 presenting a program for reform. But its influence was limited as governments failed to see the bigger picture and the connections between the non-profit sector, government and business. Mark Lyons compared it to the 'invention' of the business sector. As he said on an ABC Radio *Background Briefing* program broadcast in 2004:

> Before the 1960s people didn't talk about business, they didn't
> see that when they talked about big pastoral companies, or
> talked about small corner-store retailers, High Street retailers,
> they did it separately, they did not, before the 1960s, talk about
> business, and see that all of these were actually connected.[35]

Regardless of repeated and sustained attempts to persuade governments to address these issues, they remain largely ignored.

Recruitment and retention of volunteers

Despite the generally buoyant volunteering statistics released in 2001 and again in 2007, and with more Australians volunteering than ever before, the malaise in certain traditional sites of volunteering continues. This is one of the paradoxes of volunteering today. Certain areas, particularly to do with the environment and climate change, are doing very well. So too are the 'cultural industries', many of which rely on volunteers. Cultural organisations such as museums, art galleries, arts festivals, botanic gardens, amateur theatre, zoos, community radio and television broadcasting are all reporting a strong demand from people wishing to volunteer their services. Although these volunteers only make up about 6 per cent of Australian volunteers, they make an invaluable contribution to Australia's cultural life in both rural and urban areas.[36] Event and niche volunteering which makes events such as the Sydney Mardi Gras so successful also continues to flourish. Celebrating its 30th anniversary in February 2008, the Mardi Gras remains largely predicated on the volunteer efforts of its supporters and participants. Conversely, organisers of the World Youth Day Sydney 2008 were relying on attracting at least 8000 volunteers to assist with customer service, crowd marshalling and accommodation services for the July event. Volunteers were being enticed with an 'exclusive special audience' with the Pope if they successfully completed all their designated shifts.[37]

Some, however, have continued to argue that volunteering is in decline.[38] The voluntary welfare sector appears particularly vulnerable. Shifting employment patterns, workforce participation, retirement, family and caring responsibilities, and changes in the non-profit sector itself all have an impact on the profile, source and use of volunteers. Combined with increasing bureaucratic imposts, such as police checks when working with children and the aged, food handling requirements and occupational health and safety regulations, volunteer recruitment and retention has suffered. Many traditional areas of volunteering especially the older, well-established organisations such as Meals on Wheels and the Australian Red Cross, have felt the squeeze. Ageing volunteers and the inability to attract younger generations has meant that either services have been outsourced (such as the commercialisation of Meals on Wheels in some instances) or the structure of the organisation itself (such as the closure of Red Cross branches, once the bedrock of the organisation) has been re-shaped to accommodate these shifts. Many school canteens and uniform shops, once largely the preserve of volunteer mothers, have been commer-cialised or closed due to lack of volunteers. Other organisations, such as the Smith Family in New South Wales, have re-invented themselves by moving away from the traditional models of charity and volunteering towards social enterprise; in the case of the Smith Family, focusing on educational outcomes for disadvantaged children through its Learning for Life programs.[39]

Volunteer fire fighting is another traditional area of volunteering that has suffered from a declining and ageing membership.[40] In South Australia alone, the Country Fire Service (CFS) has lost 3000 members in ten years. One way of addressing the problem has been to encourage the recruitment of female fire fighters, who currently make up between 12 and 24 per cent of Australian fire fighters.[41] In 2006, a survey that included Rural Fire Service volunteers in a rural New South Wales grain belt community, new members to the Victorian Country Fire Authority, and a women's volunteer survey from the South Australian CFS found that there were both 'perceived and actual obstacles for women to become volunteer fire fighters'.[42] Apart from issues of child-care and employment demands, the findings confirmed what was already well known in the paid workplace: that gender and cultural diversity could adversely affect female workers in a male-dominated industry. The survey found that problems of sexual harassment and discrimination based on gender were endemic in the volunteer fire fighting sector, with 'almost intractable problems posed by deeply entrenched male chauvinistic prejudices in organisations generally'.[43]

Other difficulties concerned the restructuring of emergency services and the adverse treatment of volunteer fire fighters by governments. For example, in the wake of the disastrous 2003 Canberra bushfires that destroyed over 500 homes, killed four people and cost over $350 million, volunteers felt excluded from discussions and were given less operational independence. The problems were so deeply entrenched that in March

2007, brigade captains and their volunteer crews withdrew their labour in spectacular fashion. In front of television cameras, they drove around thirty fire trucks to the ACT parliament, threw the keys into a bucket and walked away.[44] The issue was finally resolved four months later, but these public disputes between volunteers and their government administrators reveal that volunteers sometimes have to resort to employer/employee style tactics in order to resolve sensitive workplace issues.

The recruitment and retention of volunteers continues to cause concern in the area of sports officiating, including referees, judges, scorers and umpires. In 2004, it was estimated that 27 per cent of the total population aged over fifteen, or 4.3 million Australians, were engaged in organised sport of some kind, and around one million of these people were volunteering their time as coaches, officials, referees and the like.[45] Sport has always been a central aspect of Australian culture, and the increasing awareness of the role it can play in arresting the current obesity epidemic makes the role that volunteers play in organised sport at the grassroots level more important than ever. The ABS reported that between 1997 and 2001, the number of sports officials declined by 26 per cent. A 2002 Australian Sports Commission study suggested that this attrition may be caused by 'harassment and abuse' of officials by players and spectators, as well as a lack of support, lack of career path and general human resource management issues.[46] As Russell Hoye pointed out, the Australian sports system is highly dependent on volunteers and there is a 'potential fragility' if these volunteer numbers decline.[47] Sporting organisations have been particularly affected by increases in insurance that directly affect both participation and volunteering, as well as younger Australians trending away from organised sports to more informal patterns of participation.[48]

Faith-based volunteering

In other areas, the picture is not so bleak. The importance of volunteering to religion, and its overall resilience, has been evident in recent years despite the general decline of religious identity and church attendance in Australia since the 1960s.[49] According to the ABS, the level of religious volunteering has been steadily climbing, and this view is supported by the

'Giving Australia' report, which found that people who identified with a religion carry out more volunteering than Australians who say they have no religion.[50] Researchers such as Lyons and Nivison-Smith have argued that 'people who become active in some form of religious group associated with their congregation are more likely to volunteer, and to volunteer for non-religious causes'.[51] This confirms Leonard and Bellamy's study, which found that 'volunteering within the congregation is not an obstacle to volunteering in the community' but rather the reverse is true.[52] Volunteers within the thousands of congregations across the denominational divide not only contribute locally to their own constituencies but are also involved in a range of advocacy and social justice issues such as Aboriginal reconciliation and assistance with refugees, as well as assisting with disaster relief both in Australia and overseas.

Across Australia there are many hundreds of organisations of varying sizes, with religious affiliations, that rely on volunteers. Some of Australia's largest and longest-standing charities fall into this category, such as the Salvation Army, St Vincent de Paul, Brotherhood of St Laurence and Anglicare. But there are also many hundreds of small groups such as the Sisters of Charity Outreach. Established in 1990 at St Vincent's Hospital in Darlinghurst, Sydney, Sisters of Charity Outreach began with a small group of volunteers, one paid staff member and four Sisters of Charity. This organisation was formed largely in response to the decline of the order of the Sisters of Charity, the first Catholic nuns in Australia, who originally arrived from Ireland in 1838 to assist the poor and destitute women of the colony of New South Wales. Today, Sisters of Charity Outreach offers a comprehensive program of services including counselling, court support, an eastern area visiting program, emergency accommodation and a parent support program in western Sydney, plus it runs a gift shop in St Vincent's Hospital itself.[53]

The profile of the Sisters of Charity Outreach has changed over time, reflecting the broader shifts in volunteering discussed throughout this book. In 2003, there were 200 volunteers, twelve full-time staff members and ten Sisters of Charity. When it began, 96 per cent of volunteers were women with 61 per cent over sixty years of age. By 2003, the female figure had dropped to 81 per cent and only half were over sixty. Importantly, the cultural and linguistic diversity of volunteers was changing, with 27 per cent of volunteers from this category, up 11 per cent.[54]

Baby boomers and an ageing Australia

As discussed in chapter 7, the importance of older Australians and especially the baby boomers as a valuable volunteer resource was recognised in the last decades of the twentieth century. The long-term consequences of the ageing population continue to be a priority for Australian policy makers. The Western Australian government and Judy Esmond conducted a research project 'to identify the "motivators and barriers" to volunteering and strategies to encourage baby boomers to volunteer'.[55] Under the acronym 'Boomnet' (Boomers Organised Openness Meaningful Needs Education and Time), the report concluded that the size of the baby boomers cohort alone (those born between 1945 and 1965) meant that the non-profit sector would experience a surge in volunteer numbers in years to come. However, their expectations, needs and views in regards to volunteering were different to previous generations. The most recent ABS statistics indicated a drop in the volunteer rate of fifty-five to sixty-four-year-olds (the older baby boomers) between 2002 and 2006. Although women only dropped marginally (from 39.5 per cent to 38.2 per cent) men went down from 36.5 per cent to 29 per cent. The younger boomers (forty-five to fifty-four years age group) were stable at 40 per cent. They are still busy with children (as many had children later in life). Baby boomers are generally more likely to be looking for fulfilling roles related to their skills or interests, they want flexibility, less regulation but better volunteer management and better jobs. They may also have other priorities, such as travel, and research on the impact of volunteering and the 'grey nomads' (people aged over fifty caravanning around Australia) is underway.[56] Tellingly, in terms of ethnic diversity, the Boomnet report found, among other things, that Indigenous and ethnic communities were involved in volunteering but often it went unrecorded because of its informal nature.[57]

Over the past ten years, there has been a huge debate about the costs of an ageing population. As a result, some researchers have attempted to give an economic value to the caring and volunteering activities of older people. A recent study by de Vaus revealed that Australians aged over sixty-five years contribute almost $39 billion per year in unpaid caring and volunteer work. If one includes those aged between fifty-five and sixty-four, the contribution increases to $74.5 billion per annum.[58] Jeni Warburton has argued that older volunteers are an important resource and there is increasing research to suggest that volunteering can help with healthy and productive ageing.[59] Indeed, older Australians who volunteer tend to have better psychological health, higher life satisfaction and even longer lives.[60]

There are still widely held negative assumptions and stereotypical attitudes towards older Australians. For example, in April 2005, the Productivity Commission released a report, *Economic Implications of an Ageing Australia*, in response to a request by the Australian government to examine the labour supply, productivity and fiscal implications of Australia's ageing population trends over the next forty years. The report found that the 'profound ageing' of Australia would reduce economic growth at the same time as intensifying demands for public services, such as health care, aged care and the aged pension. In other words, older Australians would seriously imbalance the economy and suck the country dry. This population imbalance, the report concluded, could not be made up through immigration or fertility increases.[61] The report was based purely on economic terms and economic indices – it was all about measuring and predicting GDP and the future 'burden' of ageing. But it hit a nerve and the media, politicians and commentators were all breast-beating over the 'ageing' problem in a particularly negative way.

The Productivity Commission's extensive 300-plus page report devoted only three pages to volunteering, and basically said that volunteering would not make any difference, presumably because volunteering is not a measured part of GDP. As discussed in chapter 1, this has been a matter of debate for years now, to impute a dollar value on volunteering and place it within the national accounts. But governments appear no closer to working out ways to include it or to measure it in a meaningful way. So volunteer work remains uncounted and outside GDP estimates. If volunteer work were included as part of GDP, the contribution of ageing

Australians would be seen very differently. Volunteering Australia said as much in its submission to the Productivity Commission but it appears that this report was ignored.[62]

New technologies, business partnerships and corporate volunteering

Other major initiatives to influence and change volunteering in the new millennium include the development of the internet, business partnerships, corporate volunteering, the development of social entrepreneurship, corporate social responsibility and sustainability, as well as involving Australians from diverse cultural and linguistic backgrounds. The internet began to be widely used ten years ago. It was argued that this 'information superhighway' would bring people closer, break down cultural barriers, and make knowledge accessible across the world. The internet has certainly made a difference to volunteering, in terms of amplifying its visibility in the general community. Almost all volunteer organisations today have websites, and increasingly use the internet for a range of activities. In Australia, this is especially important as we struggle with distance and our federal system, which can hinder the voluntary sector and volunteers, especially when they are nationally based. With pro bono support from the Boston Consulting Group and an IYV Commonwealth government grant, Volunteering Australia established Australia's first national volunteer recruitment website (www.govolunteer.com.au) as a means of disseminating information such as vacant positions within community groups and charities, as well as a portal for those looking for volunteering opportunities. Launched in June 2000 by Michael Long, well known volunteer and AFL footballer, the site now boasts 50 000 hits per month. The response from both those seeking to volunteer and organisations wanting to recruit volunteers was positive from the beginning.

The internet also has particular advantages for people who wish to volunteer but are not sure how to find out more. Younger Australians, particularly from Gen Y down, who have been brought up with the internet are forging new relationships with groups like the Inspire Foundation to promote volunteering among younger Australians.[63] Not only has the internet provided an effective and efficient tool to inform and engage volunteers through organisational websites that include information and policy data, but it can inform and educate with planning, motivation, evaluation, resources, administration, health and safety, insurance, supervision and training. The internet has also enabled whole new generations of volunteers, especially younger Australians, to volunteer their skills online. Online volunteers can assist with a range of jobs such as creating websites, translating documents and assisting organisational outreach. Similarly non-profit organisations can use websites for online surveys, to inform members and volunteers.

Large for-profit companies are also increasingly using the internet to engage with community groups and volunteers. For example, in January 2008, the National Australia Bank launched an internet-based forum called 'volunteer X change', whereby NAB employees can exchange 'skills-based intellectual tasks' with charities and groups, without leaving their work desks.[64] This virtual volunteering initiative has added a new capacity to corporate volunteering and will certainly be the beginning of new ways of volunteering in the future.

The internet has also become a very useful tool for advocacy groups, and for many volunteers it is becoming the new communication tool of choice. For example, GetUp! is a new grassroots, independent advocacy group with thousands of members across Australia. Another new federated lobby group, the National Federation of Parents, Families and Carers was formed in 2007, as Australia's 'first national voice for parents, families and carers'. 'Good use of online technology' was seen as a valuable tool for effective participation, and not accepting or initiating 'government funding for the core functions of this national voice' was seen as essential if its independence from government was not to be compromised.[65] This aversion to government funding is empowering these new internet-based voluntary organisations.

Substantial efforts are also being made to reach out to Australians from culturally and linguistically diverse backgrounds to ensure that their contribution to volunteering is recognised. Currently, about 26 per cent of people born overseas volunteer in formal organisations but when 'informal' volunteering – that is, helping out friends and extended family – is taken into account, the figure is certainly much higher.[66] The focus now is to investigate differences in perceptions of volunteering within different cultural groups and for voluntary organisations to establish practices to become more socially inclusive.

Other major objectives of the IYV global agenda were to facilitate the involvement of and create closer relationships with the business sector. Although it has been said that there are no more 'unlikely partners than the community, government and business', this is an area that has considerable potential.[67] Many international and national companies have joined forces with the non-profit sector, developing practices and procedures to form partnerships. This is so that businesses can be seen as socially responsible corporate citizens. Major companies, such as the National Australia Bank, now sponsor events such as National Volunteer Week and volunteer awards at all levels of government are becoming increasingly popular. One of the other major strands of the partnership rhetoric is to encourage and support employee volunteering in terms of community development and social responsibility. As discussed in chapter 3, this type of corporate volunteering has a long history in Australia and flourished during World War II. But it largely fell into abeyance and it is only now in the twenty-first century, that the concept (widely practised in the United States) is being encouraged in Australia as one way to not only increase volunteering but also to replenish community spirit and community engagement.

This is a growth area and there are now businesses such as 'goodcompany' that 'connects skilled professionals with charitable organisations in need of pro bono assistance'. Established in 2001 by Kate Kennedy, after a pilot program in 1999, and operating in Melbourne and Sydney, this employment agency for volunteers has, as its website boasts, 5500 registered volunteers on the books that have assisted over 600 groups with an equivalent labour cost of $7 million.[68] 'goodcompany' also runs regular networking events, a newsletter and has a savvy and very professional website where potential volunteers and community groups can register and be paired up.

Conclusion

These new ways of engaging volunteers are profoundly changing the landscape of Australian volunteering in the twenty-first century. But Australians, too, are still committed to traditional ways of volunteering when the need arises. The Tampa incident in 2001 and the reaction of Australians towards the Federal government's treatment of refugees may have been muted initially but enough people were mobilised to become volunteer activists, many for the first time. As Julian Burnside wrote, 'In August 2001 I became an activist accidentally, inadvertently. With no previous experience, I found myself on a mission to end Australia's mistreatment of boat-people'.[69] In other areas, especially the environment and climate change, Australians continue to flock to a range of volunteer groups, such as Al Gore's Climate Change Leadership Program. Hundreds of Australians have volunteered to become climate change presenters as part of the Australian Conservation Foundation's Climate Change Project.

Throughout this book, I have argued that there is a unique Australian way of volunteering. Bound up with a close association with pragmatic governments and influenced by the structures of our federal system, volunteering continues to be an integral part of who we are as Australians. We are a largely independent, autonomous, resilient and an inherently democratic people. Sometimes we do get it wrong. But we generally put our hands up and reach out when the need arises, with or without the assistance of government.

Conclusion: Looking to the future

*If we can find the right answers to these challenges then historians
may well look back to the first half of the 21st century as the Age of
the Volunteer.*[1]

Justin Davis Smith

In March 2006, Justin Davis Smith, Chief Executive of Volunteering
England, suggested that volunteering was 'the embodiment of the Spirit
of the Age', as people increasingly felt alienated from the political process
and wanted to take matters into their own hands to remedy society's
problems. Although there were a number of issues to overcome, including
how to push the boundaries of volunteering without compromising its
independence and not devaluing it, Davis Smith suggested that it was
possible we were entering the 'age of the volunteer'.

It is too early to speculate whether this optimism can be applied to
Australia. Although some of the practices of the third way, so much a
part of the philosophy of British New Labour, have been attempted here
in Australia, the lingering vestiges of economic rationalism, as well as the
cultural differences and government responses, are quite different. Apart
from two states, South Australia and Western Australia, governments
have been excruciatingly slow in recognising the important role of volun-

teering and the third sector. As argued throughout this book, Australian governments have never really taken volunteering, or the non-government sector within which it largely sits, seriously. The Federal government has never developed a clear philosophical position towards volunteering. At the top level of government there is a certain arrogance and ignorance towards volunteering that is very hard to dislodge. Similarly with business (although the situation has shifted in recent times, with a move towards an acknowledgement of corporate social responsibility with companies recognising the benefits of corporate volunteering strategies and developing partnerships with the non-profit sector), the recognition, valuation and visibility of volunteering is limited.

When the Rudd Labor government was elected in November 2007, after eleven years of a Liberal/National party coalition government, there was cause for cautious optimism. Not only did the Labor party take a volunteering policy to the election but Senator Ursula Stephens was appointed Parliamentary Secretary for Social Inclusion and the Voluntary Sector. Finally, here was a Federal government committed, it seemed, to volunteering. Stephens's appointment was, it was argued, in recognition of 'the important role of the millions of volunteers, who make Australia a fairer, safer and more sustainable place' and it was stated that the Australian government was 'committed to building a new partnership with the non-profit sector'.[2]

The Federal government got off to a good start by removing the highly unpopular 'gag' clauses that prevented non-profit organisations from publicly criticising government policy. But with Ursula Stephens's position coming under the auspices of Julia Gillard's portfolio (Deputy Prime Minister and Minister for Employment and Workplace Relations; Minister for Education; Minister for Social Inclusion), and the actual Minister for Volunteers, Jenny Macklin, leading another mega portfolio of Families, Housing, Community Services and Indigenous Affairs (FACSIA), the impact of true reform of volunteering policy is diffused. It remains to be seen whether the rhetoric will translate into a coherent and lasting volunteer philosophy and platform with tangible and lasting results, or whether it is just more smoke and mirrors and political spin with little real fundamental change.

The Prime Minister's use of the term 'volunteering' during the 2020 Summit, held in April 2008, casts further doubt. I'm not sure that he really understands what volunteering is about and I questioned this at the time.[3] It was a very astute political manoeuvre for Kevin Rudd to get 1000 of Australia's 'best and brightest' 2020 Summiteers to volunteer their services for free. He was at pains to point out that invited guests 'volunteered' their time, and that the summit was at no cost to taxpayers. To follow this logic to its natural conclusion, however, it is evident that Rudd perceives volunteering as getting something for nothing. This 'volunteering' spirit was also applied to the scores of public servants who provided essential administrative support to the Summit, which was packaged as a professional development opportunity. How much was volunteering and not simply unpaid overtime is a moot point.

In terms of volunteering policy, however, more problematic is one of the 'top ideas' to come out of the 2020 Summit – that of a Community Corps, which offers students HECS debt relief through volunteering or community service. The origins of this idea are unclear but, in May 2004, a similar suggestion was made by Victorian Liberal Senator Mitch Fifield in his maiden speech to parliament.[4] Rudd thought the idea of a Community Corps had merit and warranted further investigation, and it was listed as one of the key outcomes in the Summit's Final Report.[5] This clearly reveals Rudd and his government do not understand volunteering. As mentioned in chapter 1, the ABS definition of volunteering is 'someone who willingly gives unpaid help, in the form of time, service or skills, through an organisation or group'. The idea that students, through a so-called Community Corps, could pay off their HECS debt by volunteering is fraught with difficulties. There are so many questions – how would the students' volunteering be valued or counted? What hourly rate for what type of jobs would be allocated? Why wouldn't students simply get a paid job to pay off their HECS debt? I doubt that such initiatives will encourage students to volunteer; quite the reverse. There is little difference between this and other mutual obligation policies where the unemployed receive benefits in return for volunteering, or prisoners undertake community service instead of going to jail. These policies are not considered volunteering and the peak bodies, such as Volunteering SA, are very clear on this.[6] If there is a policy problem with the enormous HECS debt faced by Australian students, then perhaps the Federal government should look at addressing the whole concept of HECS rather than asking students to give even more through volunteering. Students already undertake volunteering through a range of campus activities such as sport and societies, and studies show that many younger Australians already undertake community service. What more do we want from them?

What this example reveals is that pragmatic governments continue to use volunteering for their own political needs. They have always taken volunteers for granted. Governments have relied on volunteers innovating and fostering new ideas, only to come in, take over and absorb concepts, often taking the credit, with the volunteer influences lost over time. Throughout our history, significant government policy has been developed around the innovations of the volunteer sector, without governments ever having to develop clear, coherent policies towards volunteers. Who remembers, for example, that before the Department of Veterans' Affairs (formerly called the Department of Repatriation) was established in 1917, assistance to soldiers and their families was provided by the voluntary sector and volunteers, through organisations called patriotic funds or war charities.

This book has attempted to rectify the situation by placing volunteers and volunteering centre stage of our history. For years, researchers have bemoaned the 'invisibility' of volunteering, the lack of recognition and acknowledgement in terms of its economic and social contribution to Australian society. Volunteering has always been in the shadow lands, sitting somewhere between the cut and thrust of paid work and markets, and the private domestic economy. Genuine understanding and commitment to reform is long overdue.

What we need now in Australia is a new revitalised and reinvigorated whole-of-government approach to all aspects of volunteering, from Federal right down to local government. Volunteering is not only about social welfare and disadvantaged communities, it is about the environment, sport, literature, the arts, and heritage – the things that make life worthwhile, to paraphrase Bobby Kennedy.[7] Currently, volunteering policy at both Federal and state level is spread over multiple government departments, which causes confusion and lessens its impact and importance. A compact with the sector, a Federal Minister for Volunteering with her or his own Office or Department (following the British example of the 2006 Office for the Third Sector), is now essential. So too is a Commission on the Future of Volunteering, akin to the UK version that would provide a long-term vision for the future of volunteering in Australia, as well as increased funding for research and evaluation. Leaders in the third sector, too, need to focus on their deficiencies and embrace change.

The other major current impediment in Australia is the lack of commitment to regulatory reform in the areas of charities, fundraising, incorporation, and the non-profit sector generally. Repeated calls for a regulatory body for the third sector, with a role similar to that played by ASIC with business, have gone unanswered. Again and again over the past ten to fifteen years, half hearted approaches to reform in this area have been stymied and reports shelved. Any Federal government which purports to be serious about volunteering needs to commit to detailed and long-term national legal and regulatory reform.

If governments want to see volunteering 'grow' and expand, to enable the benefits of volunteering to reach all Australians, then they have to be pro-active and supportive of new ways of engaging with the disadvantaged and disempowered in our community. Volunteering can play a key role in the development of social inclusion policy, but both Federal and state governments need to provide adequate funding and resources to enable volunteer organisations at the grassroots level to function properly. This means reducing impediments to volunteering by improving the regulatory environment by, for example, providing free national police checks for all volunteers across Australia. Funding processes and procedures should also be streamlined and extended to three year cycles to provide stability and coherence to volunteer programs, in order to prevent wastage of volunteer resources and effort through the ever-burdensome obligations of incessant funding round applications.

Government and business in partnership could fund a public relations campaign to educate and inform Australians about the value of volunteering and its benefits to society. This could involve a hard-hitting documentary series (one of Joy Noble's ideas) that shows the breadth and diversity of volunteering in our community as well as its crucial role in keeping the country going. Raising public awareness at all levels of society and educating through volunteering literacy is paramount. Finding out which groups in our society may not be as actively involved in volunteering, and why, and then providing the necessary tools, framework, infrastructure and funding to encourage new programs and ways of engagement for all in our society is part of the challenge of the future.

Fundamentally, however, volunteering needs to become not only visible but valued. Volunteer awards, smart uniforms and ticker-tape parades are not enough. As with paid labour, volunteering needs to be defined, collated, examined and included in all official economic data and statistics such as the GDP. Volunteering should be listed as one of the national key indicators in the 'labour force and demography' category to accurately measure and truly reflect the place of unpaid labour in Australia's social and economic data. Just as we are in the process of setting up complex carbon trading systems to assist with climate change, so too should we establish structures to recognise the economic contribution of volunteering. What about a volunteer index, 'volunteer bank' or 'volunteer stock exchange' where all volunteer activity, be it in the non-government, business or government sector, is recorded and available for scrutiny and evaluation.

Many challenges lie ahead for Australian volunteers in the twenty-first century. As I have shown in this book, volunteering is embedded in our culture, and Australians have always volunteered, mobilising at local, state, national and international levels for an endless range of causes. The time has now come to officially recognise this Australian way of volunteering in tangible, meaningful ways. Then, perhaps, we too can say that the twenty-first century is the age of the volunteer.

Notes

Preface

1 Melanie Oppenheimer (2002) *All Work. No Pay. Australian Volunteers in War*, Ohio Productions, Walcha and Jeni Warburton & Melanie Oppenheimer (eds) (2000) *Volunteers and Volunteering*, Federation Press, Sydney.
2 'Vita Activa' series on volunteering on ABC Radio National *Life Matters* program; <www.abc.net.au/rn/lifematters>. (See past programs for series.)
3 Jill Roe, 'The Australian Way', in Paul Smyth & Bettina Cass (eds) (1988) *Contesting the Australian Way. States, Markets and Civil Society*, Cambridge University Press, Melbourne, p. 79.

Part I

1 Jillian Oppenheimer (1986) 'Munro, Grace Emily (1879–1964)', *Australian Dictionary of Biography*, vol. 10, Melbourne University Press, Melbourne, p. 613.
2 Jillian Oppenheimer (2003) *The Gordon Girls*, Ohio Productions, Walcha, p. 119.
3 Elizabeth Kenworthy Teather (1994) 'The Country Women's Association of New South Wales in the 1920s and 1930s as a Counter Revolutionary Organisation', *Journal of Australian Studies*, 41, pp. 67–78.

Chapter 1

1 Joy Noble & Fiona Johnston (eds) (2001) *Volunteering Visions*, Federation Press, Sydney, pp. 151–52.
2 Australian Bureau of Statistics (2007) *Voluntary Work, Australia, 2006*, ABS, AGPS, Sydney, July.
3 Marilyn Waring (1988) *Counting for Nothing*, Allen & Unwin, Wellington, p. 6.

4   Michael Bittman (1995) 'Occasional Paper. Recent changes in unpaid work', ABS, May, p. 1.

5   Duncan Ironmonger, 'Measuring Volunteering in Economic Terms in J. Warburton & M. Oppenheimer (eds), *Volunteers and Volunteering*, Federation Press, Sydney, 2000.

6   That is up from 704.1 million hours in 2000. ABS (2007) *Voluntary Work, 2006*, AGPS, Canberra, July.

7   See José Harris (2003, 1997) *William Beveridge. A Biography*, Clarendon Press, Oxford, pp. 453-61.

8   William Beveridge (1948) *Voluntary Action. A Report on the Methods of Social Advance*, George Allen & Unwin, London, p. 10.

9   Ibid.

10 Frank Prochaska (1988) *The Voluntary Impulse. Philanthropy in Modern Britain*, Faber and Faber, London; Geoffrey Finlayson (1990) 'A Moving Frontier: Voluntarism and the State in British Social Welfare, 1911-1949', *Twentieth Century British History*, vol. 1, no. 2, p. 184; and Geoffrey Finlayson (1994) *Citizen, State and Social Welfare in Britain, 1830–1990*, Clarendon Press, Oxford.

11 Richard M Titmuss (1997) *The Gift Relationship. From Human Blood to Social Policy*, original edition with new chapters, The New Press, New York, p. 7.

12 Richard Titmuss (1971) 'Why Give to Strangers?', *The Lancet*, 16 January, p. 125.

13 Quoted in Jill Hardwick & Adam Graycar (1982) 'Volunteers in Non Government Welfare Organisations in Australia: A Working Paper', SWRC Reports and Proceedings, no. 25, September, p. 32. The term volunteerism is used throughout this book rather than voluntarism. Volunteerism, first coined in the 1970s, refers to volunteering and volunteers.

14 Pierre Bourdieu, 'The forms of Capital', in J Richardson (ed.) (1986) *Handbook of Theory and Research for the Sociology of Education*, Greenwood Press, New York; and J Coleman (1990) *Foundations of Social Theory*, Harvard University Press, Cambridge, Mass. See also Robert D Putnam (1993) *Making Democracy Work: Civic Traditions in Modern Italy*, Princeton University Press, Princeton and Robert D. Putnam (1990) *Bowling Alone: The Collapse and Revival of American Community*, Simon and Schuster, New York.

15 Anthony Giddens (1998) *The Third Way. Renewal of Social Democracy*, Polity Press, London.

16 See also 'Putin Fights Public Enemy No 1: Volunteers', *The Australian*, 25 February 2008. Organisations like Soldiers' Mothers, run by volunteers to assist young conscripts and their families fight for their civil rights, have had their activities severely curtailed through new laws restricting their operations and increased bureaucratic red tape.

17 Eva Cox, 1995 Boyer Lectures, 'A Truly Civil Society', Lecture 2. Raising Social Capital <www.ldb.org/evacox.htm>, viewed 19 May 2008.

18 United Nations General Assembly (2001) *Support for Volunteering: Report of the Secretary-General*, New York, United Nations, pp. 2-3.

19 Eva Cox, 'The Light and Dark of Volunteering' in Warburton & Oppenheimer (2000), pp. 140-49.

20 A. Petriwisky & J. Warburton (2007) 'Redefining Volunteering for the Global Context: A Measurement Matrix for Researchers', *Australian Journal on*

Volunteering, vol. 12, no. 1, p. 9.

21 Mark Lyons & Andrew Passey (2006) 'Need Public Policy Ignore the Third Sector? Government Policy in Australia and the United Kingdom', *Australian Journal of Public Administration*, vol. 65, no. 3, September, p. 90.

22 Justin Davis Smith (2000) 'Volunteering and Social Development', *Voluntary Action*, vol. 3, no. 1, Winter, p. 11.

23 The data comes from the latest ABS study, (2007) *Voluntary Work, Australia, 2006*.

24 Petriwisky & Warburton (2007).

25 Margaret Tennant (2007) *The Fabric of Welfare. Voluntary Organisations, Government and Welfare in New Zealand, 1840-2005*, Bridget Williams Books, Wellington.

Chapter 2

1 Anne Bourdillon (1945) *Voluntary Social Services: Their Place in the Modern State*, Methuen, London.

2 A version of this discussion can be found in my earlier work, especially 'An Overview of the Voluntary Principle in Australia', in J Warburton & M Oppenheimer (eds) (2000) *Volunteers and Volunteering*, Federation Press, Sydney, pp. 9-18.

3 For a detailed discussion of the early colonial settlement and its problems, see, for example, Brian Dickey (1987) *No Charity There. A Short History of Social Welfare in Australia*, Allen & Unwin, Sydney; Stephen Garton (1990) *Out of Luck. Poor Australians and Social Welfare*, Allen & Unwin, Sydney; Anne O'Brien (1988) *Poverty's Prison: The Poor in NSW 1880-1918*, Melbourne University Press, Melbourne; Anne O'Brien (2005) *God's Willing Workers. Women and Religion in Australia*, UNSW Press, Sydney.

4 David Green & Lawrence Cromwell (1984) *Mutual Aid or Welfare State. Australia's Friendly Societies*, George Allen and Unwin, Sydney.

5 Arthur Marwick (1988) *Total War and Social Change*, Macmillan, Basingstoke.

6 Mark Lyons (2001) *Third Sector. The Contribution of Nonprofit and Cooperative Enterprises in Australia*, Allen & Unwin, Sydney.

7 Cora Baldock (1990) *Volunteers in Welfare*, Allen & Unwin, Sydney, p. 24. This was confirmed by other researchers. See, for example, V Milligan, J Hardwick & A Graycar (1984) *Non-Government Welfare Organisations in Australia: A National Classification*, SWRC Reports and Proceedings, No. 51, Sydney, p. 96.

8 National Organization for Women Task Force on Volunteerism (1973) November, reprinted in *Ms Magazine*, February 1975, vol. 3, no. 8, p. 73.

9 A Cantor (1978) 'The Sheltered Workshop', *Lilith*, vol. 5, p. 20, quoted in Jill Hardwick & Adam Graycar (1982) 'Volunteers in Non Government Welfare Organisations in Australia: A Working Paper', SWRC Reports and Proceedings, no. 25, Sydney, p. 5.

10 Ibid., p. 7.

11 Ibid., p. 8.

12 FG Castles (1989) *Australian Public Policy and Economic Vulnerability*, Allen & Unwin, Sydney, p. 42.

13 For America, see, for example, Robert H Bremer (1988) *American Philanthropy*,

University of Chicago Press, Chicago; Susan J Ellis & Katherine H Noyes (1990) *By the People. A History of Americans as Volunteers,* Jossey-Bass Publishers, San Francisco and Oxford. For Canada, People in Action. National Advisory Council on Voluntary Action (1977) 'Report of the National Advisory Council on Voluntary Action to the Government of Canada', September; Janet Lautenschlager (1992) *Volunteering. A Traditional Canadian Value*, Voluntary Action Program, Department of Canadian Heritage, Ottawa.

14 Margaret Tennant (2007) *The Fabric of Welfare. Voluntary Organisations, Government and Welfare in New Zealand, 1840–2005*, Bridget Williams Books, Wellington.

15 This project, established through the Centre for Civil Society Studies, has collected data on thirty-nine countries in an effort to analyse civil society and its impact across the world. See www.jhu.edu/~cnp, viewed 20 April 2008.

16 Jill Roe (1998) 'The Australian Way' in Paul Smyth & Bettina Cass (eds), *Contesting the Australian Way. States, Markets and Civil Society*, Cambridge University Press, Melbourne, pp. 69–80.

17 Paul Smyth & Bettina Cass (eds) (1998) *Contesting the Australian Way. States, Markets and Civil Society*, Cambridge University Press, Melbourne, p. 8.

18 William & Janet Beveridge (1949) *On and Off the Platform. Under the Southern Cross*, Hicks, Smith & Wright, Wellington and Sydney, p. 70.

19 Russel Ward (1958) *The Australian Legend*, Oxford University Press, Melbourne.

20 Merle Curti (1961) 'Tradition and Innovation in American Philanthropy', *Proceedings of the American Philosophical Society*, vol. 105, no. 2, April 21, pp. 146–56.

21 See, for example, Janet Lautenschlager (1992).

Part II

1 Melanie Oppenheimer (1999) Red Cross VAs. A History of the VAD Movement in New South Wales, Ohio Productions, Walcha.

Chapter 3

1 Quoted in Melanie Oppenheimer (2002) *All Work No Pay. Australian Civilians in War*, Ohio Productions, Walcha, p. 122. Much of this chapter is a synthesis of my ideas taken from this book. See also Melanie Oppenheimer, 'Volunteers in Action: Voluntary Work in Australia, 1939-1945', PhD thesis, Macquarie University, 1997.

2 *Official Yearbook of the Commonwealth of Australia*, no. 41, 1941, p. 733. It puts the unemployment figure at 12.5 per cent in July 1939.

3 Oppenheimer (2002), p. 76.

4 Ibid.

5 Quoted in Oppenheimer (2002), p. 86.

6 Ibid., p. 86.

7 Melanie Oppenheimer, 'McKerihan, Sir Clarence Roy (1896-1969)' (2000) *Australian Dictionary of Biography*, vol. 15, Melbourne University Press, Melbourne, pp 247-48.

8   See Oppenheimer (2002).

9   See Oppenheimer (2002), chapter 5.

10 Memorandum from Director of Personal Services, Department of Army, Military Board to Defence Liaison (Voluntary Organisations), undated, circa November 1940. A817/1 59A, National Archives of Australia (NAA), Canberra.

11 Citation by General Blamey for Goward's OBE in a cablegram sent by SM Bruce, High Commissioner in London, 23 March 1942. AA1973/3362/1 H15, NAA, Canberra.

12 Oppenheimer (2002), chapter 9.

13 *Sydney Morning Herald*, 20 April 1945.

14 *Queensland Parliamentary Debates* (1942–43), vol. CLXXIX, p. 1328.

Chapter 4

1   Extract from a Report on the Work of the Ministry of Post-War Reconstruction, undated c. 1944/45. MS3939/10/2 Ministry for Post-War Reconstruction Memorandum (2 of 3). Papers of Lloyd Ross, National Library of Australia (NLA), Canberra. Parts of this chapter are based on my article published in 2005, 'Voluntary Action and Welfare in Post-1945 Australia. Preliminary Perspectives', *History Australia*, vol. 2, no. 3, pp. 82.1–15.

2   Susan Keen (1999) 'Associations in Australian History: Their Contribution to Social Capital', *Journal of Interdisciplinary History*, vol. xxiv, no. 4, Spring, pp. 639–59.

3   See Minute Books of Walcha Horticultural Society, Local History Centre, Walcha.

4   See Melanie Oppenheimer (forthcoming), 'Eleanor Manning (1906–1986) Guide Leader', *Australian Dictionary of Biography*, vol. 18, Melbourne University Press, Melbourne.

5   Biographers of Lloyd Ross have not focused on his interest in community and voluntarism. See Stephen Holt (1996) *A Veritable Dynamo: Lloyd Ross and Australian Labour, 1901–1987*, UQ Press, Brisbane, and Mark Hearn (1992) 'Means and Ends: The Ideology of Dr Lloyd Ross', *Labour History*, no. 63, November, pp. 25–42.

6   Lloyd Ross (1945) 'Building Community and Nation', *Meanjin*, vol. 4, no. 1, pp. 5–8.

7   David Maunders 'A Study of the Community Centre Movement in Australia, 1943–1955. Its Contribution to Education and an Evaluation of the Effect of Government Policy', MA thesis, School of Education, La Trobe University, 1980, p. 7.

8   Ministry for Post-War Reconstruction Memorandum, MS3939/10/2, NLA, Canberra, p. 2.

9   Extract from a Report on the Work of the Ministry of Post-War Reconstruction, undated c. 1944/45, 1 typed page 9. Community Building. Memos to Dr Coombs, MS3939/10/1, NLA, Canberra.

10 Terry Irving, David Maunders & Geoff Sherington (1995) *Youth in Australia. Policy Administration and Politics*, Macmillan, South Melbourne, p. 33.

11 Quoted in Deborah Brennan (1994) *The Politics of Australian Childcare*, Cambridge University Press, Melbourne, p. 39.

12 Maunders (1980), p. 166.

13 Speech given by Lloyd Ross, 27 April, undated circa 1945. MS 3939/10/5, NLA, Canberra.

14 The Co-operative Advisory Council (1945), *Community Centres. A Vital Social Need*, Sydney.

15 John Laurent (1994) 'This Meeting is Now Closed': The Social Significance of the Institutes in Retrospect', in P Candy & J Laurent (eds) *Pioneering Culture. Mechanics' Institutes and School of Arts in Australia*, Auslib Press, Adelaide, p. 370.

16 Kathleen Gordon (1943) *Community Centres*, AGPS, Canberra and quoted in Maunders (1980), p. 76.

17 National Fitness Council of NSW (1946) *Community Centres*, NFC, Sydney, p. 3.

18 Ibid., p. 15.

19 Talk by Professor GV Portus, 'The Significance of Nuriootpa to Australia', broadcast by 5CL, 8.45 pm, 26th September, published in Common Cause (1945) *A Township starts to Live*, Common Cause Publication, p. 35.

20 There have been a number of histories of the Fellowship of Australian Writers including Len Fox (ed.) (1989) *Dream at a Graveside. The History of the Fellowship of Australian Writers 1928–1988*, FAW, for the 60th anniversary of the organisation. See also, for example, Peter Kirkpatrick (1992) *The Sea Coast of Bohemia: Literary Life in Sydney's Roaring Twenties*, UQ Press, Brisbane; Leslie Heath (1993) 'John Le Gay Brereton, The University and Australian Literature', *Notes and Furphies*, no. 31, October, pp. 3–7; Carole Ferrier (ed.) (1992) *As Good as a Yarn with You*, Cambridge University Press, Melbourne; Drusilla Modjeska (1981) *Exiles at Home: Australian Women Writers, 1925–1945*, Angus and Robertson, Sydney; Jane E Hunt (2004) '"Following" Women: Sydney Women Writers and the Organisational Impulse', *ACH: The Journal of the History of Culture in Australia*, vol. 23, pp. 175–99.

21 Patrick Buckridge (1998), 'Clearing a Space for Australian Literature, 1940–65' in Bruce Bennett & Jennifer Strauss (eds) *The Oxford Literary History of Australia*, OUP, Melbourne, pp. 171-72.

22 For information on Mary Matheson (she married banker Thomas Matheson in 1934) and the Children's Library Movement, see *Australian Dictionary of Biography* entry on the three sisters – Judith Godden (1988), 'Rivett, Eleanor Harriett (Nell) (1883–1972)', *Australian Dictionary of Biography*, vol. 11, Melbourne University Press, Melbourne, pp. 401–03.

23 Donald Ingram Smith (1945) 'How They Did It', no. 2. *The Children's Library Movement*, ABC, Sydney, p. 1, Mitchell Library, Sydney. This is an unpublished script from the series of documentary broadcasts on community projects. This was broadcast on Monday 28 May 1945.

24 ABC (1946) *History of the Children's Library Movement Written for Radio Broadcast by a Former Member of the Staff*, ABC, Sydney; and Donald Ingram Smith (1945).

25 Ralph Munn & Ernest R Pitt (1935) *Australian Libraries: A Survey of Conditions and Suggestions for Their Improvement*, Australian Council for Educational Research, Melbourne, pp. 23–24.

26 Carl Bridge (1986) *A Trunk Full of Books. History of the State Library of South Australia and its Forerunners*, Wakefield Press, Adelaide, p. xvi.

27 ABC (1946), p. 31.

28 Alison Gregg (1993) 'The Hope of the Future: The Kindergarten Union and the Campaign for Children's Libraries in Western Australia', *Issues in Education Research*, vol. 3, no. 1, pp. 17–33.

29 There has been less interest in writing the history of the Children's Book Council than other literary organisations such as the Fellowship of Australian Writers but a couple have been written, again by those involved in the organisation, such as Eve Pownall (1980) *The Children's Book Council in Australia, 1945–1980*, Reading Time Publication No. 4, and June Smith & Margaret Hamilton (eds) (1995) *Celebrate with Stories. The Children's Book Council of Australia 1945–1995*, Margaret Hamilton Books, Sydney.

30 Much of this comes from Smith & Hamilton (1995), pp. 9–13.

31 Quoted in Pownall (1980), p. 3.

32 Although the title of Children's Book Council was not used until 1947, the first Children's Book Week in November 1945 is generally regarded as its official beginning.

33 See CR Bull, 'Children's Book Week 1945. A Summary', in Children's Book Week (Exhibition programs etc), 3 pages, Mitchell Library, Sydney.

34 John Metcalfe, 'International Children's Book Week', talk on 2BL, 12 November 1945, Mitchell Library, Sydney.

35 Western Australia was unceremoniously told they were no longer needed once the State Library of Western Australia muscled in – the Western Australia CBA was not re-formed until 1975.

36 Smith & Hamilton, (1995), p. 22.

37 Ian Britain (1997) 'Barry Humphries and the "Feeble Fifties"', in John Murphy & Judith Smart (eds) 'The Forgotten Fifties. Aspects of Australian Society and Culture in the 1950s', *Australian Historical Studies*, no. 109, October, p. 9.

38 Geoffrey Bolton (1995) 'Two Pauline Versions' in Scott Prasser, JR Nethercote & John Warhurst (eds) *The Menzies Era. A Reappraisal of Government, Politics and Policy*, Hale & Iremonger, Sydney, p. 33.

39 Stuart Macintyre (1999) *A Concise History of Australia*, Cambridge University Press, Melbourne, pp. 227–28.

40 John Murphy & Judith Smart (1997) 'Introduction', in Murphy & Smart, p. 1.

41 Britain (1997), p. 6.

42 See Mavis Thorpe Clark (1986) *No Mean Destiny. The Story of the War Widows' Guild of Australia, 1945*–85, Hyland House, Melbourne, and Susan Keen (1999), p. 654.

43 See, for example, Quota (1969) *Quota in Australia. A History of the 13th District*, Quota, Katoomba.

44 See www.soroptimistinternational.org, viewed 24 May 2008.

45 David Hilliard (1997) 'Church, Family and Sexuality in Australia in the 1950s' in Murphy & Smart, p. 135.

46 Anne O'Brien (2005) *God's Willing Workers. Women and Religion in Australia*, UNSW Press, Sydney.

47 Hugh Hunt, Executive Director, The Australian Elizabethan Theatre Trust, *Annual Report 1957*. See www.theindependent.org.au/AETT-annual-report-1957.pdf, viewed 20 March 2008.

48 Family Welfare Bureau, Annual Report, 31 March 1954, p. 3. A2421/T1

G1272/3/8, NAA, Canberra.

49 Ibid., p. 19.

50 Ibid., pp. 4–5.

51 Ibid., p. 13. The funds from the Repatriation Commission were in fact from the defunct Australian Comforts Fund, now controlled and dispersed by Repatriation, so technically not Commonwealth money at all.

52 Ibid., p. 2.

53 Ann-Mari Jordens (1997) *Alien to Citizen*, Allen & Unwin, Sydney, p. 45.

54 May Pillinger, Statement No. 2, 1 July 1954, Letter to Mr RW Carswell, Deputy Commissioner, Repatriation Commission, A2421/T1 G1272/3/8, NAA, Canberra.

55 Letter from Pillinger to Deputy Commissioner Carswell, 21 March 1956, A2421/ T1 G1272/3/8, NAA, Canberra.

56 Ann Marie Jordens (1995) *Redefining Australians*, Hale & Iremonger, Sydney, p. 26.

57 Geoffrey Sherington (1980) *Australia's Immigrants. The Australian Experience*, George, Allen & Unwin, Sydney, p. 147.

58 Rosalie A James, Annual Report Greta Holding Centre, NSW, June 1952–June 1953. Social Worker annual reports – NSW. A445/1 276/3/2, NAA, Canberra.

59 A Calwell (1949) *Tomorrow's Australians*, 14 February and quoted in Gwenda Tavan (1997) '"Good Neighbours": Community Organisations, Migrant Assimilation and Australian Society and Culture, 1950–1961', in Murphy & Smart, p. 78.

60 Jordens (1995), p. 77.

61 Tavan (1997), p. 79.

62 There is an ongoing debate about whether migrants volunteer to the same degree as other Australians. This will be discussed in chapter 7.

63 Quoted in Jordens (1997), p. 151.

64 Ibid., p. 151.

65 Ibid., p. 158.

66 Report by B Tipper, social worker, Social Worker Annual Reports – NSW. A445/1 276/3/2, NAA, Canberra.

67 Quoted in Oppenheimer (1999), p. 145.

68 Ibid., p. 136.

69 Ibid, p. 138.

70 Secretary General, ARC, Leon Stubbings, February 1957, quoted in Oppenheimer (1999), p. 140.

71 Michael Wright (2001) '"Brass Hats … from Sydney": Volunteerism, Contested Space and the Organisation of Fire Suppression in the Blue Mountains, 1950–1960', *Labour History*, no. 81, November, p. 55.

72 Ibid., pp. 65–70.

73 Ian Davison (1997) 'Welcoming the World: The 1956 Olympic Games and the Re-presentation of Melbourne', in Murphy & Smart, p. 65.

74 Letter from Honorary Secretary-Treasurer, James SW Eve to JA Lyons, PM, 15 November 1937, British Empire Games. A461/8, NAA, Canberra.

75 *Oxford Dictionary of English* (2003).

76 'Australian Olympic Federation Bulletin, 1/1954', [Melbourne Olympic Games,

1956], Australian Olympic Federation Bulletins, AA1967/379, item 6, NAA, Canberra.

77 'Allowances to sports associations', Minutes of 45th meeting of finance and general purposes committee, Friday 15 June 1956. [Melbourne Olympic Games, 1956]. Organisation Committee – Executive Committee – Agenda and Minutes. AA1967/379, 2, part 2. NAA, Canberra.

78 'Australian Olympic Federation Bulletin, 1/1954', [Melbourne Olympic Games, 1956], Australian Olympic Federation Bulletins, AA1967/379, item 6, NAA, Canberra.

79 XVI Olympiad Official News Service, No. 9, December 1955 (published by the Organising Committee for the XVI Olympiad, Melbourne), p. 3. [Melbourne Olympic Games]. Australian Olympic Federation Bulletins. 111967/379, item 6.

80 Minutes of Adjourned Transport Committee, Friday 31 August 1956. [Melbourne Olympic Games]. Organization Committee – Executive Committee – Agenda and Minutes. AA1967/379, 2, part 2. NAA, Canberra.

81 Newspaper clipping, undated, unnamed, c. 1956, Guyot collection.

82 Melissa Harper (2007) *The Ways of the Bushwalker. On Foot in Australia*, UNSW Press, Sydney, p. 240.

Chapter 5

1 Transcript of interview: Beverley Symons. Women in the Anti-War Movement, 9 September 1993. Copy in possession of Ann Curthoys. I'd like to thank Ann for her generosity in sharing this material and for providing me with the printed transcripts.

2 See Bobbie Oliver (2001) '"In the Thick of Every Battle for the Cause of Labor": The Voluntary Work of the Labor Women's Organisations in Western Australia, 1900–70', *Labour History*, no. 81, November, pp. 93–108; and Margo Beasley (2001) 'Soldiers of the Federation: The Women's Committees of the Waterside Workers' Federation of Australia', *Labour History*, no. 81, November, pp. 109–27.

3 Ann Curthoys (2002) *Freedom Ride. A Freedom Rider Remembers*, Allen & Unwin, Sydney.

4 Printed on the front page of their journal, *Peace and Freedom*, vol. 3, no. 2, March 1964 by the WILPF, Australian Section.

5 See, for example, Zora Simic (2007) 'Butter not Bombs. A Short History of the Union of Australian Women', *History Australia*, vol. 4, no. 1, pp. 07.1–07.15; and Barbara Carter (1986) 'The Peace Movement of the 1950s' in Ann Curthoys & John Merrit (eds) *Better Dead than Red: Australia's First Cold War 1945–1959*, Allen & Unwin, Sydney.

6 Campaign for Peace in Vietnam, *Newsletter*, no. 3, February 1968, p. 4.

7 Campaign for Peace in Vietnam, *Newsletter*, no. 2, 15 November 1967, p. 1.

8 Ibid.

9 Transcript of interview: Margaret Eliot, Women in the Anti-War Movement, 21 July 1993, collection of Ann Curthoys.

10 Transcript of interview: Bev Symons, Women in the Anti-War Movement, 9 September 1993, collection of Ann Curthoys.

11 See *SOS Newsletter*, no. 2, June 1966, p. 5.

12 'Statement of the Aims of SOS in *SOS Newsletter*, no 4, September 1966, A1622/46 1813, NAA, Canberra.

13 Quoted in Ann Curthoys (1995) 'Shut Up You Bourgeois Bitch', in Joy Damousi & Marilyn Lake (eds) *Gender and War*, Cambridge University Press, Melbourne, p. 322.

14 *SOS Newsletter*, no. 1, September 1965, p. 2.

15 *SOS Newsletter*, no. 2, June 1966, p. 1.

16 See article in *The Bulletin*, and quoted in *SOS Newsletter*, no. 2, June 1966, p. 5.

17 Transcript of interview, Adele Pert, Women in the Anti-War Movement, 22 July 1993.

18 See Australian Voluntary Aid Organisations – Australian/Vietnamese Association of Victoria. A1838 (A1838/288) 2101/3/17 Part 1, National Archives of Australia (NAA), Canberra.

19 Ibid.

20 *Camden News*, 8 December 1971.

21 *Australian Women's Weekly*, 8 July 1970, p. 14.

22 Rosemary Taylor (1988) 'Adoption Hero Vietnam 1967–1975', *Orphans of War* Collins, Melbourne, p. 15.

23 Daniel Oakman (2004) *Facing Asia: A History of the Colombo Plan*, Pandanus Books, Canberra.

24 Opening speech by Minister for External Affairs, Paul Hasluck to ACOA Conference, 8 November 1965. A1838 2101/5/1 Part 2, NAA, Canberra.

25 *The Canberra Times*, 9 November 1965.

26 Quoted in Australian Volunteers International <www.acicis.murdoch.edu.au/hi/docs/VolunteerinIndonesia.pdf>, viewed 20 April 2008.

27 External Affairs note from Edwin Ride to Minister of Immigration, Minister Fairbairn, 25 February 1966, in A1838 2101/5/1 Part 2, NAA, Canberra.

28 Letter to Harold Holt, 20 June 1966. 'Commonwealth assistance to voluntary aid organisations'. A463 1973/1421, NAA, Canberra.

29 Billy McMahon, 'Commonwealth assistance to voluntary aid organisations'. A463 1973/1421, NAA, Canberra.

30 ACOA, *Aid to South Vietnam*, in A1838 2102/3/14, Part 5, NAA, Canberra.

31 Ivor Forsyth Wyatt (2005) *Ours in Trust: A Personal History of the National Trust of Australia (NSW)*, The National Trust of Australia (NSW), Sydney [1987], p. 7.

32 Ibid., p. 35.

33 Bill Richards (1982) *The National Trust in NSW*, Rigby, Sydney, p. 11

34 Alfred James (ed.) (2001) 'The Affiliated Societies of the Royal Australian Historical Society', in 'Much Writing, Many Opinions. The Making of the Royal Australian Historical Society 1901–2001', *Journal of the RAHS*, vol. 87, part 1, June, pp. 112–22.

35 *The Walcha News*, 23 May 1963.

36 GG Watson (1978) *Little Athletics and Childhood Socialization*, A Report Presented to the Community Recreation Council of WA, Community Recreation Council of WA, April, p. 8.

37 *Geelong Advertiser*, 4 February 2005.

38 Babette Smith (2003) *Coming up for Air. A History of the Asthma Foundation of NSW*, Rosenberg Publishing, Sydney, p. 256.

39 Ibid, p. 49.
40 Ibid, pp. 49–50.
41 *The Asthma Welfarer*, vol. 1, no. 1, July 1964, p. 4.
42 Colleen Wardell & Dr Claire Isbister (1995) 'Report on Thirty Years of the Asthma Children's Swimming Programme', unpublished report for The Asthma Foundation of NSW, April, p. 3.
43 Jenny Bryan (2007) *The Pharmaceutical Journal*, vol. 279, 13 October, p. 404; <www.pjonline.com>, viewed 1 March 2008. 'There was precious little before Ventolin for routine bronchiodilation … we used isoprenaline, but its lack of selectivity for bronchial smooth muscle meant that it caused tachycardia and there was concern that it could be linked with other asthma deaths', stated Tim Clark, professor of pulmonary medicine at the National Heart and Lung Institute, Imperial College, London. The other drugs available in the 1960s were adrenaline and aminophylline plus sedatives.
44 Smith (2003), p. 191.
45 Ibid., pp. 192–94.
46 Wardell & Isbister (1995), pp. 3–5.
47 Smith (2003) pp. 196–97.
48 RJ Lawrence (ed.) (1966) *Community Service. Citizens and Welfare Organisations*, FW Cheshire, Melbourne, p. viii.
49 TH Kewley (1973) *Social Security in Australia, 1900–72*, Sydney University Press, Sydney, p. 189.
50 GT Sambell, 'Voluntary Agencies in our Changing Environment' in Lawrence (1966), p. 12.
51 Ibid.
52 Speech by Catherine King, 'Women's Magazine', Marriage Guidance, undated SP369/1 K/5, NAA, Sydney.
53 Marriage Guidance Organisations – Canberra Conference, 22–23 February 1960. A432/79 1960/2328, NAA, Canberra.
54 LV Harvey, 'The Federal Government and Voluntary Agencies Working Together in Marriage Guidance' in Lawrence (1966), p. 81.
55 Ibid., pp. 86–87.
56 LV Harvey, Unpublished Report on Marriage Guidance Prepared for Standing Committee on the Profession of Psychology, p. 5. A432/79 1960/2328, NAA, Canberra.
57 Marriage Guidance Conference, Canberra, March 1962. A432/79 1962/2085, NAA, Canberra.
58 Paper by Dr Margaret J Rioch, 'Summary of Pilot Project in Mental Health Counselling – 15 February 1961. Adult Psychiatry Branch, National Institute of Mental Health', in Marriage Guidance Organisations – Selection and Training – Standards and Procedures, A432/79 1960/2347, NAA, Canberra.
59 Harvey in Lawrence (1966), p. 87.
60 Family Welfare Bureau, *Annual Report 1965–66*, p. 4.
61 Ibid., p. 5.
62 Family Welfare Bureau, *Annual Report, 1967–68*, p. 3.
63 Hansard, House of Representatives, 4 March 1970, *Delivered Meals Subsidy Bill 1970*, second reading, p. 62. There does seem to be some confusion about the

specific dates of the founding of Meals on Wheels in the various states.

64 Greg Crafter (2002) 'Taylor, Doris Irene (1901 – 1968)', *Australian Dictionary of Biography*, vol. 16, Melbourne University Press, Melbourne, pp 364–65.

65 Cabinet Welfare Committee, Domiciliary Services. Preliminary Report of Director-General of Social Services and Appendix A, A5882 C0786, NAA, Canberra.

66 In 1969, for Victoria it was 400 meals a day; South Australia, 200 meals a day; Tasmania, 87 meals a day, and New South Wales the scheme operated in 55 towns although no meal figure was available. Ibid., Appendix B.

67 See Cabinet Welfare Committee, Domiciliary Services. Preliminary Report of Director-General of Social Services, A5882 C0786, NAA, Canberra and 'Direct Commonwealth Subsidies to Organisations Providing Meals on Wheels', 30 June 1969, A56/9 C647, NAA, Canberra.

68 See Hansard, House of Representatives, 4 March 1970, *Delivered Meals Subsidy Bill 1970*, second reading, pp. 61–68. See also Cabinet Welfare Committee – Meals on Wheels, A446/158 1970/95232, NAA, Canberra; and Meals on Wheels A5882 C0786, NAA, Canberra.

Part III

Chapter 6

1 Quoted in Pip Kalajzich (1996) *The Battlers for Kelly's Bush*, Battlers for Kelly's Bush, Sydney.

2 Ian McNair (1975) 'A Profile of Australians – Some Characteristics and Attitudes', *Australian Quarterly*, vol. 47, no. 4, December, pp. 66–77.

3 Ibid., p. 66.

4 *Moratorium News*, vol. 1, no. 8, October 1970, p. 2.

5 Transcript of interview: Adele Pert, Women in the Anti-War Movement, 22 July 1993. Interview conducted for Ann Curthoys and in Ann's possession. See also Save our Sons, MS 3821, National Library of Australia (NLA), Canberra.

6 Mark Lyons (2001) *Third Sector. The Contribution of Nonprofit and Cooperative Enterprises in Australia*, Allen & Unwin, Sydney.

7 Ronald Henderson (1973) *A Study of Volunteers in Social Welfare Agencies in Victoria*, Institute of Applied Economic and Social Research, University of Melbourne and VCOSS, August, p. 12.

8 Ibid., pp. 1–6.

9 See Social Welfare Commission Reference Paper (1975) *The Volunteer Bureau. A Pilot Study*, SWC, Queanbeyan, p. 5.

10 Ibid., p. 6.

11 Ibid., p. 27.

12 Ibid., pp. 10–14.

13 Ibid., p. 18.

14 Ibid., p. 7.

15 See ABS, *Life Expectancy (years) at selected ages, 1901–2003/5*; <www.aihw.gov.au/mortality/date/life_expectancy.cfm>, viewed 14 March 2008.

16 SWC Reference Paper (1975), p. 23.
17 Joy Noble (2000) 'The Future of Volunteering. A Volunteer's Perspective', in Jeni Warburton & Melanie Oppenheimer (eds), *Volunteers and Volunteering*, Federation Press, Sydney, p. 151.
18 Peter Manning & Marion Hardman (undated) *Green Bans*, Australian Conservation Foundation, Melbourne, unpaginated.
19 Battlers for Kelly's Bush, Records 1969–1991. MLMSS 5549, Mitchell Library, Sydney.
20 Minute Book, Battlers for Kelly's Bush, September 1970, MLMSS 5549.
21 Kalajzich (1996), p. 56.
22 Ibid., p. 67.
23 Ibid., p. 39.
24 Ibid., p. 51.
25 Ibid., p. 3.
26 Indeed, Petra Kelly the influential founder of the Green Party in Germany, cited the Australian green bans as her guiding influence. See Bob Brown & Peter Singer (1996) *The Greens*, Text Publishing, Melbourne.
27 EG Whitlam (1975) 'People and Power – Community Participation in Federal Government', *The Australian Quarterly*, 47, no. 2, June, p. 39.
28 For a full discussion, see Melanie Oppenheimer (2008) 'Voluntary Action, Social Welfare and the Australian Assistance Plan', *Australian Historical Studies*, vol. 39, no. 132, June, pp. 167-82.
29 So said a member of the VCSS at a meeting of the Outer Eastern Region, Victoria, 6 December 1973, cited in Report by Marie Coleman, Citizen Participation in Community Planning, 1974, p. 11. Document 363, vol. 12, A3390/1, NAA, Canberra.
30 Tom O'Brien (1977) *Planning-Becoming-Development*, Centre for Continuing Education & ANU, Canberra, p. 85.
31 Press statement entitled 'Community Welfare Development' by Marie Coleman, 24 May 1973. Australian Assistance Plan. A463 1973/1522, NAA, Canberra. See also Hayden Raysmith (1972) *Report on the Community Services of Geelong*, Geelong and District Community Chest Association, Geelong.
32 Marie Coleman (1975) Voluntary Agencies and the Australian Assistance Plan, SWC, p. 2.
33 Australian Assistance Plan A463 1973/1522, NAA, Canberra.
34 Introduction, 2nd Discussion Paper, AAP, 8, Document 303, volume 8, A3390/1, NAA, Canberra.
35 SWC, 'What is the AAP?', 1976, p. 2. Document no. 414, A3390/1, NAA, Canberra.
36 Bill Hayden, Press Statement, 19 October 1973. A463 1973/1522, NAA, Canberra.
37 SWC, 'What is the AAP', 1976, p. 24. Document no. 414, A3390/1 Appendix, NAA, Canberra.
38 Press Statement by the Minister for Social Security, Mr Bill Hayden. Australian Assistance Plan for NSW, 10 December 1973. A463 1973/1522, NAA, Canberra.
39 SWC, 'What is the AAP?', 1976, A3390 414 Appendix, NAA, Canberra.
40 Ibid.

41 SWC, 'What is the AAP?', 1976, p. 6. Document no. 414, A3390/1, NAA Canberra.

42 Ibid., p. 7.

43 Sue Kenny (1996), 'Contestations of Community Development in Australia', *Community Development Journal*, vol. 31, no. 2, April, p. 105. See also R Thorpe & J Petruchenia (1985) *Community Work or Social Change? An Australian Perspective*, Routledge and Kegan Paul, London.

44 See Carol Pateman (1970) *Participation and Democratic Theory*, Cambridge University Press, London, p.1.

45 Quoted in SWC, 'What is the AAP?', 1976, p. 23. Document no. 414, A3390/1, NAA Canberra. Ralf Dahrendorf presented the BBC Reith Lecture series, later published in 1975 as *The New Liberty: Survival and Justice in a Changing World*, Routledge & Kegan Paul, London.

46 See, for example, Leonard Tierney with Helen McMahon (1979) *From Vague Ideas to Unfeasible Roles*, AGPS, Canberra; and Adam Graycar (1979) *Welfare Politics in Australia. A Study in Policy Analysis*, Macmillan, Melbourne.

47 Peter ER Jones (1975) 'The Australian Assistance Plan – Welfare (?) on the Cheap' *Australian Journal of Social Issues* 10, no. 1, pp. 63–74; and R.J.K. Chapman (1975) 'Australian Assistance Plan: A Study in Ineffective Planning', *Australian Journal of Social Issues* 10, no. 4, pp. 283–98.

48 Adam Graycar & Joanne Davis (1979) *Australian Assistance Plan. An Evaluation Report, Number Two*, AGPS, Canberra.

49 Non Government Organisations – Mountain District Co-operative Ltd – Request for grant to enable housewives to become involved in community activities, A4218/2 W/NGO 278, NAA, Canberra.

50 'The Fence that Brought New Fellowship', undated newspaper clipping, files of Non Government Organisations and Individuals. Organisation Grant, CWA – Miriwinni, A 4218 W/NGO 104, NAA, Canberra.

51 Ibid.

52 Letter/application for funding from Dulcie Menzel to Secretariat, International Women's Year, 30 January 1975. A4218/2 W/NGO 104, NAA, Canberra.

53 Ibid.

54 Letter from Dulcie Menzel to Elizabeth Reid, 19 September 1974. A4218/2 W/NGO 104, NAA, Canberra.

55 Letter/application for funding from Dulcie Menzel to Secretariat, International Women's Year, 30 January 1975. A4218/2 W/NGO 104, NAA, Canberra.

56 Ibid.

57 GC Avery & H Bergsteiner (1980) 'Survey of Voluntary Recreation Workers in NSW', *Australian Journal of Social Issues*, vol. 15, no. 1, February, p. 56.

58 Ibid., p. 62.

59 Ibid., p. 61.

60 Ibid, p. 60.

61 Ibid., p. 63.

62 Professor J Bloomfield (1974) *Recreation in Australia – Its Role, Scope and Development*, Parliamentary Paper, no. 76, Government Printer of Australia, Canberra, p. 6.

63 Ibid.

64 Ibid., p. 1.

65 Ibid., p. 6.

66 Eve Pownall (1980) *The Children's Book Council in Australia, 1945–1980*, Reading Time Publication No. 4, p. 106.

67 Roselyn Melville (2002) '*My Time is Not a Gift to Government*'. *An Exploratory Study of NSW Community Legal Centre Volunteers*, Institute of Social Change and Critical Inquiry, University of Wollongong, p. 9.

68 Sean Brawley (2007) *Bondi Lifesaver: A History of an Australian Icon*, ABC Books, Sydney, p. 236.

69 Ibid., p. 41.

70 Ibid., p. 257.

71 Ibid., p. 236.

72 Edie Kieft, sportswoman and surf lifesaver, <www.womenaustralia.info/biogs/AWE2692b.htm>, viewed 1 March 2008.

73 Brawley (2007), p. 256.

74 Family Welfare Bureau, *26th Annual Report*, 1971–72, pp. 12–13.

75 Family Welfare Bureau, *27th Annual Report*, 1972–73, p. 3.

76 Cutler Papers – Lady Helen Cutler's Speeches, MLMSS 7151/25/1–5, Mitchell Library, Sydney.

77 Melanie Oppenheimer (1999) *Red Cross VAs*, Ohio Productions, Walcha, p. 164.

78 Ibid., pp. 150–55.

79 'ARA – Over 30 Years of Experience', <www.ausref.net/cms/home/history-mission/>, viewed 20 March 2008.

80 Ann-Mari Jordens (1997) *Alien to Citizen*, Allen & Unwin, Sydney, pp. 163–64.

81 Ann-Mari Jordens (1995) *Redefining Australians. Immigration, Citizenship and National Identity*, Hale & Iremonger, Sydney, pp. 86–87.

82 Alan Stretton (1976) *The Furious Days. The Relief of Darwin*, Collins, Sydney, p. 29.

83 Oppenheimer (1999), p. 166.

84 Ibid., pp. 98–99.

85 See DL Webber (1976) 'Darwin Cyclone: An Exploration of Disaster Behaviour', *Australian Journal on Social Issues*, vol. 11, no. 1, pp. 54–64.

86 IGC Gilmore (1983) 'Education and Training in Disaster Management in Australia', *Disasters*, vol. 7, no. 1, p. 20.

87 Neil R Britton (1984) 'Conceptual Alternatives for the Analysis of Counter-Disaster Organisational Networks', in Natural Disasters Organisation, Department of Defence, *Report of Proceedings of a Research Workshop on Human Behaviour in Disaster in Australia*, 25–27 April, p. 271.

Chapter 7

1 Bill Armstrong (2001) 'International Relations' in Joy Noble & Fiona Johnston (eds), *Volunteering Visions*, Federation Press, Sydney, p. 18.

2 Mark Lyons (2001) *Third Sector. The Contribution of Nonprofit and Cooperative Enterprises in Australia*, Allen & Unwin, Sydney.

3 Justin Davis Smith, Colin Rochester & Rodney Hedley (eds) (1995) *Introduction to the Voluntary Sector*, Routledge, London and New York, p. 66.

4 Robert Fitzgerald, 'Community Advocacy', in Noble & Johnston (2001), p. 3.

5 See Michael Pusey (1991) *Economic Rationalism in Canberra. A Nation Building State Changes its Mind*, Cambridge University Press, Melbourne.

6 Quoted in Douglas Keay, *Women's Own*, 31 October 1987, pp. 8–10. See <www.margaretthatcher.org/speeches>, viewed 30 March 2008.

7 Quoted in Cora Baldock (1990) *Volunteers in Welfare*, Allen & Unwin, Sydney, p. 105.

8 Quoted in Jill Hardwick & Adam Graycar (1982) 'Volunteers in Non Government Welfare Organisations in Australia: A Working Paper', SWRC Reports and Proceedings, no. 25, September, p. 4.

9 Labour Party (1992) *Building Bridges: Labour and the Voluntary Sector*, The Labour Party, London, p. 1.

10 Anthony Giddens (1998) *The Third Way. Renewal of Social Democracy*, Polity Press, London.

11 Justin Davis Smith & Melanie Oppenheimer (2005) 'The Labour Movement and Voluntary Action in the UK and Australia: A Comparative Perspective', *Labour History*, no. 88, May, p. 117.

12 Justin Davis Smith, Colin Rochester & Rodney Hedley (eds) (1995) *An Introduction to the Voluntary Sector*, Routledge, London & New York; Jeni Warburton & Melanie Oppenheimer (eds) (2000) *Volunteers and Volunteering*, Federation Press, Sydney.

13 Jeni Warburton & Allyson Mutch, 'Volunteer Resources', in Warburton & Oppenheimer (2000), p. 37.

14 ANESBWA Records, Box 9, uncatalogued collection, ML 07/565, Mitchell Library, Sydney.

15 Ibid.

16 See, for example, Paul Kelly (1992) *The End of Certainty. The Story of the 80s*, Allen & Unwin, Sydney; Hugh Mackay (1993) *Reinventing Australia: The Mind and Mood of Australia in the 90s*, Angus and Robertson, Sydney; and Clive Hamilton (2003) *Growth Fetish*, Allen & Unwin, Sydney.

17 Hardwick & Graycar (1982), p. 2.

18 Ibid., p. 3.

19 See, for example, HM Paterson (1982) 'Voluntary Work in Australia', *Australian Bulletin of Labour*, vol. 8, no. 2, March, pp. 95–103; S Thorman (1987) *A Journey Through Self Help. An Evaluation of Self Help in Western Australia*, Western Institute of Self Help, Perth. In this study it was estimated that about 8 per cent of the population were involved in a range of self-help organisations. See also ACOSS (1996) *Volunteering in Australia*, ACOSS Papers, no. 74, April.

20 Hardwick & Graycar (1982), pp. 11–12.

21 Erica Fisher (1983) *Women's Voluntary Work*, NWAC, Canberra, p. v.

22 Ibid., pp. 3–7.

23 Ibid., pp. 14–15.

24 Joy Noble (1988) *Volunteer Management. A Resource Manual*, Volunteer Centre of SA, Adelaide, pp. 22–24.

25 Joy Noble (1991) *Volunteering. A Current Perspective*, Volunteer Centre of SA, Adelaide, p. 3.

26 Baldock (1990), p. 105.

27 Ibid., pp. 131–32.

28 Ibid., p. 43.

29 See interview in ABC television series, *A Life*, screened January 1996.

30 Industry Commission (1995), *Charitable Organisations in Australia. Overview*, Report no. 45, 16 June, AGPS, Melbourne, p. 81. See also ACOSS (1996), pp. 25–28.

31 Lyons (2001).

32 ABS (1986) *Voluntary Community Work, NSW, Preliminary*, AGPS, Canberra; and ABS (1988) *Community and Volunteer Work, South Australia*, AGPS, Canberra.

33 Noble (1991), Appendix 4, pp. 85–86.

34 ABS (1993) *Involvement in Sport Australia*, March, AGPS, Canberra; ABS (1994) *Unpaid Work in the Australian Economy, 1992*, Occasional Paper, AGPS, Canberra; ABS (1992) *How Australians Use their Time*, AGPS, Canberra. See also ABS (1993) *Work in Selected Cultural/Leisure Activities, Australia*, March, AGPS, Canberra.

35 House of Representatives Standing Committee on Legal and Constitutional Affairs (Lavarch Report) (1992) *Half Way to Equal. Report of the Inquiry into Equal Opportunity and Equal Status for Women in Australia*, Canberra, April.

36 Ibid., p. 37.

37 ABS (1995) *Voluntary Work Australia*, June, AGPS, Canberra, p. 1.

38 Ibid., p. 10.

39 ABS (1994) *Unpaid Work and the Australian Economy*, AGPS, Canberra, p. 2.

40 Quoted in Lyla Rogan (1996) 'Tides of Change in Community Services. The Industry Commission and COAG as Case Studies', in Adam Farrar & Jane Inglis (eds) *Keeping it Together. State and Civil Society in Australia*, Pluto Press, Sydney, p. 132.

41 Industry Commission (1995), p. 31.

42 Ibid., p. 30.

43 Duncan Ironmonger, 'Measuring Volunteering in Economic Terms' in Warburton & Oppenheimer (2000), p. 56.

44 Warburton & Mutch (2000), p. 40.

45 Sha Cordingley, 'The Definitions and Principles of Volunteering. A Framework for Public Policy', in Warburton & Oppenheimer (2000), pp. 73–74.

46 Ibid., p. 79.

47 RJ Lawrence (ed.) (1966) *Community Service. Citizens and Welfare Organisations*, FW Cheshire, Melbourne.

48 Quoted in Sue Keen (1999) 'Servicing Social Capital? Service Clubs in Decline', *Third Sector Review*, vol. 5, no. 1, p. 101.

49 Ibid., p. 104.

50 Ibid., pp. 104–07.

51 Sean Brawley (2001) '"Surf Lifesaving Owes No Person a Living": A Third Sector Case Study', *Labour History*, no. 81, November, pp. 75, 76 & 89.

52 Ibid., p. 81.

53 Ibid., p. 82.

54 Quoted in Brawley (2001), p. 83.

55 Sean Brawley (2007) *Bondi Lifesaver: A History of an Australian Icon*, ABC Books, Sydney, p. 288.

56 Ibid., p. 88.

57 In 2001, the expenses of the Swimming Program Coordinator totalled $7097. See Report on Asthma Children's Swimming Program, July 2002.

58 *The Asthma Welfarer* (1988), vol. 21, no. 2, p. 37.

59 Colleen Wardell, Shih-Wen Huang & Claire Isbister (2006) 'When Children with Asthma go Swimming, The Benefits Can be Many and Long-lasting', *Contemporary Pediatrics*, 1 October, <www.contemporarypediatrics.com/contpeds/content>, viewed 20 March 2008.

60 Colleen Wardell & Claire Isbister (2000) 'A Swimming Program for Children with Asthma', *Medical Journal of Australia*, vol. 173, 4/18 December, p. 647.

61 Babette Smith (2003) *Coming up for Air*, Rosenburg Publishing in association with Asthma Foundation of NSW, Sydney, p. 202.

62 *Sydney Morning Herald*, 18 January 1995, p. 3.

63 Quoted in Sol Encel & Penelope Nelson (1996) *Volunteering and Older People*, Consultative Committee on Ageing, NSW Government, Sydney, p. 22.

64 Ibid., p. 32.

65 Jeni Warburton & Sha Cordingley (2004) 'The Contemporary Challenges of Volunteering in an Ageing Australia', *Volunteering Australia*, vol. 9, no.2, p. 67.

66 Encel & Nelson (1996), p. 8.

67 'The Multicultural Contribution', in Noble & Johnston (2001), p. 98.

68 ANESBWA Records, Box 7, uncatalogued collection, ML 07/565, Mitchell Library, Sydney.

69 Encel & Nelson (1996), pp. 39–40.

70 Constitution of the 'Association of Non-English Speaking Background Women of Australia Inc', Box 1, uncatalogued collection, ANESBWA Records, ML 07/565, Mitchell Library, Sydney.

71 *Sydney Morning Herald*, 5 December 1988 ,when Matina Mottee received the 1988 Qantas Ethnic Communities Award.

72 Debbie Georgopoulos, Migrant Women Statistical Profile, BIPR, 1994, in Box 9, uncatalogued collection, ANESBWA Records, ML 07/565, Mitchell Library, Sydney.

73 *ANESBWA Annual Report*, 1996/7, Mitchell Library, Sydney.

74 ABS (1994) *National Aboriginal and Torres Strait Islander Survey, Detailed Findings*, AGPS, Canberra, p. 47.

75 Encel & Nelson (1996), p. 41.

76 'Indigenous Action', in Noble & Johnston (2001), p. 11.

77 Ian Kiernan, 'Clean Up Australia', in Noble & Johnston (2001), p. 56.

78 Ibid., p. 59.

79 Rob Youl, Sue Marriott & Theo Nabben (2006) *Landcare in Australia. Founded on Local Action*, SILC and Rob Youl Consulting Pty Ltd, Victoria [1998].

80 Stewart Lockie (1992) 'Landcare – Before the Flood', *Rural Society*, vol. 2, no. 2, August, p. 7.

81 Geoff A Wilson (2004) 'The Australian Landcare Movement: Towards "Post-Productivist" Rural Governance', *Journal of Rural Studies*, vol. 20, p. 465.

82 Joy Noble & Roger Dick (eds) (2000), *Australian Volunteers at Work: 101 Stories*, Wakefield Press, Adelaide, p. 22.

83 Wilson (2004), p. 466; Youl et al. (2006), p. 8.

84 See, for example, Philip Hughes, Alan Black, Peter Kaldor, John Bellamy & Keith

Castle (2007) *Building Stronger Communities*, UNSW Press, Sydney.

85 Simon Schama (1995) *Landscape and Memory*, Fontana Press, London.

86 Margaret Gooch (2003) 'A Sense of Place: Ecological Identity as a Driver for Catchment Volunteering', *Australian Journal on Volunteering*, vol. 8, no. 2, pp. 23–32.

87 Carr in Gooch (2003), p. 26.

88 In 1999–2000, a survey undertaken by Leichhardt Council found there was less than one hectare of bushland remaining.

89 Youl et al. (2006), p. 20.

90 Martin & Halpin quoted in Geoff A Wilson (2004), p. 463.

91 Lockie (1992).

92 Senator Bob Collins, Federal Minister for Primary Industries and Energy, 1994, quoted in Stewart Lockie (1995) 'Beyond a "Good thing": Political Interests and the Meaning of Landcare', *Rural Society*, vol. 5, no. 2–3, p. 6.

93 Neil R Britton (1984) 'Conceptual Alternatives for the Analysis of Counter-Disaster Organisational Networks', in Natural Disasters Organisation, Report of Proceedings of a Research Workshop on Human Behaviour in Disaster in Australia, 25–27 April, Department of Defence, p. 285.

94 Ibid., p. 286.

95 Margaret Rees (1998) 'Concerns Raised by Deaths of Volunteer Firefighters', 11 December, <www.wsws.org/news/1998/dec1998/fire-d11.shtml>, viewed 20 March 2008.

96 Allan Woodward, 'Protecting Communities', in Noble & Johnston (2001), p. 43.

Chapter 8

1   Robert Fitzgerald (2001) 'Community Advocacy', in Joy Noble & Fiona Johnston (eds), *Volunteering Visions*, Federation Press, Sydney, p. 10.

2   Brendan Lynch, 'Lessons from the Olympics', in Noble & Johnston (2001), p. 75.

3   Ibid., p. 71.

4   'Olympic Excitement', in Joy Noble & Roger Dick (eds) (2000) *Australian Volunteers at Work: 101 Stories*, Wakefield Press, Adelaide, p. 100.

5   Official Report of the XXVII Olympiad, 'Out and About: Volunteers, <www. gamesinfo.com.au/postgames/en/pg001411.htm>, viewed 3 June 2008.

6   Laurence Chalip (1999) 'Volunteers and the Organization of the Olympic Games: Economic and Formative Aspects', Papers of the Volunteers, Global Society and the Olympic Movement Symposium, 24–26 November, p. 4. <olympicstudies. uab.es/volunteers/chapil.html>, viewed 28 March 2008.

7   Jo Fairbairn (2001) 'Big Picture, Small Picture', *Australian Journal on Volunteering*, vol. 6, no. 1, p. 51.

8   Lynch in Noble & Johnston (2001), p. 73 and Official Report of the XXVII Olympiad, 'Out and About: Volunteers, <www.gamesinfo.com.au/postgames/en/pg001416.htm>, viewed 3 June 2008.

9   Sandy Hollway, 'State Government Strategies: NSW', in Noble & Johnston (2001), p. 111.

10 'International Year of Volunteers 2001', World Volunteer Web, <www. worldvolunteerweb.org/tools/about-us/iyv-2001.html>, viewed 20 March 2008.

11 Kathleen Dennis (2002) 'International Association for Volunteer Effort', *Australian Journal on Volunteering*, vol. 7, no. 2, p. 5.

12 Ken Allen, World President, IAVE (2001) 'The Global Agenda for Action to Strengthen Volunteering', *Australian Journal on Volunteering*, vol. 6, no. 1, p. 3.

13 Ibid., pp. 5–6.

14 Megan Costigan & Susan Woolias (2001) 'Celebrating our Quiet Achievers', *Australian Journal on Volunteering*, vol. 6, no. 2, p. 6.

15 Kylee Bates (2001) 'The National Community Council of Advice', *Australian Journal on Volunteering*, vol. 6, no. 1, p. 14.

16 See Australian Bureau of Statistics (2001) *Voluntary Work, 2000*, AGPS, Canberra.

17 Hollway in Noble & Johnston (2001), p. 111.

18 Quoted in Melanie Oppenheimer & Jeni Warburton (2000) 'Introduction', in Warburton & Oppenheimer (eds), *Volunteers and Volunteering*, Federation Press, Sydney, p. 1.

19 Jeni Warburton, Melanie Oppenheimer & Gianni Zappala (2004) 'Marginalizing Australia's Volunteers. The Need for Socially Inclusive Practices in the Non-Profit Sector', *Australian Journal on Volunteering*, vol. 9, no. 1, p. 34. See also J Warburton & C McDonald (2002) '"Compulsory Volunteering" Under Mutual Obligation Policies: Implications for the Future', *Just Policy*, no. 26, pp. 11–17.

20 Jennifer Wilkinson & Michael Bittman (2002), 'Neighbourly Acts – Volunteering, Social Capital and Democracy', *Australian Journal on Volunteering*, vol. 7, no. 2, p. 33.

21 Mark Lyons & Andrew Passey (2006) 'Need Public Policy Ignore the Third Sector? Government Policy in Australia and the United Kingdom', *Australian Journal of Public Administration*, vol. 65, no. 3, September, pp. 91–101.

22 Volunteering Secretariat (2004) 'Revisiting the Vision 2004. Valuing Volunteering – A Shared Vision', Department of Community Development, Perth.

23 Melanie Oppenheimer, 'The Protection and Rights of Volunteers', unpublished paper presented to the Volunteering NSW Conference, 24 May 2001; and Sandy Hollway in Noble & Johnston (2001), p. 112.

24 'Valuing Volunteers: The Queensland Government Policy on Volunteering, 2007–2010', p. 8.

25 For a contemporary discussion, see Sue Kenny (2000), 'Third Sector Organisations and Risk', *Third Sector Review*, vol. 6, no. 1/2, pp. 71–88.

26 Myles McGregor-Lowndes, Stephen Marsden & Carolyn Vincent (2001) 'Volunteering in the New Tax System', *Australian Journal on Volunteering*, vol. 6, no. 1, pp. 21–29.

27 Melanie Oppenheimer (2001) 'Rights and Protection of Volunteer Workers. Some Preliminary Considerations', *Australian Journal on Volunteering*, vol. 6, no. 2, pp. 139–44.

28 This Act updated the 1989 Act and the *State Emergency and Rescue Management Act 1994* (NSW).

29 Myles McGregor-Lowndes (2003) 'Australian Volunteer Protection Provisions', *Australian Journal on Volunteering*, vol. 8, no. 2, p. 43.

30 Ibid., p. 46. The other state and territory legislation includes the *Civil Act 2002* (NSW); *Volunteer (Protection from Liability) Act 2002* (WA); *Civil Laws (Wrongs) Act 2002* (ACT); *Wrongs and Other Acts (Public Liability Insurance Reform) Act*

2002 (Vic); *Civil Liability Act 2002* (Tas).

31 See the Volunteering Australia website for their quick guide to occupational health and safety laws, <www.volunteeringaustralia.org/files>, viewed 3 June 2008.

32 Mark Lyons & Andrew Passey (2006) 'Need Public Policy Ignore the Third Sector? Government Policy in Australia and the United Kingdom', *Australian Journal of Public Administration*, vol. 65, no. 3, September, p. 91.

33 Sarah Lucas, Not-for-profit roundtable, quoted on 'Not for Profit, Not for Volunteers', *Background Briefing*, ABC Radio National, 27 June 2004.

34 Senator Andrew Murray, Spokesperson for Taxation, Finance and Corporate Affairs, Action Plan, Charities & Not-for-Profits, <www.democrats.org.au>, viewed 30 March 2008.

35 'Not for Profit, Not for Volunteers' (2004).

36 Cultural Ministers Council (2003), *Australia's Cultural Volunteers 2000*, National Centre for Culture and Recreation Statistics, ABS, May, p. 18.

37 World Youth Day volunteer uniforms mark one hundred days to go, <www.wyd2008.org/index.php/en/volunteers_homestay>, viewed 3 June 2008.

38 See, for example, Mark Lyons & Charlotte Fabiansson (1998) 'Is Volunteering Declining in Australia?', *Australian Journal on Volunteering*, vol. 3, no. 2, pp. 15–21; and Mark Lyons & Susan Hocking, 'Australia's Highly Committed Volunteers' in Warburton & Oppenheimer (2000), pp. 44–55.

39 Gianni Zappala (2001), 'From "Charity" to "Social Enterprise": Managing Volunteers in Public Serving Nonprofits', *Australian Journal on Volunteering*, vol. 6, no. 1, pp. 41–49.

40 R Beatson & J McLennan (2005) 'Australia's Women Volunteer Fire Fighters: A Literature Review and Research Agenda', *Australian Journal on Volunteering*, vol. 10, no. 2, pp. 18–27.

41 Jim McLennan, Adrian Birch, Ruth Beatson & Sean Cowlishaw (2007) 'Factors Impacting on Recruiting and Retaining Australia's Volunteer Firefighters: Some Research Evidence', *Australian Journal on Volunteering*, vol. 12, no. 2, p. 59.

42 Ibid., p. 67.

43 Ibid., p. 68.

44 'Volunteers Resign en Masse', *Canberra Times*, 16 March 2007.

45 Russell Hoye (2006), 'Sport and the Third Sector: An Introduction to the Special Issue', *Third Sector*, vol. 12, no. 2, p. 9.

46 Russell Hoye & Graham Cuskelly (2002) 'Problems in Recruiting and Retaining Sports Officials: An Exploratory Study', *Australian Journal on Volunteering*, vol. 9, no. 2, p. 47.

47 Hoye (2006), p. 10.

48 Ibid., p. 11. See also Bob Stewart et al. (2004) *Australian Sport: Better by Design? The Evolution of Australian Sport Policy*, Routledge, London; Kevin Brown (2006) 'The Position of Australian Community Sporting Organisations in the Third Sector: Membership Profiles, Characteristics and Attitudes', *Third Sector Review*, vol. 12, no. 2, pp. 17–39.

49 S Bond & P Hughes (2003) '"No Religion" in Australia', *Pointers*, vol. 13, no. 3, pp. 1–5.

50 ACOSS (2005) *Giving Australia: Research on Philanthropy in Australia. Summary of Findings*, AGPS, Canberra.

51 Mark Lyons & Ian Nivison-Smith (2006) 'The Relationship Between Religion and Volunteering in Australia', *Australian Journal on Volunteering*, vol. 11, no. 2, p. 26.

52 Rosemary Leonard & John Bellamy (2006) 'Volunteering Within and Beyond the Congregation: A Survey of Volunteering Among Christian Church Attendees', *Australian Journal on Volunteering*, vol. 11, no. 2, p. 24.

53 See 'Sisters of Charity Outreach. Our First Ten Years', Sydney, 2000 and www.outreach.stvincents.com.au, viewed 12 February 2008.

54 See Indu Balachandran & Margaret Guy, 'The Challenge of the Changing Volunteer. Sisters of Charity Outreach', unpublished paper, 2004.

55 Ibid., p. 15. See the full report at www.dpc.wa.gov.au/volunteer/boom.pdf, viewed 30 March 2008.

56 Annette Maher (2007) 'The Long and Winding Road: Grey Nomad Research Update', *Australian Journal on Volunteering*, vol. 12, no. 2, pp. 108–10.

57 Department of the Premier and Cabinet in partnership with the Department for Community Development; Seniors Interests (2002) '"BOOMNET". Capturing the Baby Boomer Volunteers: A 2001 Research Project into Baby Boomers and Volunteering', *Australian Journal on Volunteering*, vol. 7, no. 1, p. 16.

58 D de Vaus, M Gray & D Stanton (2003) *Measuring the Value of Unpaid Household, Caring and Voluntary Work of Older Australians*, Australian Institute of Family Studies Research Paper No. 34, October. See www.aifs.org.au/institute/pubs/respaper/rp34.html, viewed 30 March 2008.

59 J Warburton & S Cordingley (2004) 'The Contemporary Challenges of Volunteering in an Ageing Australia', *Australian Journal on Volunteering*, vol. 9, no. 2, pp. 67–74; J Warburton (2006) 'Volunteering in Later Life: Is it Good for Your Health?', *Voluntary Action*, vol. 8, no. 2, pp. 3–15; J Warburton, J Paynter & A Petriwiskyj (2007) 'Volunteering as a Productive Ageing Activity: Incentives and Barriers to Volunteering by Australian Seniors', *Journal of Applied Gerontology*, vol. 26, no. 4, pp. 333–54.

60 Jeni Warburton, guest on ABC Radio National's *Life Matters*, 'Vita Activa 6,: Will the Baby Boomers Save Volunteering?', 5 November 2007. See www.abc.net.au/rn/lifematters/stories/2007/2078590.htm, viewed 30 March 2008.

61 Productivity Commission (2005) *Economic Implications of an Ageing Australia*, Productivity Commission, Melbourne.

62 Volunteering Australia (2004) *Submission on the Productivity Commission's Commissioned Study, "Economic Implications of an Ageing Australia"*, Melbourne, October.

63 Rosie Lewis (2001) 'GoVolunteer. Using the Internet to Help Australians Volunteer', *Australian Journal on Volunteering*, vol. 6, no. 1, pp. 53–55.

64 National Australia Bank and volunteer x change, <www.web.volunteerxchange.com/scripts/openExtra.asp>, viewed 3 June 2008.

65 National Federation of Parents, Families and Carers, <www.civilsociety.org.au/federation.htm>, viewed 3 June 2008.

66 Volunteering Australia and Australian Multicultural Foundation (2006) 'Involved and Valued? Findings from a National Survey of Australian Volunteers from Diverse Cultural and Linguistic Backgrounds', Research Bulletin, July, <www.volunteeringaustralia.org/files>, viewed 6 June 2008.

67 John Murphy, 'Creative Partnerships. Community, Government and Business', in

Noble & Johnston (2001), p. 124.

68 Goodcompany, <www.goodcompany.com.au>, viewed 3 June 2008.

69 Quoted in Joy Noble & Fiona Verity (2006) *Imagine If. A Handbook for Activists*, Wakefield Press, Adelaide, p. 1.

Conclusion

1 Speech by Justin Davis Smith at the Launch of the Commission on the Future of Volunteering, 29 March 2006, <www.volcomm.org.uk/news/TheAgeoftheVolunteer.htm>, viewed 30 March 2008.

2 'Towards a 2020 Vision for Volunteering', speech to Volunteering NSW Forum: Diversity and the Volunteer Workforce, 28 March 2008, <www.ursulastephens.com>, viewed 10 April 2008.

3 Melanie Oppenheimer (2008) 'An Idea that Serves Nobody', *The Australian Higher Education Supplement*, 14 May, p. 51.

4 Parliament of Australia: Senate: First Speeches, Mitch Fifield, Senator for Victoria, 12 May 2004, <www.aph.gov.au/senate/senators/homepages/first_speechs/sfs-D21.htm>, viewed 4 June 2008.

5 Australia 2020 Final Summit Report, <www.pm.gov/au/media/Release/2008/media_release_0279.cfm>, viewed 6 June 2008.

6 See VSA ebulletin, 4 June 2008, <www.volunteeringsa.org.au>, viewed 6 June 2008.

7 '… Gross National Product … measures everything in short, except that which makes life worthwhile.' Remarks of Robert F Kennedy, University of Kansas, 18 March 1968 – John F Kennedy Presidential Library & Museum, <www.jfk.library.org/Historical+Resources/Archives/Reference+Desk/Speeches/RFK/RFKSpeech68Mar18UKansas.htm>, viewed 6 June 2008.

Index

baby boomers 65, 121, 171, 198–200
Baldock, Cora 21, 161, 172
Bandler, Faith 85
Beasley, Margot 84
Beaurepaire, Beryl 161
Bell, Margaret 165
Beveridge, William 8–10, 25, 54
Billingham, Trevor 26, 101
Blair, Tony 10, 155
Blewett, Neal 89
Bloomfield, John 140
Bourdieu, Pierre 10
Bowling Alone 10
Bridge, Carl 60
British Voluntary Service Overseas 96
Brotherhood of St Laurence 107, 197
Brundage, Avery 80–1
Buck, Heather 127
Builders' Labourers Federation (BLF) 131
Bunbury 135
Burney, Linda 190
Bush Nursing Association 52
Bushells Employees' War Fund 41
business partnerships 200–2
bushwalking movement 83

Cairns, Ceci 91
Calwell, Arthur 71, 72
Campaign for Peace in Vietnam 87–9,
   122
Carden, Tony 93
Carr government 190
Carson, Rachel 100
Carswell, RW 70
Cass, Bettina 24
Catholic Family Welfare Bureau 108, 111
Catholic Overseas Relief 96
Catholic Womens' Association 66
Central Council of Victorian Benevolent
   Societies 19
Chaney, Fred 159
Chifley government 53, 54
Children's Book Council 62–4, 98, 141
Children's Book Week 63
Children's Library and Crafts Movement 60
Children's Library Movement 59–61, 62,
   63

Children's Swimming Program 102–4
civil defence 77–9
Clean Up Australia 26, 176
Co.As.It 74
Coleman, James 10
Coleman, Marie 125
Commonwealth Literary Fund (CLF) 58,
   98
communism 42, 86, 92, 131
Community Activities Section
   (Department of Post-War
   Reconstruction) 52, 53–5
Community Aid Abroad 96, 97
Community and Cultural Development
   Fund 21
community building, post-war 52
community centre movement 55–8,
   132–7, 141
Commonwealth Natural Disasters
   Organisation 149, 180
Co-operative Advisory Council 56
corporate volunteering 200–2
Council of Charitable Relief Organisations
   (SA) 19
Council of Social Service (NSW) 19
Counting for Nothing 7
Country Fire Authority (CFA) 180
Country Fire Service (CFS) 195
Country Women's Association (CWA)
   3–4, 19, 36, 43, 52, 63, 72, 78, 136,
   137–9, 166
Cox, Eva 11, 12
Croll, Joan 129–30
Curti, Merle 26
Curtis, Margaret 160
Cyclone Tracy 127, 148–9, 180

Dahrendorf, Rolf 136
Davis Smith, Justin 13, 162, 204
Deakin, Nick 162
Dillon, Thelma 76
disasters 76–9, 148–9, 179–80
Dixon, Brian 10
Dobson, Nancy 112
Dung, Luu Thi Tuyet 93–4
Dunphy. Myles 100
Dunstan, Don 112, 133